workers' li|

_____ reason in revolt ✓____

Contents

Editorial
1   In an Age of Barbarism
7   The left must unite Europe
12 Socialists in the General
    Election

15 The experience of the French
    left in elections
    by Colin Foster
19 The new turn of the SWP
    by Martin Thomas
30 Nature 1, Nurture 0
    by Clive Bradley
33 Factfile: Dick Whittington's
    heir by John Bloxam
38 Briefing: Who are the anti-
    capitalists by Nick Holden
40 A century of Satch
    by Jim Denham
43 China and independent
    working class politics
    by Paul Hampton
60 Sylvia Pankhurst and
    democracy
    by Susan Carlyle and Sean
    Matgamna
84 Lenin and the myth of
    revolutionary defeatism
    by Hal Draper
112 The Degradations of
    "Apparatus Marxism"
    by Jack Cleary
140 Tony Cliff and Max Shachtman
    part 3 by Paul Hampton

Forum
144 Capitalism: neither decline,
    nor progress
    by Bruce Robinson
147 A one-sided view of capitalist
    progress by Clive Bradley
148 Kosova and East Timor: an
    Australian view
    by Roger Clarke
150 We need a critical
    appreciation of Benjamin
    by John Cunningham
151 For a democratic-secular
    state! by Paul Flewers

Reviews
152 Neither capitalism nor
    Stalinism but dreamworld?
    by Colin Foster
153 Democracy's decisions
    by Brian Palmer
154 How Stalin armed Hitler
    by Matt Heaney
154 A half-critique of Cuba
    by Paul Hampton
155 But still, it moves
    by Gerry Bates
156 Genome alone?
    by Edward Ellis
157 Global police and the
    multitude by Mellisa White

Subscription information page 111

Workers' Liberty Volume 2 no. 1

Published September 2001 by the Alliance for Workers' Liberty

Editor: Sean Matgamna
Assistant Editors: Cathy Nugent, Martin Thomas
Design: Cath Fletcher, Duncan Morrison
Business Manager: Alan McArthur

ISBN: 0-9531864-2-3

What is Workers' Liberty?

The Alliance for Workers' Liberty organises to fight the class struggle on all levels — trade union and social battles, politics and the combat of ideas. We are active in workplaces, in trade unions, in the Labour Party, in single-issue campaigns, in students unions, and in debates and discussions on the left. We aim to integrate all these activities into a coherent effort for socialism.

If you want to know more about the Alliance for Workers' Liberty, write to: PO Box 823, London SE15 4NA, phone 020 7207 3997, or email office@workersliberty.org

www.workersliberty.org

EDITORIAL

In an Age of Barbarism

"Without revolutionary theory, there can be no revolutionary movement" – Vladimir Lenin

ACCORDING to the classic account by Lewis H Morgan, "barbarism" is in human history the stage between savagery and civilisation; between the stage of "savage" peoples who are hunters and casual gatherers on one side, and on the other "civilised" people who have developed cities.

In barbarism, human beings have become settled, regular producers; agriculturalists, herdsmen, handicraftsmen. Over thousands of years, these "barbarians" create all the prerequisites of civilisation. In barbarism, human beings had already developed most of the agricultural technique that would underscore human life for ensuing thousands of years, up to recent times. In barbarism the productivity of labour developed from the "savage" stage in which one human being would, like a beast eternally browsing in search of food, "produce" barely enough to stay alive and reproduce, to the stage in which it "paid" to keep war captives alive as slaves able to produce for their masters a surplus over what was needed to keep the producers alive. Classes of exploiters and exploited developed.

Barbarism was one of the great moves forward in human history. It was unavoidable; there was no progressive alternative to it. Over long ages it created the preconditions for a higher stage.

The Age of Barbarism in which we live is not unavoidable. Our neo-barbarism is not a step forward, though it contains immense steps forward. It is no necessary stage of development though in it human society continues to develop. It is characterised by being a stage in human society that has too long outlived the time in which it created the preconditions for a higher, successor system: there is a progressive alternative to it.

It is the stage in which humankind, over a period of two centuries and more, has made tremendous strides in developing its power to control nature and, physically, in terms of medicine and surgery in all their aspects, over itself, but is as yet unable to break through into the higher stage of civilisation whose preconditions now exist, and have long existed.

That stage will be characterised by rational, human, as distinct from exploitative class, control over our society; and therefore and thereby, by rational human control over nature – by a harmonious relationship with the eco-system on which everything depends.

The progressive ruination of the environment is the terrible ultimate price humankind will pay and is paying for its prolonged incapacity to put its own society under rational democratic control.

BARBARISM was characterised by progressive human control over nature, by accumulating awareness of how things worked, how natural processes could be understood, manipulated, modified, controlled and reproduced – that is, by human growth and developments in harmonious integration with nature.

Our neo-barbarism is characterised by the enormous and awesome but increasingly ruinous power over nature of a humankind that has not yet mastered its own social processes. We are still at the mercy of irrational social and political forces, even while our power to tame the irrational forces of nature, at whose mercy humankind has been throughout its existence, reaches an amazing and still increasing capacity.

Where social relations are concerned, humankind is kept in a condition of possibly suicidal macro-irrationality by the internal conflicts, contradictions and bestialities of a class society that has outlived itself: by the fact that we still live in a society controlled by an exploitative ruling class in its own interests.

In barbarism, human beings led short, brutal, insecure lives imprisoned in recurring hunger and the ever-present possibility of uncontrollable natural catastrophe – crop failure, floods, mysterious disease – and the predatory attentions of other human groups. They developed imaginative superstitions and religions that at bottom expressed a helpless incomprehension of nature and of themselves.

In neo-barbarism, uncontrolled social forces, and social forces controlled by the predators, create devastation in communities and countries such as natural calamities created in barbarism. Many, many millions of human beings, even those living in the richest countries, live lives imprisoned in want, insecurity and ever-threatening, socially-determined, avoidable catastrophe, side by side with people – close by or in countries that with modern transport systems are also "close by" – living rich lives and some of them extravagant lives.

We, too, develop superstitions that at bottom express helpless incomprehension. We send rockets into space, but immense numbers of people consult their star sign for insight into their daily lives. The dominant religion in our society is the awestruck worship of market forces and the human groups and individuals who personify their depredations. We take it for granted that tens of millions of human lives each year should be sacrificed to propitiate the forces of social chaos.

ENORMOUS areas of rot and social decadence coexist in this society, alongside tremendous, escalating, technical and economic progress.

The contrasts have for socialists become weary, heart-breaking commonplaces: millions of Third World children starve to death every year while enormous "food moutains" in Europe are destoryed every year.

Millions of people, including millions of children, condemned to live below the official poverty lines in enormously rich countries like Britain and the US, where there is vast consumption of luxury goods and gross and obscene "conspicuous consumption" by the seriously rich.

A magically expanding magic-working clinical drugs industry whose best products are priced beyond the reach of millions who need them most – not only in spectacular and dramatic crises like that created by the HIV-AIDS plague in Africa, but in the daily life of millions of the poor in rich countries like Britain and the US.

Tremendously sophisticated means of communication mainly disseminating the modern equivalent of bear-baiting, lunatic-tormenting and gladiatorial sport spectacles in a commerce-regulated and profit-driven, lowest-common-denominator culture.

The list could be endlessly extended.

Karl Marx, generalising from the experience of history, said that no society gives way to something else until it has exhausted all the potential inherent in its system of production. Karl Marx also approvingly quoted the dictum of the English political economist William Petty: "Labour is its father, the earth its mother." In the *Communist Manifesto,* Karl Marx and Frederick Engels outlined the alternative in the history of human society to the victory of the representative of historical progress: "The mutual ruination of the contending classes" takes on a new and terrible meaning in our time, in a society that progressively destroys the natural preconditions of production and is destroying the conditions of its own social existence.

The capitalist neo-barbarism in which we live is simultaneously civilisation of a very high order and yet the darkest barbarism – an inchoate and ultimately untenable hybrid. In barbarism, humankind was at the mercy of nature; in neo-barbarism, very large aspects of nature are at the mercy of the masters of human kind.

THIS age of neo-barbarism is not determined by an inadequate development of humankind's power over nature and low levels of labour productivity, or by a too slow building up of the potential for humankind to raise itself to a higher stage: it is superimposed on an economy and technology that make it unnecessary and therefore, because something better is possible, a tragic abomination.

Our neo-barbarism is defined by our incapacity to raise ourselves to a higher stage for which the economic and many of the social preconditions already exist. That is defined by the belatedness of the working class socialist revolution.

Today powerful labour movements exist all across the world. The idea that they exist to replace capitalism with a higher system, to take humankind from neo-barbarism to socialism, is not their guiding principle.

Earlier generations of socialists thought of the transition from capitalism to socialism as a much more simple business than it has proved to be, as something covering a shorter time span than it is taking.

They thought of the self-preparation of the working class to lead humankind out of capitalist neo-barbarism as a much more straightforward thing than it is. Labour movements experience not only phases of growth and political development, but also phases of destruction and defeat – such as that experienced by the revolutionary labour movement before World War Two – and of decay, decline and political regression – and then, again, periods of new growth and political refocusing.

Side by side with the long political regression of labour movements in a country like Britain, there has been tremendous growth of working class movements all across the world.

AS barbarism led to civilisation, feudalism led to the higher stage, capitalism. The bourgeoisie too spent ages as a class that needed to remake society in its own image. It took the bourgeoisie, living within feudalism and monarchist absolutist systems, hundreds of years to make itself fit to be the ruling class.

It went through many phases, experienced false starts, defeats, was led into "historical compromises" with its class-antagonists.

As a revolutionary class it had immense advantages compared to the proletariat in capitalist society. Its wealth, power, self-rule and historical self-awareness grew even within the old system; the growth of markets, the increasing role of money in the old society, cleared its way and made it socially a subordinate segment of the exploiters even before it ruled. By contrast, the working class in capitalism remains the basic exploited class: it can progress only by independent organisation and by way of its social and political awareness.

Leon Trotsky situated the labour movement of his time in the historical perspective of how the bourgeoisie had developed into a ruling class: "The Social Democracy – from whom we broke by breaking with the Second International – marked a certain epoch in the development of the working class. This was not the epoch of revolution but the epoch of reform. Future historians, comparing the bourgeoisie's course of evolution with that of the proletariat, may say that the working class, too, had a Reformation of its own.

"What was the gist of the bourgeois Reformation? At the dawn of its independent historical action, the bourgeoisie did not immediately set itself the task of conquering power but sought instead to secure for itself, within the framework of the feudal state, to alter its forms and to transform it into a bureaucratic monarchy. It transfigured religion, personalising the latter, that is, adapting religion to bourgeois conformities. In these tendencies we find expressed the relative historical weakness of the bourgeoisie. After securing these positions for itself, the bourgeoisie went on to the struggle for power.

"Social Democracy proved incapable of translating Marxism into social-revolutionary action. The role of the Social Democracy dwindled to an attempt to utilise bourgeois society and the bourgeois state in the interests of the working masses. The goal of the conquest of power, although formally set forth, exercised virtually no effect upon the actual practice. Activities were not directed toward the revolutionary utilisation of parliamentarianism, but toward adapting the working class to bourgeois democracy. This adaptation of a proletariat not yet fully conscious of its own strength to the social, state and ideological forms of bourgeois society was apparently a historically inevitable process, but it was just that and nothing more, that is a historical process delimited by the given conditions of a given epoch.

"This epoch of proletarian reformation gave birth to a special apparatus of labour bureaucracy with special mental habits of its own, with its own routine, pinch-penny ideas, chameleon-like capacity for adaptation, and predisposition to myopia."

In fact, there was a second epoch of working class reformism after World War Two. It came because of the defeat of the revolutionary movement, whose spokesman Trotsky had been, and it was made possible by the expansion of capitalism. It was in the 1940s and after, that the British labour movement experienced its reformist high point.

The threat posed by the demagogic Stalinist propaganda against capitalism on one side, and on the other the strength of the labour movement, forced the ruling class to concede welfare states to the working people. The reform labour movements bided their time within capitalism, losing drive and even reformist coherence, falling more and more under the control of college education professionals who, even in many trade unions, replaced the old leading layers rooted in day to day working class experience and, after their self-serving fashion, loyal to the working class.

The mass Communist Parities outside the Third World were distinguished from the Social Democrats not by revolutionary anti-capitalist politics – in their domestic policies they shared the political assumptions and parliamentarian *modus operandi* of the reformists – but by adherence to the USSR, the great "Socialist Fatherland" beyond the mountains that would, somehow, by its prosperity and ultimate triumph in competition with capitalism, bring about world socialism (whatever that was). The history of the CPs in the last half of the 20th century is the story of their progressive disillusionment with the USSR.

The admission by Stalin's successor Kruschev that Stalin was a mass murderer, Kruschev's bloody suppression of the Hungarian Revolution of 1956, the invasion of Czechoslovakia in 1968, the invasion of Afghanistan in 1979, the relapse to hard-faced neo-Stalinism in the mid-60s after the brief rule of the reforming Stalinist Tsar, Kruschev – all of these things eroded and progressively destroyed the faith of the CPers in the USSR. In their disillusionment they – in the first place, layers of intellectuals – rediscovered the virtues of bourgeois democracy. If Stalinism was the only alternative, then they were not mistaken that the bourgeois-democratic system was not only preferable but also the one that was historically progressive.

By the time, a decade ago, that Stalinism collapsed in the USSR, the Stalinist parties, even where they were still large and largely working class-based organisations, were typically on the right wing of the reform "socialist" spectrum.

FOR more than 100 years things other than working class defeat and the continuation of capitalism to this stage have been possible. Working class victory and the beginning of a rational socialist system was possible; but we have had defeat. As a result, we have neo-barbarism super-imposed by an outmoded bourgeois ruling class on an economically dynamic society.

Trotsky, who had helped the Russian workers in October 1917 demonstrate that the working class suffers from no inbuilt organic political incapacity, understood the crux of the crisis of human civilisation in the mid-20th century as a crisis of the labour movement. Great labour movements had been created on the perspective of preparing the working class to suppress wage labour and capitalism – a working class that would make itself the ruling class, and freeing itself from capitalism, begin to free humankind from class society. The leaderships, bureaucracies and upper working class layers of the old socialist movement had, when the first imperialist World War broke out, delivered the labour movements into the hands of their bourgeois enemy as cannon fodder and butchers of the workers of other nations.

The Communist International had been created to restore independent working class politics after the collapse of 1914. The Stalinist counter-revolution in the USSR in the 1920s tied the Communist International to the new bureaucratic ruling class in the USSR.

When, after 1929, capitalism reached the stage of convulsive semi-collapse, powerful labour movements existed that were strong enough to kick it into its historical grave. But they were everywhere tied to either the bourgeoisie, through the reform-socialist "labour movements", or to the Russian ruling class, through its Communist Parties. Trotsky wrote of their "perfidy" and "betrayal".

In the confusion created by the existence of big socialist parties that weren't socialist and big Communist Parties that weren't communist, the working class suffered murderous accumulating defeat. Trotsky organised the tiny forces that could be organised to compete, with desperate urgency, for the leadership of the working class against the perfidious incumbent leaderships. But Trotsky and everything he represented was defeated and – as we have to recognise in retrospect – defeated for a whole historical period. Capitalism renewed itself on the mass graves, on the destroyed means of production and the ruined cities of the Second World War and began a long period of expansion. Stalinism survived, expanded and then slowly asphyxiated in its own bureaucratic caul, for half a century, until, in Europe, it collapsed.

IT is impossible to tell how *long* it will take the working class to make itself ready to suppress capitalist neo-barbarism and take humankind forward. It is more easily definable in terms of things that must be accomplished.

The labour movements again need to learn by way of their own experience and by the enlightening work of socialists:

● that capitalism is neither natural nor eternal;

● that it is a historically finite system whose inner processes – the creation and recreation of a proletariat and the relentless socialisation of the means of production, of which "globalisation" is the latest manifestation – prepare its own end;

● that capitalism digs its own grave;

● that the working class, which finds no class in society "lower" than itself and which can only organise the economy collectively, that is, democratically, is the representative within capitalism of the post-capitalism future, and the only force that can suppress this neo-barbarism and replace it with something better.

Quick, seemingly miraculous, transformations in the thinking of labour movements have occurred and will occur. That workers who accept capitalism is in a condition in which her objective interests as both worker and human being are at odds with the ideas about society and the world she has been taught to accept. Once that begins to change, everything can change.

Marxism is a necessary part of this process.

Labour movements can arrive at vaguely "socialist" hopes and aspirations, just as young people can arrive at angry rebellion against capitalism. Scientific understanding of capitalism, of society, of the centrality of the working class and the politics of working class self-liberation – in short, understanding of how we can map the way from capitalism neo-barbarism to human liberation – does not arise "spontaneously". That is what Marxist theory is for – that is Marxism's irreplaceable contribution.

Writing about Russia 100 years ago, Lenin put it like this: "Social-Democracy [the revolutionary Marxist movement] is a combination of the labour movement with socialism. Its task is not passively to serve the labour movement at each of its separate stages, but to represent the interests of the movement as a whole, to point out to this movement its ultimate aims and its political tasks, and to protect its political and ideological independence.

"Isolated from Social-Democracy, the labour movement becomes petty and inevitably becomes bourgeois: in conducting only the economic struggle, the working class loses its political independence; it becomes the tail of other parties and runs counter to the great slogan: 'The emancipation of the workers must be the task of the workers themselves.'

"In every country there has been a period in which the labour movement existed separately from the socialist movement, each going its own road; and in every country this state of isolation weakened both the socialist movement and the labour movement. Only the combination of socialism with the labour movement in each country created a durable basis for both the one and the other. But in each country this combination of socialism with the labour movement took place historically, was brought about in a special way, in accordance with the conditions prevailing at the time in each country... The process of combining the two movements is an extremely difficult one, and there is therefore nothing surprising in the fact that it is accompanied by vacillations and doubts.".

And again: "The strikes of the 1890s [in Russia] revealed far greater flashes of consciousness: definite demands were put forward, the time to strike was carefully chosen, known cases and examples in other places were discussed, etc. While the earlier riots were simply uprisings of the oppressed, the systematic strikes represented the class struggle in embryo, but only in embryo. Taken by themselves, these strikes were simply trade union struggles, but not yet Social-Democratic struggles. They testified to the awakening antagonisms between workers and employers, but the workers were not and could not be conscious of the irreconcilable antagonism of their interests to the whole of the modern political and social system, i.e., it was not yet Social-Democratic consciousness. In this sense, the strikes of the 1890s, in spite of the enormous progress they represented as compared with the 'riots', represented a purely spontaneous movement.

"We said that *there could not yet be* Social-Democratic consciousness among the workers. This consciousness could only be brought to them from without. The history of all countries shows that the working class, exclusively by its own efforts, is able to develop only trade union consciousness, i.e., it may itself realise the necessity for combining in unions, for fighting against the employers and for striving to compel the government to pass necessary labour legislation, etc.

The theory of socialism, however, grew out of the philosophic, historical and economic theories that were elaborated by the educated representatives of the propertied classes, the intellectuals. According to their social status, the founders of modern scientific socialism, Marx and Engels, themselves belonged to the bourgeois intelligentsia. Similarly, in Russia, the theoretical doctrine of Social-Democracy arose quite independently of the spontaneous growth of the labour movement; it arose as a natural and inevitable outcome of the development of ideas among the revolutionary socialist intelligentsia."

Today, Marxism, scientific socialism – what in Lenin's time was called Social Democracy – is everywhere separate from the labour movement, greatly more so than when Lenin was writing. To unite Marxism with the labour movement is the task of revolutionary socialists and consistent democrats everywhere. The collapse of Stalinism gives us a better chance of doing that then we have had in 75 years.

But Marxism itself – the consciousness of the unconscious processes of society – Marxism as a guide to revolutionary action, has suffered tremendous blows in the last historical period. The supreme irony is that the collapse of Russian Stalinism, which had through much of the 20th century turned "Marxism" into the pidgin religion of a totalitarian state, should have as its first consequence the discrediting of "Marxism". That is only the first consequence. The collapse of the Russian state-fostered pidgin Marxism clears the way for the development of unfalsified Marxism. We have a considerable way to go yet to achieve that. One of the articles in this issue of *Workers' Liberty* – "The Degradations of Apparatus Marxism" – presents a detailed analysis of how decrepit what passes for Marxism can become.

The revolutionary Marxist tradition is "given" but Marxism is not. Marxism as a living force in socialist organisations and in the labour movement is not something given – it has to be fought for and won and then again fought for and won over again, and then yet again.

It has to be clarified and refined and augmented, again and again in a never-ending process. That process is, in a word, "the class struggle on the ideological front".

Lenin said it plainly and truly: "Without revolutionary theory there can be no revolutionary movement." He also said: "Practice without theory is blind: theory without practice is sterile." In a declaration of the Editorial Board of the revolutionary newspaper *Iskra*, Lenin wrote:

"The intellectual unity of Russian Social-Democrats has still be to established, and in order to achieve this it is necessary, in our opinion, to have an open and thorough discussion of the fundamental principles and tactical questions... Before we can unite, and in order that we may unite, we must first of all firmly and definitely draw the lines of demarcation. Otherwise, our unity will be merely a fictitious unity, which will conceal the prevailing confusion and prevent its complete elimination.

"Naturally, therefore, we do not intend to utilise our publication merely as a storehouse for various views. On the contrary, we shall conduct it along the lines of a strictly defined tendency. This tendency can be expressed by the word Marxism, and there is hardly need to add that we stand for the consistent development of the ideas of Marx and Engels, and utterly reject the half-way, vague and opportunistic emendations which have now become so fashionable... [Having rejected eclecticism and indifferentism, he went on:]

"But while discussing all questions from our own definite point of view, we shall not rule out of our columns polemics between comrades. Open polemics within the sight and hearing of all Russian Social-Democrats and class conscious workers are necessary and desirable, in order to explain the profound differences that exist, to obtain a comprehensive discussion of disputed questions, and to combat the extremes into which the representatives, not only of various views, but also of various localities or various 'crafts' in the revolutionary movement inevitably fall. As has already been stated, we also consider one of the drawbacks of the present-day movement to be the absence of open polemics among those holding avowedly differing views, an effort to conceal the differences that exist over extremely serious questions."

These words offer a guide to revolutionary Marxists now. They will guide the way we conduct the relaunched *Workers' Liberty*.

The fight for Marxism and for a Marxist labour movement is the fight to prepare the only force capable of taking humanity out of our age of neo-barbarism, the working class, for that task.

The left must unite Europe

THOSE who cry against a European single currency, that it would mark a fundamental "surrender" of British sovereignty, are correct. It would. A single currency will be a giant step in the direction of European unity and a decisive move towards the creation of a European state. Europe has already achieved an irreversible though uneven and incomplete level of economic integration and unity. "Europe" already determines much of what happens within the member states of the European Union. The question is not whether there will be a united Europe, but, what sort of European unity?

The creation of a properly democratic European state would be a great step forward. But the development of Europe-wide democratic institutions lags far behind the development of European economic unity.

Now national parliaments are overshadowed. Bourgeois democratic politics which within the national states of Holland, Britain, Belgium and France took centuries of popular struggles to win, have been increasingly weakened. Though the power of national Parliaments has become, in fact, more and more attenuated there is no European-wide equivalent of the National Parliament. The European Parliament has very limited powers, and in the gap between growing "European" power and the shrinking real power of the parliaments of the EU component states, Europe, not too far now from forming a common state, is governed by haggling in the Council of Ministers.

Europe today is what it is because its unification is historically belated and because it is being united by the bourgeoisie and not by the working class. During the decades in which the European bourgeoisie has been integrating Europe to the point where a European state is the next logical step, opposition to European unity, "under capitalism", has been one of the pillars of much of the European left, a left that under Stalinist and nationalist influences had uncoupled from the historic goals of the uncorrupted real left. To put it back in perspective we must start with the fact that European unity, even now, lags decades behind the objective need for it. We must look back over the history that has shaped the European Union.

BY the beginning of the 20th century Europe needed unity because the existing big nation states were too small for the enormous economic dynamic which had developed within the borders of the bigger ones. The economies of the great European states, in the first place that of Germany, were stifling within their too-narrow national boundaries. The question posed by history was: who would unite Europe, the bourgeoisie or the working class?

The unification of Europe – under the German jackboot – had been the programme of the Kaiser in World War One, as it was later to be of Hitler. The Kaiser failed. In 1919, the victorious powers imposed a predators' peace on Germany and thereby laid the basis for a second World War, two decades later. In 1940 at the beginning of that war, Hitler succeeded in achieving European unity. From the Pyrenees, on the borders of the Iberian peninsula, north to the borders of Sweden and east as far as Poland. Hitler united most of Europe. It was a Europe of peoples united by chains rather than bonds of international solidarity, a Europe of enslaved peoples yoked together by conquering German armies, not a Europe of free nations that had voluntarily come together in a United States of Europe.

Yet – and sixty years later there can be no doubt of it – that European unification, even under Hitler, was a horribly distorted expression of a great historical necessity. It is now forgotten, but demoralised segments of the old European left – the mirror image of the contemporary left wing opponents of European unity under the bourgeoisie – justified collaborating with Hitler on the grounds that this unification of Europe was, ultimately, progressive work, though history would have to clean it up. It was a variant of the thinking of those on the left such as the ex-Trotskyist Isaac Deutscher, who attributed historically progressive work to Stalinism, despite its horrors.

How did the bourgeoisie, which presided over two Europe-ruining world wars in the first half of the 20th century, come to bring Europe within sight of a United States of Europe?

THE Anglo-American invaders of Europe in 1944-5 came to destroy German hegemony and to break down the walls of the Nazi prison-house of nations which Europe had become. All across Europe, the invaders were supported by uprisings of peoples seeking national self-determination — French, Belgians, Italians, Poles, Serbs, Czechs. A hundred and thirty years earlier, the French Empire of Napoleon Bonaparte had evoked a similar nationalist reaction against itself in Spain, Prussia and other parts of Europe. After Germany was beaten and overrun, the peoples of Europe outside of Stalin's new East and Central European empire reverted to independent nation-states under the protection of the USA.

Indeed, one consequence of Hitler's brutal German-imperialist attempt to override the peoples was to stoke up a new intensity of self-liberating nationalism and its malignant extension, chauvinism, all across Europe. In the East, ethnic Germans were its main victim. Germans to the number of perhaps 13 million were driven out of East Prussia (nine million), Czechoslovakia (three million), Yugoslavia (half a million) and other areas where Germans had lived for hundreds of years.

Much of Europe was in ruins. Old states were being rebuilt. European-wide political unity, even in areas outside USSR control, was politically impossible — less possible even than it had been before Hitler's rapist "unification".

Recent European history worked to make political unity impossible; yet European unity was not only necessary, but for the bourgeoisie unpostponable. Russia had control of nearly half of Germany and of much of Eastern and Central Europe. It was universally believed, there would be war with Russia, whose vast army would, with Germany disarmed and divided, advance quickly from the centre to the Western end of Europe. An attempt in the late 1940s to create a single West European army proved still-born. (In fact, the prospect of a third World War gave way to the prolonged balance of nuclear terror after the USSR developed an atom bomb in 1949.)

At this point, the European bourgeoisie (the British stood aside) started work to lay the ghosts of recent European history by drawing on the experience of German history. Most of the big and little early 19th century German states had been drawn together inside a customs union (17 states in all), the Zollverein, from 1834. The basis was thereby laid over decades for the unification of most of Germany, under Prussian predominance, in 1871. Prodded by the US and afraid of the antagonistic USSR, the bourgeoisie of Western Europe resolved on a "Zollverein" strategy for uniting Western Europe. Work to create economic unity — and eventually the rest would follow. And so it is following, slowly, unevenly.

First, they created in 1951 the Coal and Steel Community (Germany, France, Italy, Belgium, the Netherlands, Luxembourg). They signed the Treaty of Rome in 1957, under which there would be a series of moves over time to eliminate internal tariffs and make common external tariffs. In 1973, the UK, Denmark and Ireland adhered to the EC; in 1981, Greece; in 1986, Portugal and Spain; in 1995, Sweden, Austria and Finland. There are now 15 states in the European Union — almost all of Western and Northern Europe. Expansion to the east is in prospect.

This movement towards union had bypassed the insoluble political obstacle presented by the recently re-won, precious sovereignties of the states and concentrated on economic knitting-together. The independent states of the EU still stand half a century later, but, while the facade and the many different doors are preserved, the economic walls separating the states have been largely eliminated.

But this Europe, which is at its core economically united, politically still resembles a shanty-town: something thrown together higgledy-piggledy. Democratic politics hobbles far behind economic unification. Over time, a ramshackle growth of Europe-wide political and economic institutions has grown up alongside and on top of the institutions of the nation-states, piecemeal, unfinished.

Half-united Europe is run by a bureaucracy responsive to the needs of the bourgeoisie. Though it increased its powers not so long ago, the European Parliament is only a feeble shadow of what a sovereign parliament should be. It does not have effective control over the civil servants or the Council of Ministers. Relations between the component states and the EU are disablingly ill-defined. In short, much that the nationalist and other critics of the EU say against it is true.

THE European Union is a great cartel, confronting the underdeveloped countries as a preda-

8

tor and confronting migrant workers from outside its walls as "Fortress Europe". Many things about it outrage the spirit even of serious liberal democracy, not to speak of the spirit of international socialism. It is stamped in the image of the bourgeoisie which has achieved it. The fact that the European working class, which would have unified Europe and created a fully-democratic Socialist United States of Europe, was defeated in the decades before World War Two has determined that.

Yet, even politically, despite all that needs to be said against the present EU, Europe is more united than at any time since the breakdown of the Western Roman Empire 1,500 years ago. Undesirable aspects of the European unity which the bourgeoisie has created notwithstanding, it is much better than the older Europe of separate, often hostile and sometimes warring nations. Before 1945, by which time much of Europe had been reduced to ruins inhabited by starving people, European history had more resembled what happened in ex-Yugoslavia in the 1990s than what it has been in the last half-century. The basis exists now as never before for working-class unity all across Europe; for a Europe-wide working-class struggle to create a democratic and socialist United States of Europe.

There is a great deal to object to in this quasi-united bourgeois Europe. But it is where we are. What policy will best serve working class interests within this EU of the bourgeoisie?

THERE are two basic lines of possible policy. Build on what the bourgeoisie has built and unite the working class across the EU to fight the bourgeoisie for democratic and social reform and in the course of doing that build towards the possibility of socialist transformation by working-class revolution on a European scale. That means:

● Fight to democratise the EU by way of scrapping existing bureaucratic structures and replacing them with a sovereign elected European Parliament;

● Fight to level up working class living standards, and for a plan to eliminate unemployment and social exclusion (cut the working week, expand public services);

● Fight to rebuild a European international socialist movement.

Such an approach does not commit socialists to support, or forbid us to oppose, any specific bourgeois measures. Support for European unity does not have to imply backing what the dominant capitalists and their servants do, or the way that they do it – for example the Maastricht Treaty. It does not commit us to vote yes in the referendum that the British bourgeoisie may hold on the question of a single currency. It does commit us to European unity and to opposing politically all those who advocate the break up of the European Union and the restoration of the old, long-bankrupt, European bourgeois national-state system. It does commit us to counterpose working class measures on a European scale to the bourgeois system.

That is one clear line of response to where the working class movement is in the evolution of Europe. The alternative is to respond to the bourgeois character of the existing process of European unification by advocating regression to an outlived earlier stage of bourgeois rule – the era of competing and sometimes warring European national states. It is to stand for a political version of the "Irish" joke in which a man asked for directions responds, "Well, if I were you, I wouldn't start from here at all..." It is to want to go back to a decades-past stage on the road and start again. It is not desirable; and it is not possible either. Despite its advocates' sometime concern with working class self-defence, this is a *reactionary* policy. It is a break with the best traditions of the working class movement and of Marxism.

THE unification of Europe was a policy of the working class left long before any sort of union became the policy of the ruling bourgeoisie. Trotsky raised the call for a United States of Europe in the middle of the First World War. In 1923 the Communist International adopted the slogan for the Socialist United States of Europe.

Marxists, including Trotsky, rightly dismissed feeble bourgeois talk (in the '20s) of a capitalist united Europe as utopian. It took the Second World War, the destruction of large parts of Europe and the long-term threat of USSR conquest before bourgeois quasi-unification, in the form described above, became possible.

Because of the successive series of defeats the working class movement suffered at the hands of fascism, Stalinism and plutocratic "democracy" we have not the Socialist United States of Europe advocated by revolutionary socialists, but the quasi-democratic bureaucratic European Union of the bourgeoisies — that is the way that history has answered the objective need to unite the European economy. *Socialists now start from that.* We cannot start from anywhere else!

ISSUES similar in principle have confronted labour movements for over 150 years. There is a strong Marxian tradition on such questions. The bourgeoisie industrialised much of Europe in the 19th century. In the long term, they were creating the precondition of socialism — a high level of labour productivity and thus the possibility of abundance for all and the elimination of ruling classes and class exploitation. In the lives of many millions and of whole generations they created industrial hell-holes and foetid slums. They worked young children to death. They tore down all the old defences of the working people. The pioneer new technology, that of the British cotton industry, made it profitable for the cotton kings to get their raw material by way of black slavery in the USA, where chattel slaves were worked to death in seven or eight years of hard labour to feed machines run by the child and woman wage-slaves in the cotton mills.

Some early working-class rebels and good-willed observers wanted to "rescind" industrialisation and go back to an earlier historical stage. Describing such ideas as "reactionary socialism", *The Communist Manifesto*, the foundation stone of modern socialism, proposed instead that the working class should in the short term organise to protect themselves and in the longer term aim to win political power and, by way of that power, take over industrial society, humanise it and use it to build a socialist society. There was no other way to build a socialist society, a humane working-class system, except on the basis of the economic achievements of the bourgeoisie: socialism is in history the child of bourgeois society. Thereby, *The Communist Manifesto* established the basic working-class approach to bourgeois society and its development — to simultaneously fight it in self-defence and in the longer term aim to build on its achievements.

FUNDAMENTALLY the same issues arose at the start of the 20th century. Imperialism bestrode the world. Great trusts and cartels united with powerful states to fight other states and their industries for markets and colonies. In response, there arose a movement against these "unacceptable" manifestations of capitalist development. Proposals were made to break up the giant industries, to unscramble and undo what the organic evolution of capitalism was doing. In America, such ideas were made law, and Standard Oil was broken into parts — most of which then developed into giant corporations... It was, even if desirable, simply not possible to roll the film of capitalist development backwards.

Lenin, Luxemburg, Trotsky and that whole generation of revolutionary Marxists mocked at the ideas of the "trust-busters" and denounced their programme as a petty-bourgeois utopian aspiration to "devolve" capitalism back to a stage it had long passed, never to return to. Lenin saw the gigantism of capitalist organisation as a potentially progressive work of social integration and organisation: the answer to its exploitative and brutally capitalist character was for the working class to win political power, and by expropriating the bourgeoisie take over the economy and put it under humane, rational working class control.

Historically the knitting-together of peoples and states is one of the great progressive works of capitalism. But, as with "globalisation" now, it proceeds universally, inhumanely, destructively — in short, in a bourgeois way.

To say, as some do, that because socialism is now possible, therefore capitalism is completely reactionary and must be opposed when it tries to unite Europe, is both foolish and sectarian. Who says? Who knows that? Who decides and how? Capitalism does not come to a dead end: for example, the microchip revolution over the last two decades is a tremendous capitalist-era addition to humankind's power over nature and potentially over its own social affairs. These and other contemporary technological advances will be taken over by the working class, which develops and redevelops with and within capitalism and its constantly changing technologies. Capitalism develops and, in its own bourgeois way, continues to socialise production. It continues to create the material basis for socialism.

THOUGH it will always remain itself, capitalism will go on developing until the working class, led by the socialist movement, overthrows it. The European Union represents a necessary development. It is reversible only by regression to economic chaos and probably war.

Fighting the bourgeoisie within their system, conducting the working-class struggle for trade union and social rights, for the best achievable wages and conditions, for the fullest democratic rights and procedures, and ultimately for the overthrow of capitalism and its replacement by socialism, socialists in Marx's tradition know only one viable anti-capitalism: the conquest of political power by the working class and the transformation of advanced capitalism into the beginning of socialism. Anything else is reactionary anti-capitalism in the muddled form of a utopian drive to go back to stages capitalism has outgrown – in relation to Europe, back to the system, that, two times in the first half of the 20th century brought Europe to ruin and devastation and turned it into a vast abattoir for tens of millions of human beings.

THE predominant position on the left in Britain has for decades been to "oppose" the European Union as such and to champion "British withdrawal". Often it is implied that this has something to do with socialism, or that it would better the prospects for socialism in Britain. But the immediate alternative to British capitalism *in Europe* is British capitalism *out of Europe*. The alternative to the EU is an independent capitalist Britain, or, rather, one oriented more to the US than to Europe.

It is nonsense to sloganise: "No to Europe", "No to Maastricht", "No to the single currency", or whatever and link such slogans with "Yes to the Socialist United States of Europe". The road to the Socialist United States of Europe has to be the road of building European working-class unity, the road of class struggle, the road of fighting one's own bourgeoisie and one's own nationalism and chauvinism, in the spirit of Karl Liebknecht and Rosa Luxemburg, who raised the cry in 1914: "The main enemy is at home."

Anybody who thinks that "Britain out of the EU" means the Socialist United States of Europe or that a campaign for British withdrawal can be part of the struggle for the Socialist United States of Europe is a fool or a liar, or both. The notion that these British nationalist ideas can play any positive role in rousing British workers against either the British or the European bourgeoisie has been shown by decades of bitter and shameful experience to be utter nonsense. The right, and the forces of working-class disunity, gain from such nationalism, not the left.

WHEN the bourgeoisie unite Europe and integrate the European capitalist economy, in their own way and for their own objectives, socialists who learn from Marx, Engels, Luxemburg, Lenin and Trotsky can not propose to roll the film of history backwards, or want Europe to regress to the old "Balkanised" system of antagonistic bourgeois states and alliances. The way forward lies not in a vain and reactionary attempt to unscramble capitalist Europe back into its component parts but in a campaign to democratise it, and for a Socialist United States of Europe.

Nor can we want the British working class to stand aloof from the working class of Europe. We seize the chance to unite the European working class; we propose that the working class should set as its goal the creation of a fully democratic Europe, the overthrow of the bourgeoisie and the creation of the Socialist United States of Europe.

Socialists advocate not British withdrawal from the European Union but the creation of a democratic European parliament, with full powers; British socialists need to unite with European socialists to win it. A EU-wide working-class campaign for such a democratic transformation would help show the working class its own immense strength and convince it of the feasibility of radical social transformation.

BUT how will such a European parliament be achieved? By piecemeal evolution? That is slow, uncertain and blind. It leaves both power and initiative in the hands of the bourgeoisie and their bureaucrats.

When great democratic states have been in the making, a Constituent Assembly or Parliament has been called to work out constitutional arrangements for the new state. That is what the USA and revolutionary France did 200 years ago; what England did at the dawn of Parliamentary sovereignty, over 300 years ago. It is what Europe should do now. The European Union needs a Constituent Assembly.

A European Parliament should be elected to work out a constitutional framework for the United States of Europe. In that way the boundaries between the present national parliaments and the future sovereign European parliament, and similar perplexing questions, can be democratically and publicly worked out.

Campaigning for such a "Constitutional Parliament", the labour movement and the left across Europe would undercut the rightists, the chauvinists and the unreconstructed Stalinists who make legitimate criticisms of the chaotic European political structures the basis for a reactionary attack on European unity and incoherent propaganda for an impossible and reactionary historical regression; whose political work, in practice, whatever they may intend, amounts to trying to make the working class not a progressive but a reactionary alternative to the bourgeoisie.

European unity is better than any other capitalist alternative; the fight for European unity is an irreplacable part of the fight for European socialism. By arguing for a Constituent Assembly the serious pro-European left can point simultaneously the way forwards to a democratic Europe, and towards the Socialist United States of Europe.

Socialists in the General Election

THE Socialist Alliance in the June 2001 General Election gave voters in 98 constituencies the chance to vote for "socialism" and against New Labour. On average, 1.62% of the people who voted in each constituency did so.

We have something to congratulate ourselves for in having organised such a widespread public challenge to Blairism. The Socialist Alliance has little else to congratulate itself for. With very few exceptions our impact on the electorate was not noticeably greater than that which any half-way presentable socialist candidate would have made in any suitable constituency at any time in the last hundred years.

So far, the main significance of the Socialist Alliance lies in its impact on the left, where it has brought a number of tendencies together in a loose collaboration, rather than in its impact on the working class electorate or the broad labour movement. So far, the latter is slight.

Blairism is still at high tide in terms of parliamentary seats. It dropped only 10 seats. But this masks a great deal of disillusionment, and millions of lost votes. Swathes of those who flocked to Blair in 1997 with hope, however faint and faltering in their hearts, simply did not vote in the 2001 General Election. Many of those non-voters were traditional working-class Labour voters, people who have come to think that Labour is no longer, even minimally, their party.

One measure for the performance of the Socialist Alliance is its striking failure to attract more than a tiny proportion of those ex-Labour voters, or of the Labour voters who stayed Labour this time only with extreme reluctance.

The Socialist Alliance did very much worse in the circumstances than we could reasonably have hoped to do.

One factor was the generally low level of confidence and morale in the working class, which works against all large new enterprises. But, beyond that, the brutal truth is that the Socialist Alliance waged a campaign that was shaped and limited by the politics and by the organisational practices of the SWP, which was by far the predominant force within it. It ran a campaign that was, essentially, sectarian towards the broad labour movement.

The central fact of recent working class history, the thing that made an electoral challenge to the Labour Party both necessary and plausible, is the hijacking of the old Labour Party by the Blairites. The labour movement has thus been deprived of its own representation in Parliament for the first time in the last 100 years.

What should, in response to that hijacking, have been the central rallying cry of the Socialist Alliance, labour representation, the need for working class MPs, played very little part in the campaign. Outside of Nottingham East, where the campaign was shaped by

Workers' Liberty and other non-SWPers, and a few other areas, this was something that was, at best, given an occasional mention in small print or the tail-end of speeches here and there.

This campaign was not focused on the biggest event in British working class politics for decades. It did not highlight the need for new measures to secure labour movement parliamentary representation. Instead, the campaign had a curiously timeless quality.

It was motivated on the need for a "socialist alternative". In fact, under headlines about being a "socialist alternative", Socialist Alliance leaflets proposed a few reforms and resistance to New Labour. Instead of striving to convince, and engage working-class voters in honest political debate about why they should no longer vote Labour, and how voting Socialist Alliance could be part of rebuilding a working class political force, the leaflets were designed to advertise the Socialist Alliance as having a collection of policies which the SWP thought would look attractive to ex-Labour voters.

To "front up" the Alliance, they systematically chose showbiz figures, journalists and lawyers, the sort of people that a conventional advertising campaign would use to endorse a product, rather than figures who could symbolise a drive for working-class political representation. Working-class voters are understandably, and reasonably, sceptical of advertising material.

Where a campaign more focused on restoring working class representation was mounted – in Nottingham East and Manchester Withington – the results were among the best achieved (apart from the special cases such as that of the well-known ex-Labour MP, Dave Nellist, in Coventry, and the challenge to Tory defector Shaun Woodward in St Helens) in votes – and also in activist and labour movement impact.

The bulk of the leaflets were shaped by the SWP-dominated national office of the Alliance. The content of the leaflets was, quite apart from the lack of focus on labour representation, largely routine SWP agitation stuff. This was the SWP in reformist mode, rather than its "f**k capitalism", "one solution, revolution" mode. But it was unmistakably the SWP, with its characteristic view that elections and politics are scarcely proper concerns for socialists, and that the fundamental purpose of agitation is to advertise "the party" to the working class.

Even on that level there was disorientation and lack of focus. Albeit in special circumstances, the victory for a local doctor in Kidderminster, who campaigned to save the local hospital, showed how the future of the NHS should have been central to our campaign. Even the need to restore full freedom for trade unions received far less than its proper attention in the campaign.

The "timelessness" and the routine-agitation quality of the Socialist Alliance leaflets reflected the politics of the SWP. It reflected both their general approach to political agitation, and their failure to grasp what has happened in recent working-class politics. In their view – spelled out in the article written by John Rees in _International Socialism_ 90 to orient their members for the Socialist Alliance campaign – "it is an error to suppose that the Labour Party has fundamentally changed its nature. No, the Labour Party has [not] fundamentally changed its character. It is still the political expression of the trade union bureaucracy and it enjoys the support of most organised workers. It is, as Lenin described it, a 'capitalist workers' party'. The fundamental strength of the unions and the strength of their ties with the Labour Party remain considerable."

The whole business of the Socialist Alliance is, therefore, in the SWP's eyes, just another scene in the age-old drama of people "breaking from reformism"; and being reformist, for them, is defined as being "members of, or deeply committed to the values of, the Labour Party..."

The second biggest, albeit semi-detached, group in (or, rather, semi-attached to) the Socialist Alliance, the Socialist Party – formerly Militant – makes the opposite mistake. The SP thinks the old Labour Party is entirely defunct and dismisses even the residual links with the trade unions. This despite the protests by trade union leaders against New Labour's policies of privatistion, showing the union link to be still a potential focus of struggle. But at least they have registered that there is something radically new in New Labour. The SWP have not.

That stops the SWP grasping that labour representation is the central immediate question in working class politics. Their decision to stand candidates for the first time in 20-odd years had more to do with calculation about themselves, and worries about being gazumped by other left factions, than with calculation about what has happened to the Labour Party and therefore to working class political representation.

The blighting effect of SWP predominance on the Socialist Alliance campaign did not stop at politics. Their organisational sectarianism created a certain amount of disruption in the latter period of the campaign, when they suddenly decided that Socialist Alliance campaigners would not canvass door-to-door. Leaflet door-to-door? Yes. Yes, indeed! Do it again and again! Talk to potential voters? No!

This was not just a judgement about the use of resources, of the sort that was reasonable in areas where the Socialist Alliance had very few activists. It was a Party Line, centrally decided and imposed almost everywhere that they were numerically predominant. One high point of this anti-canvassing drive was in Islington South and Finsbury, where the candidate was a *Workers' Liberty* supporter, Janine Booth. There they tried to impose the ban on canvassing through a binding vote of the local Socialist Alliance: there would be NO canvassing! This, to put it delicately, was downright eccentric.

Even SWPers were reduced to speculating about what was going on. Was it just that they wanted to control the flow of new contacts? (Those who responded to a leaflet would contact a central address, rather than talking to a possibly non-SWP individual.) Were they afraid that the doorstep reality would demoralise young SWPers hyped up on "revolution is near" fantasies? Or did they really believe that there were voters waiting only for a leaflet advertising the Socialist Alliance to drop through their letterbox in order to rally to us – and so many of them that there was really no time to talk to them?

The problem is not just the SWP. Very few decisions in the Socialist Alliance have been pushed through only by an SWP numerical majority, or by SWP predominance in the national office. The other groups in the Socialist Alliance have chosen to go along with the SWP. All of them, for example, disagreed with the SWP on canvassing; none of them have argued the issue vigorously within the Alliance.

The Socialist Party has been content to let the SWP run the main Socialist Alliance operation so long as the SP maintains autonomy for its own electoral activities as a sort of semi-attached annexe to the Alliance. The CPGB and Workers' Power have chosen to focus on rather abstract controversies about whether the Socialist Alliance should be more "political" (as against "economistic"), more "revolutionary" (as against "reformist"), or more of a "party" (as against "alliance") – controversies which have little grip on the day-to-day political choices of the Socialist Alliance, and in which the critics are, anyway, by no means always entirely right as against the SWP.

The ISG has adopted the role of friendly adviser to the SWP on how to be non-sectarian, with the manner of an elderly uncle counselling a cherished, vigorous but headstrong nephew. All these groups seem to desire above all to become the "loyal opposition" whose arguments will be accepted by the SWP as meriting attention.

Most of the prominent, unaffiliated activists in the Alliance seem to have chosen a broadly pro-SWP stance – in return getting some individual leeway, and maybe even the chance of some influence on chosen issues – as preferable to what they perceive as the available alternative, being marginalised.

Whatever the explanation for the SWP-imposed "party line" on canvassing, the point is that this strange nonsense and the effects the SWP attempts to impose "the line" had on the campaign – in Islington South, for example – is another measure of how far we have to go before we have in the Socialist Alliance a politically coherent, democratically structured, electorally credible force. That is another way of saying that the left needs to sort itself out. Part of that self-sorting will have to be a learning of the lessons of the General Election campaign in time for next year's local government elections.

Of course, it will take time. No-one could have expected that the left would realign itself instantly or without controversy. But time alone will not sort us out. Only political argument and conflict will. In the months leading up to the Socialist Alliance conference in December, fruitful and relevant controversy should flourish, instead of being smothered under calls to get on with organising for the next demonstration or appeals to our natural inclination to console ourselves by thinking that the General Election result was not so bad after all.

The experience of the French left in elections

By Colin Foster

IN France, unlike Britain, municipal elections attract as much interest as national polls. In the municipal elections of 11 and 18 March 2001, there was a higher turnout (66% at the second round) than in Britain's general election of June 2001; and the revolutionary left scored impressively. *Lutte Ouvrière* (LO) averaged 4.37% over 128 municipalities, and elected 33 municipal councillors. The *Ligue Communiste Révolutionnaire* (LCR), standing in a variety of lists under titles like "100% on the left", got 36 municipal councillors, and those lists, 91 of them, averaged 4.52%. There were 175 municipalities in total where far-left lists of candidates were presented – 44 of them have both LO and LCR-supported lists – covering about 18% of the electorate.

Other recent left election results in France have been equally, or more, impressive - 5.3% in the presidential election of 1995, and 5.2% in the Euro-elections of 1999. How were they achieved? What can we in Britain, much newer to serious electoral activity, learn from France?

France's political system has many differences from Britain's which make simplistic transposition of formulas from one country to another inadvisable. In France there has never been anything like the Labour Party's near-monopoly on working-class political representation. Political party organisation generally is weaker in France than in Britain, allowing all sorts of local peculiarities and splinter-group activity. The Communist Party (CP) used to be an exception, but its once-famous discipline and monolithism has been a thing of the past since the end of the 1980s at latest.

Voting is not by Britain's simple but minority-suppressing "first-past-the-post" system. There are complicated semi-proportional arrangements for local government elections; for a while in the 1980s there was proportional representation in parliamentary elections; and voting is generally in two rounds. The worst-scoring candidates from the first round, and those who withdraw voluntarily in order to assist better-scoring allies, are eliminated from the second, run-off, round. Communist Party and Socialist supporters can vote far-left in the first round, to register a protest, and then return to their own party in the second round.

Besides all that, ever since the great general strike of May-June 1968 the far left in France has been more widely known – reported more by the media, recognised more as an element of the political spectrum – than it is in Britain. In presidential elections it gets a good deal more media time and space than the left is ever likely to get in Britain in the foreseeable future.

The far left's first electoral foray was to run Alain Krivine of the LCR for president in June 1969. He did badly, getting 1.05% of the vote. This proved that to run a well-known candidate associated with a popular cause does not guarantee good results. Krivine was famous from May-June 1968. Evidently, however, the vast majority of the supporters of the great general strike voted for the CP (21%), the Socialist Party (5%), or the left-Socialist PSU (3.6%).

Krivine's campaign was very "revolutionary", very "far-left". No doubt that went down well with the tens of thousands of people, mostly young, with whom the LCR were immediately in contact. With the working-class millions it was different. LO, already much better implanted in the factories than the LCR was, though as yet with a much lower general public profile, supported Krivine, but reported that the workers they talked with in the factories found Krivine's TV speeches wild or incomprehensible.

The lesson was reaffirmed in the 1974 presidential election. Krivine stood again and got only 0.36% of the vote. This time LO also stood their own candidate, Arlette Laguiller. Although she was prominent in a strike that year at the bank where she worked, Crédit Lyonnais, and she attracted some special attention by being the first woman candidate ever for president of France, Laguiller was not nearly as well known to the general public as

Krivine, and her organisation, LO, was smaller and less well-known than the LCR. She won 2.35% of the poll.

Laguiller adopted a different approach from Krivine. She made no secret of being a revolutionary, but she emphatically did not make socialist revolution her election platform. Though she said where she stood on issues when asked, she did not offer a long "shopping list" of demands. Her trademark was (and is) to start all her speeches and television slots with the greeting: "Working women! Working men!" – in place of the traditional opening phrase of General De Gaulle, president from 1958 to 1969, "Frenchmen! Frenchwomen!" Why was she standing? In order to allow workers to express their class opposition to or defiance of the established parties.

Since 1974, LO has deliberately promoted Laguiller as their public spokesperson – their presidential candidate at every election, the signature on their paper's editorial every week, the author of all their statements to the press. It is not exactly "personality politics", however. An unflamboyant middle-aged bank clerk, Laguiller has gained her public profile as a straightforward, unpretentious voice for working-class interests and working-class politics.

Laguiller's eventual "breakthrough", the 5.3% she won in the 1995 presidential election, cannot be put down mainly to cumulative effort in building up her profile. There was no gradual build-up. For twenty years, from 1974 to 1994, LO's other results were all poorer than the 2.35% of 1974. Laguiller won 2.30% in the presidential election of 1981, and 1.99% in 1988; LO's results in other elections varied between 1.11% (legislative elections, 1981) and 2.28% (Euro-elections, 1994).

The high point in the interim was an effort at left unity, in the 1977 municipal elections. Across 56 municipalities – admittedly, only a small, and of course selected, part of the electorate – 3.78% of the vote was won by joint lists of LO, the LCR, and the OCT (a semi-demi-quasi-Maoist-cum-Trotskyist group, which was formed by a split from the LCR in 1970 and later collapsed back into the LCR). In the Euro-elections of 1979, an LO-LCR list won 3.08%.

The Union of the Left, an electoral coalition centred round the Communist Party and the Socialist Party, had been formed in 1973, and much of French politics in the 1970s revolved around whether the coalition would hold together and when and how it would oust the Gaullist right wing, who had been in power since 1958. It did so in May 1981. The Union of the Left promised a markedly more radical programme than any other mainstream-left coalition or party in Europe at that time - sweeping nationalisations, shorter working week, etc. People danced in the streets. In the legislative elections that followed the Left's presidential victory, LO was reduced to 1.11% of the vote.

Until 1981 LO and the LCR had had a broadly similar policy for the second round of elections. Once their own candidates were put out of the race, they supported the candidates of the bigger parties with roots in and links to the organised working class, the Communist Party and the Socialist Party. In the 1980s, this changed. After legislating a few reforms in its first couple of years, the Union of the Left in government did a sharp turnabout in 1983. Its policies were soon almost indistinguishable from the Right's. In fact, between 1986 and 1988, and again between 1993 and 1995, the Left was effectively in coalition with the Right - Mitterrand, the Left's president, ruled in alliance with a right-wing prime minister and parliamentary majority. Since 1997, the Left's prime minister, Lionel Jospin, has ruled in alliance with the Right's president, Jacques Chirac.

LO responded by ceasing to support the Communist Party and the Socialist Party on the second round. The policy was less drastic than it sometimes sounds. LO did not positively call for abstention or a boycott on the second round. It indicated that it had no objection to its voters backing the CP and the SP on the second round (as most of them did), only it could not positively recommend them to. And LO's stance was aimed more at appealing to the more hardbitten members and supporters of the CP – who detested the Union of the Left – than at preaching a general principle of not voting for reformists.

The LCR has, just this year, "caught up with" this policy, saying rather mealy-mouthedly that now it will leave its voters "free to decide for themselves" what to do on the second round. Through the 1980s and 90s, though, it emphatically advocated a CP or SP vote on the second round. This was one factor making LO-LCR unity in elections difficult for most of that time, though there were joint LO-LCR lists in the municipal elections of 1983 (2.16% of the vote).

A more important one was that, as the CP decayed and threw off dissident factions, and different Green groupings emerged, the LCR threw itself into protracted efforts to concoct some sort of new broad left-wing party out of the splinters. LO was scornful of these efforts, and in fact they produced absolutely nothing.

One major debacle was the 1988 presidential election. Pierre Juquin, a former CP leader who had recently quit the party, put his name forward and made a few left-wing speeches. The LCR rushed to support his campaign as a vehicle, so they thought, for pulling together a broad new left. In the event Juquin ran a lacklustre campaign, saying nothing notably more radical than the official CP candidate. The LCR were left as forlorn footsoldiers. The supposed "broad left" Juquin scored only 0.1% more than the avowedly Trotskyist Laguiller.

A lesson of general application, perhaps, is that a serious and patient orientation to the mass base of the traditional working-class parties should not be confused with deferential illusions in once-prominent individual leaders of those parties when they cut loose, even on a vaguely left-wing basis.

Come the 1995 presidential elections, the LCR was still wallowing in confusion. Some of its members wanted to support Laguiller. Others wanted to back the Green candidate, Dominique Voynet (a leftish talker, though since 1997 a minister in a not-very-left-at-all government). Yet others said that the LCR should advise people to vote radical-left – either Laguiller or Voynet; or even either Laguiller, or Voynet, or the CP candidate, Hue – without stating a preference within that spectrum. A few even wanted to back the Socialist Party candidate, Lionel Jospin, straight off. No one policy could command a majority, so the LCR was left with no official policy at all on polling day.

Laguiller won 5.3%, or 1.62 million votes, a score unprecedented for a revolutionary working-class candidate in Europe for many decades. Plainly the reason for this breakthrough was not left unity. (The third of the big left groups in France, the hyper-factional Parti des Travailleurs, which has had occasional electoral sallies of its own over the years – 0.39% for a presidential candidate in 1988, for example – commented only that Laguiller, in its eyes, was as bad as Chirac!)

Nor, as we have seen, was the good score due simply to a cumulative build-up of political profile. It cannot really be put down to a general rise in working-class militancy or shift of opinion to the left, either. The presidential election was won by Jacques Chirac, the candidate of the right; his main rival, the Socialist Party's Lionel Jospin, felt no great need to "talk left"; and the total for all the left-of-Jospin candidates, Laguiller, Hue and Voynet, at 17%, was only slightly up on the 15% left-of-SP vote in 1988. The great mass-strike movement of November-December 1995 came after the presidential election, not before.

One novelty in 1995 is that Laguiller added to her bedrock message the advocacy of an "emergency plan for the workers and the unemployed", a deliberately honed-down package of transitional demands. She called for the expropriation of profit-making enterprises which cut jobs; a stop to government subsidies to big business, an increase in tax on profits and wealth, expansion and more jobs in public services, and a general increase in wages and social benefits; and she explained all these as first measures of workers' control over the economy.

The idea caught on, but to attribute the big rise in the far-left vote entirely to that is surely to overestimate the power of slogans. In any case, in the municipal elections later in 1995, LO, with exactly the same politics, won only 2.8% – better than in any previous municipal campaign since the joint LO-LCR-OCT effort of 1977, but much less than the presidential 5.3%.

Rising discontent among CP members – many of whom would say openly that they were voting for Laguiller, without any intention of following that up by leaving the CP and joining LO – was another factor, but again cannot be the whole of it. The CP vote, against long-term trends, went up slightly between the presidential elections of 1988 and of 1995, from 6.9% to 8.7%.

In any case, the electoral breakthrough happened – maybe due to a combination of rising working-class resentment which the established parties were slow to recognise, a further erosion of CP discipline, and a politically well-focused LO campaign. LO followed it up by raising the call for a broad new workers' party, but in such a dour and highly-conditional way that it was almost impossible for anything to come of it. Nothing did come of it except the expulsion from LO, in early 1997, of a faction who took the "new workers' party" call more seriously than the rest. Paradoxically, the main far-left force to gain from the general revival

17

after 1995 was not LO, but that same LCR which had been so disoriented at the time of the presidential election.

Despite LO's relatively disappointing score in the 1995 municipals, a joint LO-LCR list for the Euro-elections in 1999 got 5.2% of the vote, and five Euro-MPs. And, as we have seen, the municipal elections this March yielded 4.37% for LO, 4.52% for lists supported by the LCR.

The impression that the LCR outscored LO — which would be unprecedented — is, as we shall see, not quite accurate, but without doubt this is the LCR's best-ever election result by a large margin.

In French municipal elections, it is necessary to stand a full list of candidates in each municipality in order to stand at all, though, on the semi-proportional system used, it is certain that no more than the top two or three names on any minority list have any chance of being elected. LO, therefore, in order to stand in its 128 municipalities, had to find no fewer than 5,300 candidates — in other words, many more candidates than it has members, or even organised sympathisers. LO had to canvass door-to-door, not just to win votes, but in order to find its candidates in the first place.

Less determined groupings have an obvious incentive to combine with each other to put up lists. Thus the LCR-supported lists were an enormously varied patchwork of coalitions, some led by the LCR and more or less reflecting its politics, others only having a few LCR names somewhere down a list led by people with quite other politics. At least five lists were joint lists of the LCR and the local CP. (LO has also run occasional joint lists with local CP groups in the past, though not this time.) The cumbersome titles of some others indicate the variety: in the 11th arrondissement of Paris, for example, the list was entitled: "Paris 100% on the left, for real change in Paris and in the 11th, list supported by Citizens' Alternative, the LCR, and trade-union and campaign activists of the 11th." Plainly a snappy signboard is not a precondition for electoral success in France... (Nor, to judge from election leaflets reproduced by LO in a special issue of its magazine dealing with the elections, is smart graphic design. LO, however, has over the years developed an effective line in posters and small stickers with short one-sentence comments — 20 words or so — rather than slogans.)

In the past such coalition-building efforts by the LCR have brought little joy, often winning smaller scores than direct candidates of the LCR itself. This time the LCR stood in its own name in 55 cantonal (smaller local-government) elections, and won an average of 3.07% — better than its previous scores, but less than the 4.52% average in the municipals, and less than LO's average of 5.01% in the cantonals where it stood.

Over the past couple of years the LCR's activity has refocused onto what the LCR itself can do now — with allies where appropriate rather than on vapid projections of a future new broad left party. Its leaders have shelved plans to give their organisation a new and blander name, Revolutionary Democratic Left, and the LCR has developed a more vigorous tone to its politics. That must have helped.

LO, scornful of the LCR's coalition-building efforts in the past, has been equally scornful this time. It freely concedes that it was a first "real success on the electoral level for the LCR". But, LO protests, "rallying together some ecologists, some anti-globalisers, some anti-neo-liberals, and a few others, and baptising them 'objectively anti-capitalist' even though they do not call themselves that, is perhaps easier today, but it is not the road that we want to take. The relative success of the LCR is not the success that we wish for.

"We do not consider it a political success in the sense of the building of a proletarian revolutionary party, a party which will be 100% communist and not 100% 'on the left'... 'left' and 'right', these days, are very devalued terms, or even devoid of sense."

Does "communist" have a clearer positive sense than "left", after 70 years of Stalinism? We may doubt it. And we may question whether LO's orientation to the more hardbitten core of CP activists is necessarily a better tactical choice (and tactical choice it is) than the LCR's to different left-wing sensibilities.

LO's bedrock argument for a positive working-class political profile, as against the LCR's penchant for the "anti-capitalist" or "anti-neo-liberal", does however have much to vindicate it, both in terms of basic politics and in terms of electoral results over the longer term. And its preference for a terse, honed-down class message has much to recommend it over the LCR's bias towards filling its leaflets with a welter of good causes.

The new turn of the SWP

By Martin Thomas

"Sometimes differentiation is essential if a revolutionary organisation is to survive in an unfavourable political environment... In the 1980s... the SWP [took] refuge in the Marxist tradition as protection against the right-wing climate in society" (Alex Callinicos SWP internal document).

"The SWP tailored its approach accordingly, placing a high priority on insulating its members from the rightward drift in the movement, and stressing the virtues of the revolutionary tradition as a bulwark against pessimism and defeatism" (John Rees, International Socialism no.90).

BUT now, so the SWP says, since the Seattle protests against the World Trade Organisation in November-December 1999, the tide has turned. "Revolutionaries will have to... shake off the habits they developed during the 1980s and the first half of the 1990s, when right-wing ideas were in the ascendant and it was therefore essential to protect Marxist ideas and organisation from a hostile political environment... [Now] it is more often through being the most dynamic and militant force in building the movement... that we distinguish ourselves and draw new people towards us. Of course, this process leads to arguments, but these develop from the concrete situation rather than being produced by some abstract 'duty' to disagree with everyone else..." (Callinicos).

Tony Cliff, then the leader of the SWP, argued from April 1978 that the class struggle was in a great "downturn". From about 1979-80 the "downturn thesis" shaped SWP activity. The trade union movement had become bureaucratised right down to shop-steward level. Large political enterprises, like the rank-and-file rebellion in the Labour Party which exploded between 1979 and 1982, were meaningless froth, doomed to failure, because there were no large working-class industrial struggles to underpin them. Socialists should spurn the "time-consuming wrangles" in the Labour Party and (after 1982) attempts to build rank-and-file movements across unions. Instead they should "build the party" in "insulation" by advocating "the Marxist tradition", recruiting students, and focusing on such small industrial battles as did exist.

No more of that now! The SWP are now anxious to be the "best builders" of all sorts of movements. Where they used to use almost exclusively SWP events to "rally their troops", now they rally them for more broadly-sponsored activities. Even if the initiative is primarily SWP they take pains to give it a broader front. They are relaunching rank-and-file papers in trade unions, with non-SWPers on the editorial boards, and getting involved in the union left opposition groups.

They bill their new initiative, "Globalise Resistance", as "the broadest possible anti-capitalist movement bringing together NGOs, students, trade unionists and direct action activists of all shades". In the left-wing coalition that fought 98 seats in the June 2001 parliamentary election, the Socialist Alliance, the SWP claim to be the greatest champions of making the Alliance broad and welcoming to reformists keen to fight for immediate socialist priorities as well as to revolutionaries.

Thousands of socialists have common-sense reasons to welcome the SWP's turn, if only for the increase it brings in ordinary human civility within the left. But the bustling let's-not-argue, let's-get-on-and-build-the-movement approach begs some questions. What exactly is "the movement"? How do we decide how and what to build, if not by argument?

In the final parts of this article, I will look at the logic and implications of the general turn announced by Callinicos and Rees, away from "taking refuge in the Marxist tradition" and towards being "the best builders". First, however, I will look specifically at the two main areas where the SWP has made its new turn: the "new anti-capitalism", and the Socialist Alliance.

1

THE demonstration in Seattle against the World Trade Organisation in November-December 1999 has inspired many thousands across the world. It has provided a focus and model for the beginnings of a new generation of radicals, disgusted by the arrogance of exultant big capital and free of the depression soaked into many of their elders by the defeats of the 1980s and the triumph of private-profit economics in Eastern Europe and the USSR.

Seattle and its sequels have helped galvanise some trade-union action, too. In Sydney, in June 2001, unions responded to plans by the New South Wales state Labor government to cut workers' compensation for injuries on the job by organising a picket of Parliament to stop Labor MPs going in to vote for the plans. Blockades by anti-capitalist demonstrators outside the World Economic Forum in Melbourne last September, and outside stock exchanges this May, must have helped inspire this action.

But a series of demonstrations, even good ones, to "shut down" the IMF, the World Bank, the G8, and so on, do not amount to a strategy, or a solid basis for an ongoing movement. And they certainly do not amount to a "new mood" right across the working class. Strike figures in Britain are still near their lowest levels since records began. Trade-union membership has suffered a more protracted and serious decline than ever before, and it is not yet certain that it has "bottomed out". The modest showing for the Socialist Alliance in the June 2001 general election and the huge abstention rate (41% overall, and much higher among the working class and among youth) indicate a low general level of working-class political confidence. In several other countries – France, the USA, South Korea, Indonesia, all in their different ways – the current trends are more promising than in Britain, but in none of them is working-class political confidence positively high.

To recognise the facts is not to bow down to them, to fail to see the exceptions, contradictions, or signs of movement, or to think that change cannot come quickly. Nor is it an excuse for dawdling or a sniffy attitude to the "new anti-capitalist" activists. But a realistic grasp of where we are, and how far we have yet to go, is a necessary part of orienting ourselves politically, both in the bigger picture and with the "new anti-capitalist" youth.

"Comrades, the revolution has begun!" So George Monbiot told the "Globalise Resistance" fringe meeting at the National Union of Students conference in spring 2001, and the SWP applauded him enthusiastically. Even taking Monbiot's claim as a flourish, not to be interpreted too literally, it just is not true.

If the SWP was cheering for "revolution" not so much in the belief that it had really begun, but in the hope of bringing it closer, then that is not much better than dressing in green to make spring come. If there is no revolution under way – and there isn't – then to pretend helps no-one. In fact it works against doing what can and must be done.

If revolution of some sort really were brewing, then the job of Marxists would be not to cheer for it but to fight for clarity on what sort of revolution, made by whom. In Portugal in 1974-5, when there really was revolutionary ferment, every windbag and opportunist was for "revolution". The Socialist Party – the main political prop of bourgeois power, as it turned out – called itself "revolutionary socialist". The leader of the main liberal bourgeois party called himself a "Leninist". The job of Marxists was to cut through the bluster and focus on the substance – independent working-class politics.

However important, inspiring and valuable the demonstrations, socialist revolution cannot emerge just from more and more demonstrations to "end this" and "shut down that". Working-class revolutions are distinguished from all previous revolutions – where the people come out on the streets, and fight heroically, but have no means of systematically planning and collectively controlling the results – by mass organisation, preparation, and consciousness. The Marxist concept of socialist revolution is distinguished from anarchist and populist (all-the-people-together) concepts by its understanding of the centrality of independent working-class organisation, preparation and consciousness.

In *International Socialism* 90, John Rees writes: "Anti-capitalist movements are giving a particular coloration to every other movement of resistance against the system... Trade unionists are now being thrust into a politicised world..." But the "new anti-capitalist" moods and mobilisations are nowhere near definite enough, and big enough, to define the "world" for trade unionists. They are in fact moods and mobilisations – encompassing a vast variety of groups, from the social-democratic/liberal petitioner across to the wildest direct-actionist, with many socialists or potential socialists as well – rather than a single movement with a cohesion sufficient to set the frame for trade unionists.

To think otherwise is to have our proportions all wrong. The workplaces, the trade unions, and the working-class neighbourhoods are the big picture, and the "anti-capitalist" moods and mobilisations a valuable leaven and source of activists – not vice versa . A real "new movement" – a revitalised workers' movement – will be built through painstaking activity in the workplaces and on the doorsteps, and through thorough discussion and education, not through any amount of loudspeakering about the "spirit of Seattle".

Beyond the demonstrations, Alex Callinicos claims the Tobin Tax movement in France, ATTAC, as the prime example worldwide, of a "more or less organised political milieu where a new left is beginning to take shape". But what sort of class demand is the Tobin Tax? This proposal for a small percentage tax on foreign-exchange transactions, made by the very mainstream US economist James Tobin, is certainly more welcome than calls for cuts in public-service spending, or increased indirect taxes on working-class consumers. We do not need to hector or denounce Tobin Tax supporters. We do need to formulate an independent assessment of the issue from a working-class viewpoint, rather than just throwing in every halfway impressive-looking manifestation of "anti-capitalism" as evidence for incipient revolutionary insurgence.

The Tobin Tax it is neither a realistic interim "quick-fix" – to be effective, it would have to be implemented by every major government in the world acting simultaneously, or else foreign-exchange business would simply move to sites without the tax – nor a step towards mobilising the working class against the bosses, nor a fundamental challenge to the privileges of capital.

If the working class were strong and coordinated enough worldwide to enforce the Tobin Tax, then it would be strong and coordinated to focus on measures much more central to class relations – and it should do so.

Transitional demands along those lines might include: international union rights, enforced by demanding a "made by union labour" mark on all goods handled; opening the books of the multinationals; information and veto powers for international shop stewards' committees over multinationals' investment plans; action by international shop stewards' committees to demand "levelling up" of wages and conditions; aid from rich countries to poor ones under the control of workers' and community organisations in those countries, and along the lines of workers' reconstruction plans worked out by those organisations; taxing the rich in countries where industry is shutting down to finance workers' reconversion and reconstruction plans there; and so on.

Without sectarianism or pedantry, it is the job of Marxists to criticise, explain and argue politics. Against global big capital? Yes. But "global good, local good"? "Big bad, small good"? "Multinational bad, national good"? "European Union bad, nation-state not so bad"? No. For us, the real axis is workers against capital, not "ordinary people" against "the multinationals". We are not against globalisation, or European integration, or a European single currency. We are for a workers' struggle for social levelling-up and political democracy across Europe, against the bosses' social levelling-down and bureaucratism. We are for workers' globalisation against capitalist globalisation.

The SWP, however, uses its picture of the "new anti-capitalist" mobilisations as "almost a revolution" to rationalise a different approach: on the one hand, frantic instructions to build the movement as wide as possible, and not to risk political criticism or discussion in case they slow things down; on the other, abstract counterpositions of "revolution" to "reform". The space in between, which should be filled by politics, it leaves empty.

One example: in May 2001, in Australia, the collectives set up around the "new anti-capitalist" blockade of the World Economic Forum in Melbourne in September 2000 organised a follow-up activity – blockades of the Stock Exchange buildings in the main cities. What demands should the blockades make? The ISO, Australian satellite of the SWP, argued that we should make no demands at all – only some general slogan like "our world is not for sale" – because otherwise we would "narrow down the movement".

And what does "revolution" mean if the street demonstrations in Seattle, Prague and Nice are already almost a revolution? Slogans like the SWP's "Rebel! Resist! F**k capitalism!" or

"Anti-capitalism: reform or revolution?" point not in a Marxist direction but towards a more militant version of anarchist and populist concepts.

The SWP also claims that to point to "destroying the IMF" or "smashing the WTO", rather than to "reforming" them, is to grasp the gist of revolution as against reform. But this misses the point. Of course the IMF and the WTO are vile capitalist institutions. What else would they be, when their job is to coordinate the capitalist world market? If they could somehow be separated off from the body of capitalism and "smashed" separately, it would get us no further forward. Either the big capitalist governments would set up replacements, different in detail but similar in essence. Or they would not — in which case capitalism would regress into a world of trade blocs and high trade barriers. To change world capitalism from the "top" — IMF, WTO — downwards is possible neither by "reform" nor by "smashing".

"In any case," as Lenin wrote in 1917, "the slogan of the moment on the eve of the new revolution, during it, and on the morrow of it, must be proletarian organisation." There is no substitute. It means, not being stand-offish towards the "new anti-capitalist" youth, but understanding that the workplaces, the unions, and the labour movement are central.

2

THE Socialist Alliance is an electoral coalition, involving the Alliance for Workers' Liberty, five other left groups, and a number of individual activists or more-or-less long-standing local circles, alongside the SWP. The SWP is the dominant force in its national office. It stood a slate in the Greater London Authority elections of 2000, and 98 candidates in the General Election of June 2001.

Its origins go back before Seattle. Talks for an electoral coalition of the left in the 1999 Euro-elections started late in 1998. The main initial participants were the Alliance for Workers' Liberty, the Socialist Party, and the Independent Labour Network which had been set up by the left Euro-MPs sacked by New Labour, Ken Coates and Hugh Kerr. The ILN would never come to much, but that was not clear at the time. After a while, the SWP joined in. It went as far as agreeing a joint manifesto for the London Euro-elections.

When the SWP peeled off, at a late stage, and instead supported Arthur Scargill's Socialist Labour Party in the Euro-elections, the remaining groups decided to back off from running candidates. But connections remained. And choices remained for the SWP.

If they did not get involved in the process of building a left electoral coalition, they would sooner or later see an effective one formed without them. They would be gazumped — stuck with voting Blair-Labour "without illusions" while others presented an attractive alternative. Or they would have to try to outdo such a coalition in direct competition — and probably fail. In the late 1970s the SWP ran a number of by-election candidates, only to retreat in confusion when they were easily outscored in direct competition by a much smaller group, the IMG (forerunner of Socialist Outlook). The quasi-anarchist politics expressed by the SWP in such slogans as "One solution, revolution!", "F**k capitalism", or "General Strike Now!" do not make for effective electioneering.

Only one choice remained for the SWP: to join the Socialist Alliance and hegemonise it. They have done that. But the Socialist Alliance is almost exclusively a regroupment of an older generation of activists. Its talk in its leaflets, on the streets, and on the doorsteps is not of "Reform or revolution" or "F**k capitalism". On the contrary, it orients — through necessity and good sense — to core immediate working-class issues of public services, jobs, housing, wages, conditions. The SWP, far from contesting that orientation, has used its weight to push the Alliance towards a downright minimalist "old Labour" bias. And the Alliance's electoral results, far from signalling the emergence of a big new left, have given sober proof of how marginal the left still is: 1.62% average over the 98 constituencies.

The Alliance's electoral activity, even with its poor results, makes sense if we understand the transformation of Labour politics under Blair. Building on the trade unions' defeats under the Tories, he has transformed the Labour Party profoundly, from the top down, to silence working-class voices within it and thus largely to abolish working-class political representation in Britain. Our job, as socialists, is to fight to reconstitute working-class political representation on a new basis, both by stirring up the trade unions to use their remaining positions within the New Labour structures to assert themselves politically despite and against Blair and — given the narrowness of those structures — by promoting pioneer socialist and independent working-class candidates in the open electoral arena.

But how does all this make sense in the SWP's scheme? Their own accounts of what they are doing with the Socialist Alliance are full of muddle. Here, where the SWP's aerated generalisations come up against the hard facts of numbers, votes, and trade-union decisions, the contradictions are glaring.

They claim that the Socialist Alliance is just another of the "dimensions" along which "the anti-capitalist movement manifests itself". Reviewing those "dimensions", Callinicos writes: "The Socialist Alliances and the Globalise Resistance conferences in Britain have brought together two overlapping constituencies — those inspired by the anti-globalisation movement and Labour Party supporters disillusioned by the experience of the Blair government." He adds: "The way the Socialist Alliances in Britain have brought together revolutionaries from hitherto bitterly opposed Trotskyist tendencies alongside left reformists from a traditional Labourist background in very effective common activity is an indication of the kind of realignments under way. This is part of the larger flux characteristic of the anti-capitalist movement itself."

Rees: "The anti-capitalist movement is of... central importance to the crisis of reformism. It provides an alternative ideology and an alternative political home for reformist activists. This home too may only be temporary, but it is at least a house where those breaking from reformism to the left and revolutionaries can co-operate to build a stronger movement... The same general point can be made about the Socialist Alliances that have tried to provide an electoral alternative to the left of New Labour." He describes what he sees as the target group which the Socialist Alliance should organise: "a large floating population of left wingers, many of whom have already left or been driven out of the Labour Party, and others who remain members but keep their heads down, who are looking for a socialist alternative to Blairism. They are enthused by the new mood of resistance symbolised by the anti-capitalist demonstrations and share its values..."

Rees argues further that it is an "error" to suppose that "the Labour Party has fundamentally changed its nature". No, "the Labour Party has [not] fundamentally changed its character. It is still the political expression of the trade union bureaucracy and it enjoys the support of most organised workers. It is, as Lenin described it, a 'capitalist workers' party'... The fundamental strength of the unions and the strength of their ties with the Labour Party remain considerable." Moreover: "It seems premature... to conclude that Blair is more right wing than all his political ancestors. Neither are the policies of the Labour Government more right wing than those of Jim Callaghan's government in the 1970s."

For Rees, what is happening with the increasing working-class alienation from New Labour, and the increasing willingness of an important though as yet relatively small layer of activists to look for working-class electoral alternatives, is not a matter of New Labour moving to the right and away from the working class. It is a matter of the working class and the activists, "enthused by the new mood of resistance symbolised by the anti-capitalist demonstrations", moving to the left, indeed "breaking from reformism to the left".

How Rees squares this with his off-hand comment on "the evident contempt with which New Labour treats the unions", I do not know. However right-wing and treacherous previous Labour governments were, they did not do that. On the most abstract level Labour is still residually a bourgeois workers' party. But its shift within that general formula has been huge.

A further attempt by Rees to define the post-Seattle "new left" which the SWP sees the Socialist Alliance as targeting explains a bit of the confusion. "Thousands of new activists are moving into political activity... The majority of these activists are clearly not revolutionary socialists... But neither are they convinced reformists in the sense that they are members of, or deeply committed to the values of, the Labour Party... They are likely to share many of the sentiments of more openly committed anti-capitalist activists..." (emphasis added).

With the "new anti-capitalist" mobilisations, the SWP takes direct action on the streets, or a desire to "smash" the IMF, as proof of almost-revolutionary politics. With the Socialist Alliance, it takes "breaking from Labour" as proof that people are "breaking from reformism from the left", and becoming, at least, suitable house-mates for the revolutionaries. The "dialectical" thought seems to be that any set of politics, however limited or indeed reformist, becomes *de facto* a "break with reformism" as long as it can attract people "enthused by the new spirit of resistance" and thus help them "break from Labour". All the Alliance really needs, politically, is a skilled team of graphic designers and slogan-writers, and a dictionary of old Labour policies for them to work from... Discussion, debate, developed policies – those are for "sectarians".

Where serious discussion cannot be sidestepped, in the unions, the SWP is utterly disoriented. In May, the Fire Brigades Union voted to democratise its political fund by opening up the possibility of the union giving money to candidates in line with union policy standing against New Labour. The SWP rushed out a Socialist Alliance broadsheet headlined "Making the break with New Labour" and calling on readers to put resolutions in their union branches to "make the break with New Labour". To disaffiliate? But the FBU had not disaffiliated. And for unions to disaffiliate now, rather than insist on using their voices at Labour Party conference and in the National Executive to challenge the Blair Government's plans to privatise public services, would be a cop-out rather than a militant action. To the SWP, it seems, anything that can be called a "break with Labour" is a quasi-revolutionary step. In the real world, a union "breaking with Labour" in that way might well just be enlarging its options to make alliances with the Lib-Dems.

Anti-Labourism, in British politics, is no more sufficient in itself than "anti-corporate" feeling is in world politics.

3

THE general scheme for Marxist tactics sketched by Callinicos and Rees, so we saw at the start of this article, is: in downturns, "take refuge" and "insulate" yourself in the Marxist tradition; in upturns, tone down criticisms, be more pragmatic, and distinguish yourself by being the "most dynamic and militant force in building the movement". In both phases, what the scheme omits is thought-out politics. In the first phase, the "Marxist tradition" is supposed to "insulate" the activists from the uncongenial politics around them, rather than equipping them to intervene; in the second, general "anti-corporate" feeling or anti-Labourism will do service for politics, so long as they seem to "build the movement".

Marxist theory is not a species of thermal underwear, to be worn to keep warm in winter but put back in the drawer when the mass-action spring arrives. It is not a dogma or a revelation, but a guide to action; action, in its turn, is a guide to theory. Upturns in struggle increase the urgency of attention to Marxist theory, rather than decreasing it.

High class struggle generates more action requiring guidance, more choices and turning-points, richer experiences to learn from, wider confidence and keenness to explore ideas. When "socialism" and "revolution" become the "conventional wisdom", we need more, not less, theoretical sharpness, in order to cut through the waffle, deceit, and ambiguity.

On the other hand, times when the working-class movement is emerging for the first time, or beginning to re-emerge from depression, are those when Engels' "pragmatic" recommendations are apt. "The great thing is to get the working class to move as a class; that once obtained, they will soon find the right direction, and all who resist... will be left out in the cold with small sects of their own... Our theory is not a dogma but the exposition of a process of evolution, and that process involves successive phases... What the [theoretically-educated socialists] ought to do is to act up to their own theory... to go in for any real general working-class movement, accept its *faktische* starting point as such and work it gradually up to the theoretical level by pointing out how every mistake made, every reverse suffered, was a necessary consequence of mistaken theoretical views in the original programme; they ought, in the words of *The Communist Manifesto*, to represent the movement of the future in the movement of the present. But above all give the movement time to consolidate, do not make the inevitable confusion of the first start worse confounded by forcing down people's throats things which at present they cannot properly understand, but which they soon will learn."

It is true that a solid base of theoretical understanding is more necessary to sustain morale in disappointing times than in times of upsurge; that Marxist organisations have to put more "against-the-grain" effort into theoretical education in low times than in high; and that when class struggle is warming up anew, we often have to unlearn habits of stiffness and reserve forced on us in previous cold times. But if those are drops of truth in the scheme sketched by Callinicos and Rees – "theoretical" in downturns, "pragmatic" in upturns – they are drops in a bucketful of error.

If theory is a guide to action, then the wider and richer the possibilities of action, the more urgently relevant theory becomes. For Callinicos and Rees, evidently, theory is something else. It is more a substitute for action than a guide to it. It is an instrument for holding together an organisation in hard times. It serves socialists somewhat as the Bible is supposed to serve Christians, by giving us comforting words which afford "refuge" and "insulation" from the wicked world around us.

Lenin famously wrote: "Without revolutionary theory there can be no revolutionary movement. This idea cannot be insisted upon too strongly at a time when the fashionable preaching of opportunism goes hand in hand with an infatuation for the narrowest forms of practical activity." The background was "upturn" – the rapid but diffuse expansion of working-class militancy and of the Marxist movement in Russia at the end of the 19th century. The opportunism Lenin was concerned with was, in his words, "not an ailment that comes with decline, but one... that comes with growth," a time when "the wide spread of Marxism was accompanied by a certain lowering of the theoretical level".

The Callinicos-Rees view of theory is a neat mirror-image of a view of "calls to action" criticised by Lenin at the same time. He polemicised against one Martynov, who wanted to separate off "agitation" as a special and prioritised form of socialist activity, meaning "the call upon the masses to undertake definite, concrete actions" as distinct from overall "revolutionary explanation". For Lenin, "the 'call', as a single act, either naturally and inevitably supplements the theoretical treatise, propagandist pamphlet, and agitational speech, or represents a purely executive function." Theory and the various forms of socialist advocacy, smaller-audience and more complex or larger-audience and simpler, were all parts of one integrated, consistent whole. Martynov separated off "calls to action" because he wanted to stress "measures that 'promise certain palpable results' (or demands for social reforms...)" at the expense of broader socialist argument.

For the SWP, theory, propaganda, agitation, and calls to action all become detachable, separable instruments of "party-building". Theory is useful to keep the activists together in hard times; calls to action enable them to promote themselves as the best and most militant builders of the movement in good times. And it is perfectly permissible that "tactics contradict principles", as the SWP's longtime leader Tony Cliff put it when justifying their turn to "Britain out of Europe" agitation in 1971. For authentic Marxism is substituted what Sean Matgamna, in a previous issue of this magazine, has called "Apparatus Marxism", Marxism as a wardrobe of alternative costumes which the "party" apparatus puts on, takes off, or combines according to gate-receipt calculations.

On one level, it could be said that the SWP's approach simply enlarges out of all proportion the "normal" distance there must always be between fundamental theory and daily agitation. Immediate slogans can never be read off from basic theory straight away, with no more ado. Some element of judging what is best to "catch the mood" is always necessary. But this "enlargement" makes the distance so great as to lose sight of the Marxist notion that the job of revolutionaries is to strive constantly for greater accuracy, consistency, and overview in politics, and replace it by a manipulative approach. It shapes a "party" which has no will for or training in consistent politics – one which will therefore waver and shilly-shally in any complex and difficult test – and one which acts in the "movement of the present" not as a consistent and principled representative of the "movement of the future" but only as a narrow-minded competitor for factional advantage.

In a Marxist understanding, we need a revolutionary party because we need those activists who have committed themselves in advance of the rest of the working class to work together, consistently and systematically, to clarify our ideas and to make those ideas available, amidst and against the welter of bourgeois ideas, to the working class as it comes forward in struggle. "The Communists, therefore, are on the one hand practically, the most advanced and resolute section of the working-class parties of every country, that section which pushes forward all others; on the other hand, theoretically, they have over the great mass of the proletariat the advantage of clearly understanding the lines of march, the conditions, and theultimate general results of the proletarian movement."

The SWP, however, operates with a quite different view of the need for a revolutionary party as primarily the need for centralised organisation. This has recently been summarised in *Socialist Review* no. 248 by Chris Bambery.

"Again and again the working class has been defeated not because it lacked strength, but because it lacked the centralised leadership and clarity of the ruling class. In the last instance capitalist power rests ultimately with the general staff of the armed forces and the elite troops they control. To take power we need our own general staff, its own centralised organisation and leadership...

"Only a revolutionary party can provide the centralised organisation and leadership without which the struggle will end in defeat. [The revolutionary party's] task is to act as a stimulus to workers' struggles, and to give them a coherence and direction which they would otherwise lack, to aim them at the apparatus of capitalist state power. Socialist organisation is forced to mirror the centralised structures of the capitalist state it is out to overthrow."

The argument here completely misses the difference between the working-class socialist revolution and previous revolutions. All revolutions stem from mass struggles and require, in some form, in some way, and at some point, a centralised leadership to pull together the energies of those struggles and use them to overthrow the existing state power and replace it by a new one.

The workers' revolution is different because in it the revolutionary mass force, the working class, is not just the means by which a new exploiting class replaces an old one. It emancipates itself. It is not just a source of miscellaneous destructive energy to be harnessed by a general staff. It can generate its own coherence and direction. It can create its own "counter-state" (workers' councils). But it also needs far more clarity of thought than previous revolutionary classes, because it must reconstruct society consciously. Clarity of thought always requires study and long-term effort. But the working class lives in capitalist society as its basic slave class, deprived of leisure and education, bombarded daily with bourgeois ideas. Mass struggles generate an instinctive striving towards different ideas – but that striving can find shape in an adequate counter-theory only if the activist minority who become committed to revolutionary struggle in advance of the rest of the class have set themselves to studying, educating, and clarifying alternatives to bourgeois ideas, and making those alternatives available.

Forget all that, regard the revolutionary party only as an apparatus to "centralise" struggles, and the use of theory, propaganda, agitation and calls to action all as detachable instruments for "party-building" makes perfect sense. Every gambit to expand and to hold together the organisational machine which will centralise the struggles is good; every criticism on grounds of political logic is mere "sectarian" pedantry.

That was true in the 1980s, when the SWP annoyed many by its reckless "insulated" factionalism. It also true in the year 2001, when the SWP impresses and pleases many, in the wider left and in its own ranks too, by its new desire for "broadness".

4

I DO not argue that the SWP's turn is merely a controlled shift from one sets of sails to another, with the same ship and the same voyage, or that it has what the US military call a clear "exit strategy". Significantly, the turn is not – despite what the passages I have quoted from Callinicos and Rees suggest – the SWP shifting from what it sees as "downturn" in the class struggle to what it sees as "upturn". It is, on the contrary, a rather frantic and incoherent effort to replace failed attempts at an orientation for the "upturn" with what the SWP leaders hope will be a more successful package. It was Tony Cliff's last bequest to the SWP before his death in April 2000, and it is not at all clear that his heirs know what to do it.

The SWP dropped full-strength "downturnism" as long ago as October 1984. Four weeks into the 1984-5 miners' strike, Tony Cliff wrote: "The strike... is like a car that stalls at every set of traffic lights... The miners' strike is an extreme example of what we in the Socialist Workers' Party have called the 'downturn' in the movement." The SWP cried disaster for the strike at every turn, and refused to join the miners' support groups ("left-wing Oxfam"). By October 1984, though, it had to do a partial and unacknowledged U-turn. During the real "downturn", after the miners' defeat, the SWP's "downturnism" never had the same brio as it had during the relatively fizzy 1979-84!

The SWP explicitly announced the end of the "downturn" and its replacement, so they reckoned, by a "new mood of anger", as far back as June 1988. In March 1991 they saw "a clear shift in the political situation... major opportunities for us to grow as a revolutionary party... deepened discontent"; in October 1992 they considered the downturn so far behind them that they launched the call "General Strike Now!" on the back of two big demonstrations against pit closures; and in February 1994 SWP placards on a big student demonstration in London read "Paris 1968, London 1994".

If anything, the SWP's whoop-it-up claims for a "new mood" are rather more moderate now than they were 10 years ago. What is different is that then they hoped to build on the new mood simply by taking the "downturn" SWP, with its "insulated" self-obsession, and shifting the tone of its agitation. It worked for a while. Then recruitment sagged. Cliff, always ready with improvisation, had tried out a different tack as early as 1993, when he set his German co-thinkers to launch a loosely-defined, action-oriented faction inside the Social-Democratic youth (*Linksruck*). What the SWP is doing now could be called "the *Linksruck* turn in Britain", only adapted to different circumstances.

Even in Germany, where it won a good few new recruits, the "*Linksruck* turn" scattered a large part of the (longstanding) organisation the SWP had there beforehand. Though the weight of the SWP's apparatus, and its position as the biggest group on the far left, give it more protection through inertia than a smaller group in another country could have, to try even a modified version of the same sort of turn on the SWP itself is more than a routine tactical recalibration. The shift from one variant of "Apparatus Marxism" to another is not nearly as simple an operation politically as it is abstractly and intellectually. It may well mean the SWP entering crises from which many interesting new things will emerge. But it is not, in and of itself, a shift towards a more authentic Marxist conception of building a revolutionary party. Not even a small one. Not even a beginning.

Evidence? I cite four items. One, the SWP's proclaimed concepts of how to organise itself for its new tactics. Two, the SWP's excommunication of the ISO-USA. Three, the SWP's concept of "the united front without political debate", exemplified by its agitation against the Kosova war. And four, the way that the SWP, and the desire of others on the left to see the SWP as "reformed", has shaped the internal life of the Socialist Alliance, as exemplified in the argument about canvassing in the 2001 general election campaign.

5

● IN an orientation document circulated shortly before the June General Election, the SWP Central Committee said: "We have abandoned the old party branches, which only involved a minority of comrades, because these have often been in practice sectarian barriers to our wider intervention... They tended to involve only a small number of members in attendance and activity, while the majority of members have not seen them as the centre of their activity... There is no going back to the old structures... Many comrades are involved in many activit[ies] and meetings every week and therefore have little time or inclination for small internalised meetings." And instead? Despite abandoning branches, the SWP still wants "very detailed direction of our work and interventions:" "Our organisation needs to be... highly centralised". The "high centralisation" and "very detailed direction" is to be achieved through full-time district organisers and their district committee members distributing *Socialist Worker* to every member and giving them "a clear direction and push... which involves polemical arguments where necessary."

The right to detailed discussion of politics in "small internalised meetings" is thus made a monopoly of the Central Committee and, under it, the district committees. If the ordinary members want to do more than be "pushed" by the district organiser – if they have any "polemical arguments", or just unresolved questions, of their own – then too bad. Those who want "small internalised meetings" – branch meetings, of the sort almost every working-class movement known to history has had – only condemn themselves as not "being involved in many activities", or as positively desiring "sectarian barriers to wider intervention".

In short, the membership loses any right of collective discussion and control. Indeed, the proposed structure hardly allows for a membership at all, in the sense of a defined collective. Its concession to the principle of a collective membership is monthly district meetings. But these are "open to people [non-members] working closely with us" – while, at the same time, as the whole drift of the document makes clear, it is taken for granted that many members will not attend. It may well turn out, in fact, as the contradictions of the SWP's policy develop, that these district meetings gain real life. But in the scheme as it comes down from Central Committee, outside the activist core in each district, there is only a cloud of individuals, each more or less responsive to the "direction and push" from above.

In the dispute which led to the split in the Russian Marxist movement between Bolsheviks and Mensheviks, Lenin famously lambasted the Menshevik leader Martov for declaring that: "We could only rejoice if every striker, every demonstrator, answering for his actions, could proclaim himself a Party member." The idea that every striker could be a Marxist party member, said Lenin, was "complacent daydreaming" and "opportunist phrasemongering" which dissolved the specific tasks of the party into the general development of the class. The SWP eerily reproduces Martov with a claim that: "We want people who can organise a post office strike even if they can't make a meeting on a Wednesday night, or..." – and this makes it clear that the argument is not just about Wednesdays rather than a time which may be more manageable for a worker with difficult shifts or family circumstances – "... protest over tuition fees even if they do nothing outside the college". Every fees protester should be considered an SWP member! This is not only "opportunist phrasemongering", but demagogy which cuts against any concept of an educated Marxist party.

● The SWP expelled its most important international co-thinker group, the ISO-USA, from its international network in March 2001. It did this in a way that contradicts all claims that the new SWP turn means greater openness to political debate. If anything, there is less openness, and more brittleness in the face of halfway serious political challenge, than there was in the depths of the "downturn" . The alleged crime of the ISO-USA ? "Degeneration" and "ossification into a sect". The evidence? Nothing more drastic than a mildly less gung-ho, and more critical, attitude to the "new anti-capitalist" militancy than the SWP's. The debate on this question? Minimal.

Read the ISO's Ahmed Shawki. He quotes Alex Callinicos covering his bases by admitting that the "new anti-capitalist" milieu contains leading figures who oppose extreme free-marketeering but not capitalism in general, and comments: "So the anti-capitalist movement is actually made up of people who are against capitalism and are for it? So what we really are saying is that the movement has a dynamic which can lead it in the direction of anti-capitalism, but is not there yet. So what sense is there to continue to describe the whole movement as anti-capitalist? The real question – which is not asked or answered – is how we can help move it in the direction of revolutionary conclusions instead of proclaiming that it has already arrived there."

Whatever the problems with Shawki's politics here, they are not outrageously aloof. Much of what he writes about Seattle and after could come straight from the SWP press. ""The enthusiasm for Seattle was immense – and rightly so – most of all among the left, both in the US and internationally. Though the radicalisation didn't start there, Seattle came to symbolise the new resistance, which could be seen in many expressions everywhere." The difference amounts to no more than the ISO insisting that what they prefer to call "the global justice movement" is only part of "the new resistance", and that socialists need to intervene with arguments rather than just be "the best builders".

None of this was debated openly in the SWP's press. The SWP finally – after the excommunication – published a polemic against the ISO on its web site, but without giving any of the ISO's side of the argument. Can critical minorities in the SWP – or critical minorities in broader movements which the SWP controls, if the time comes that the SWP finds them too troubling – realistically expect any better treatment than the ISO?

● According to Callinicos, the SWP "stumbled on" the use of "the united front approach" most appropriate for these new times "more or less empirically during the Balkan War of 1999". It did not make what Callinicos considers to have been the mistake that the ISO-USA made, of trying to "attack illusions in the United Nations as an alternative to NATO, sympathy for Serbian nationalism, and opposition to Kosovan self-determination". That was a "sectarian attitude towards other forces opposed to the Balkan war".

Why? Because the United Nations should be supported as an alternative to NATO? Serbian nationalism is progressive? The Kosovars have no right to self-determination? Or the questions of Kosovar rights, and Serbian ambitions, were irrelevant, tangential, or marginal to the Kosova war? Callinicos argues none of these propositions. He evades them. It was smart tactics to surf on those illusions, that nationalism, and those anti-Kosovar prejudices, in order to build "the widest possible movement" in which the SWP could "draw new people towards us" by "being the most dynamic and militant force in building the movement". That, for him, is primary. To a Marxist, "sectarianism" means private, small-group considerations being allowed to override our responsibilities to develop the broader class struggle. To Callinicos, it means something almost exactly opposite – letting programmatic politics (based on responsibility to the broader class struggle) impede or hinder what seems to be smart tactics for his small group.

Callinicos's concept here, the "united front without politics", is not Lenin and Trotsky's idea of the united front, as united action between revolutionaries and reformists for central immediate working-class goals in the course of which the revolutionaries can more effectively criticise the reformists. It is far closer to the Stalinist notion of the popular front, where the "revolutionary party" sets itself up as the champion of unity at all costs and the arch-enemy of "divisive" debate, but seeks to siphon out recruits by virtue of organisational weight and prestige.

● In its orientation document circulated just before the June General Election, the SWP Central Committee called on its district organisers to ensure that all SWP members got a "clear direction and push... which involves polemical arguments where necessary..." And which issues were so thorny that this "polemical argument" might be necessary? "E.g.," the document continued, "over canvassing."

In the last weeks of the General Election campaign, the SWP launched a drive in the Socialist Alliance to stop canvassing and put all resources into mass leafletting. It considered this a prime issue where full-time organisers should apply pressure to bring its members into line.

I believe the "anti-canvassing" drive damaged the election campaign and the Alliance . My concern here, however, is not so much with the substantive issue as with the way that the SWP and its allies dealt with it, and the implications for the political life of the Socialist Alliance.

The anti-canvassing drive was launched through an email circular on 23 May. Grant for the sake of argument that the SWPers running the national Socialist Alliance office were alarmed at a lag in leafletting and felt there was an emergency where the tight election deadline gave no time to discuss widely. What did they do when faced with criticism and dissent?

Instead of responding with political debate, they filled the air with secondary and *ad hominem* arguments. The pro-canvassers only wanted to canvass because that would help us sell papers. We were lying about how much leafletting had been done. We were pessimistic. We didn't understand the "new mood" in the working class. And, very soon: why were we making such a fuss?

A *Workers' Liberty* representative raised the issue in the Socialist Alliance executive after the election, and asked the SWP to explain. One comrade complained we were being "divisive"; another, that we were suggesting that the only factor keeping the Socialist Alliance vote down to a disappointing 1.62% was "subjective", and that canvassing would have been a cure-all; a third, that we were "bludgeoning" the SWP. None of these were SWP. The SWP members present did not even have to pretend to offer a reply.

It is all rather like the old Cold War "police-state liberalism": since we have freedom here, not like the Stalinist states, therefore, say nothing that may cause difficulties to the government. Since we have a new SWP, willing to talk pleasantly and patiently and even be flexible on this or that issue, therefore do not say anything that causes a fuss with them. Yet in the Socialist Alliance, too, the SWP's fundamental concept is the "united front without political debate". To allow them to pursue it without challenge is not only to compromise the possibility of the Socialist Alliance developing a real political life of its own; it is also to forgo the possibility of that real political life, once developed, reacting back on the SWP, applying pressure to the contradictions in its new turn, and thus making something positive out of them.

29

Nurture 1, Nature 0?

By Clive Bradley

THE movie *Amadeus* sees the precocious Mozart through the eyes of his rival, Salieri. For their first proper meeting, when Mozart arrives at the Court, Salieri has composed a little piece of music. Mozart thanks him, plays back the thing from memory, and then, having commented that a particular chord change "doesn't really work", proceeds to improvise on the theme, vastly improving Salieri's original. Salieri turns to the audience and tells us: "I think it was then that I first decided to kill him."

It would be hard to dispute that the difference in talent between Mozart and Salieri was genuine, and something they were respectively born with. Mozart didn't "learn" to be the genius Salieri could never hope to be. And this difference goes to the heart of the long-standing debate between theories of "nature" and "nurture" explaining human behaviours and capacities. After World War Two, and reacting to the horrors of Nazi biological approaches to human beings, a dominant view held that human nature is entirely, or mainly, determined by "environment", or "culture". More recently, modern genetics has challenged this, in numerous ways.

So the announcement by the different teams working on the human genome that human beings are made up of far fewer genes than previously thought has thrown new light on this debate. Against previous guesses of 100,000 genes in the human genome, scientists now say there are between 30,000 and 40,000. This is upsetting, on one reading, because there are, in that case, only a bit more than twice as many genes making up a human being as making up a fruit fly. The complexities of human behaviour would seem not to be automatically shaped by our genes.

What, then, of Mozart and Salieri?

Of course there is much about human beings which is genetically shaped. We are organisms – same as any other – and what makes us human organisms rather than, say, fruit flies, or chimpanzees, is, biologically speaking, our "genome", the sum total of the bits of DNA called "genes". Raise even a very intelligent chimp in a human community and it will still be a chimp.

Where the argument has always been controversial is in reference to human behaviour. As genetics has matured as a science, wide-ranging claims have been made for the power of genes to explain behaviour, in a number of different ways, and with differing degrees of emphasis. "Behaviour genetics" has looked to find genetic influence on, for instance, sexual preference, alcoholism and other addictions, aggressiveness and propensity to violence, obesity, risk-taking, intelligence, and so on. Sometimes this has been simply through studies of related people (best of all identical twins), where a statistically significant correlation of such relatives sharing a "trait" is shown to declare a hereditary, and therefore genetic, influence. Sometimes it has gone on from there to try to identify the specific gene or "genetic marker" (bit of a chromosome) responsible.

Evolutionary biology, under a number of pseudonyms (the most famous is "sociobiology"), has focused not on differences between individuals in this way, but on common human characteristics which are claimed to have been shaped by evolution.

From whichever point of view, none of the scientists (or journalistic popularisers) of such theories would describe themselves as "genetic" or "biological" determinists, though their critics often do. But their studies have been presented as a challenge to what is sometimes called the "Standard Social Science Model", supposedly favoured by sociologists, social anthroplogists, Marxists and feminists, in which biology is allowed no part in explaining what human beings think, feel and do. Thirty thousand genes might be only a third of the number previously hoped for, but it's not few enough seriously to undermine the approaches these schools have outlined.

As the extreme example of Mozart shows, it's plainly common-sense plausible that elements of an individual's behaviour and ability are inherited. But there are methodological, or philosophical, problems with the ways in which behaviour genetics has approached its subject.

Take the famous "gay gene" discovered by Dean Hamer and his team in the early nineties. (In fact Hamer claimed only to find a genetic marker for male homosexuality, but I'll say "gay gene" for short because this is how it's popularly known). Whatever the reliability of Hamer's results, which have been contested, those results can only ever show a correlation between two phenomena.

Hamer showed that a statistically high number of male homosexuals share the "gay gene" (Xq28), suggesting their sexual preference is inherited through their mothers. He did not show either that Xq28 caused their sexuality (it might be a gene for something else completely with sexual orientation as a side-effect). Nor did he show that most men with this gene are gay. It was never part of the claim that Xq28 alone makes a man gay, or that you can't be gay without it. A statistically high correlation is only that. Sometimes scientists and their popularisers mistake correlation for cause. But even if they don't, a theory – in this case of sexuality, needs to integrate these results into an overall picture.

This is true of all the areas where such "high" (very rarely more than 50%) influence for identified or putative genes has been claimed.

Perhaps more important that that, though, the qualities or types of behaviour subjected to such analysis are usually treated as more or less obvious, unproblematic. What is "homosexuality"? Ask a tribesperson in Papua New Guinea, assuming you could translate it, and he or she would have no idea what you are talking about.

Stephen Jay Gould, in his book *The Mismeasure of Man*, which chronicles the frequently racist assumptions of intelligence testing through history, criticises even modern, state-of-the-art research into intelligence on these grounds, which he calls "reification" (making something into a "thing", although it is not one). Different types of intelligence are tested for, which are then averaged into "g" or "general intelligence". "G" is then treated as if it is measurable, and can be inherited. But "g" isn't a real thing, it's a statistical convenience, an average.

This problem runs through most behaviour genetics. It's true that if you read both behaviour geneticists and their critics carefully, on one level they often seem to say the same thing about how much we know. Yet is there is often a dramatic difference in emphasis. Writers like Hamer, or Matt Ridley (in his book *Genome*, for instance) enthuse about the discoveries of modern genetics. Gould, or his colleague, Harvard geneticist Richard Lewontin, put great stress on the limits of our knowledge and the dangers of "reductionist" (concentrating on "ultimate" causes without looking at complex interaction) or "atomist" (looking only at 'bits') reasoning.

On the evolutionary front, "sociobiology", or as it's often called now "evolutionary psychology", has become extremely popular, infiltrating pop culture with television documentaries called things like *Why Men Don't Iron*. Since as a species we evolved in our modern form in stone age Africa, the argument runs, human beings are, basically, stone age hunter-gatherers. One typical assertion which follows is that men hunt and women gather, which explains differences between the sexes (men don't iron because the palaeolithic savannah didn't require them to... well, iron).

There are more and less sophisticated versions of such theories (for an unbelievably crass and offensive one, see Thornhill and Palmer's *A Natural History of Rape*). The fundamental objection, put forward by scientists and others, is that it doesn't take account of the complexity of human culture, transmitted as it is through language and social practices, giving instead tendentious and ideological justifications for inequalities.

The relatively small size of the human genome does not spell death either for behaviour genetics or Darwinian narratives. It throws into sharp relief a point made by many scientists, on both sides of the debate, that genes operate in extremely complex ways, interacting with each other and with other biological – and in the case of human beings at least, social and cultural – processes. "Nature" and "nurture" is a simplistic distinction. The question, for an account of human nature, is to explain how nature and nurture interrelate.

Genes, and inherited characteristics, clearly play a role: human beings aren't "blank slates" purely shaped by "environment". There are common features of what makes human beings human, and many of these are probably to do with evolutionary history. Which, though? And to what extent?

There is no doubt that there remains, both in genetics and evolutionary biology, a way of looking at life, and at human beings in particular, which suffers from the "reductionist" and "atomistic" methods of reasoning condemned by Stephen Jay Gould and others. "Genetic determinism" in its full-blown sense is largely to be found only in the media, or in popular crudifications of these approaches. But in a softer sense, they remain.

That we only have two and a half times as many genes in our genome as a fruit fly is not the end of the story. (It still makes us a lot more complex.) But it demands of us a recognition that it is, indeed, a complex and subtle thing to be human, and that "the environment" plays a part at all sorts of levels.

We are not merely the outer expression of a genome; our biology is not simply destiny. We are, as human beings, free to make and remake our world.

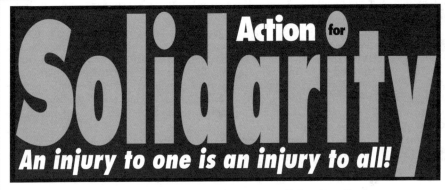

FACTFILE

Dick Whittington's heir

By John Bloxam

ROBBED of the official Labour candidacy by Tony Blair, Ken Livingstone defied the New Labour leaders and in the summer of 2000 was elected Mayor of London. No sooner was Livingstone installed as Mayor than he created a Tory-Liberal-New Labour "popular front" government for London.

The most "left-wing" plank in his election platform had been opposition to Blairite plans to privatise London Underground.

His record, as distinct from his reputation, for many years, at least, did not identify Livingstone as a leftist. Yet he had the support of many left-wingers in the Labour Party and trade unionists. This made a limited sense even for those, like us, who were inclined to expect nothing in the way of socialism or working class politics from Livingstone: if he successfully defied the New Labour machine and gave the Blairites a bloody nose, as he did, this might well encourage others to stand up to them.

But in fact many who would identify themselves as left-wingers went much further, and indulged in the fantasy that Livingstone was a left-wing candidate.

Nobody had any respect-worthy reason for believing that. Class struggle politics disappeared from Livingstone's agenda, if they were ever seriously part of it, in the early 1980s.

In 1981, he broke with Labour's class struggle left, organised around *Socialist Organiser*, of whose editorial board he had been a founding member, and the Socialist Campaign for a Labour Victory which published *Socialist Organiser*. In the same year he became GLC leader. Instead of the politics of confronting the newly elected, still shaky and unpopular Thatcher government, using left-controlled local government as fortresses of the class struggle left, Livingstone sought a softer, safer option. When the Tory government imposed cuts, Livingstone chose to duck out of confrontation by raising local taxes in an attempt to compensate for the cuts. This passing on of the cuts was incompatible with mobilising the local government electorate to fight the Tory cuts.

Livingstone still talked "left", gave GLC money to selected politically correct good causes, made gestures towards conducting an independent GLC foreign policy – on Ireland for example – and thereby helped make up Mrs Thatcher's mind to abolish London-wide local government. But this was instead of, not part of, a policy of confrontation with Thatcher, using the GLC as a base from which to mobilise working class resistance to the Tories.

It is one of the strangest things in British labour movement history that such a struggle was not mounted in the three years in which Thatcher was seriously unpopular, before the South Atlantic war with Argentina turned the British political situation in Thatcher's favour. Nonetheless, that is what happened. No small part of the responsibility for making it happen belongs to Ken Livingstone and his then allies such as "Red Ted" Knight, leader of Lambeth Council in the 1980s.

As the Tories imposed union-shackling laws, used the slump that began in 1980 to devastate working class communities that were centres of opposition to them, and moved towards confrontation with the miners, the dominant Livingstone segment of the GLC left acted as if all this scarcely concerned them. By the time – 1984-5 – the miners were locked in conflict with the brutal state power thrown at them by Thatcher, Livingstone and the rest of the local government left, who had come to office breathing revolutionary socialist fire, and boasting of what they would do to the Tories, were in London holding hands with dissident Tories – like former Prime Minister, Edward Heath – Liberals and showbiz celebrities, trying to prove how "cuddly" and non-threatening they could be.

Livingstone is an intelligent, engaging, media-friendly personality, a politician more in an American than British mould. In a world in which most New Labour MPs have the force and personality of an unused white paper cup, Livingstone comes across as a thinking, independent human being. But he is not something that people concerned with the working class, the labour movement, or socialism can afford to go on kidding themselves about. The following is an outline of the facts of Livingstone's career.

In **March 1969** Ken Livingstone joined Norwood Labour Party. He was in his early 20s. This was a time when the left, especially the young left, was streaming out of the Labour Party in disgust with the Wilson Labour government.

1971: Livingstone is elected a councillor in Lambeth, and becomes its vice-chair of housing.

1973: Livingstone is elected GLC councillor for Norwood; he becomes a member of the Inner London Education Authority.

1974: Livingstone is elected to the executive of the Greater London Labour Party; he becomes Vice-Chair of Housing Management at the GLC but resigns in 1975 in protest at rent and fare rises and cuts.

1976: Livingstone becomes prospective parliamentary candidate for Hampstead Labour Party.

1977: Labour loses control of the GLC.

1978: Livingstone is elected to Camden council. In July 1978 he signs the founding statement of the Socialist Campaign for a Labour Victory which includes opposition to cuts, rent and rate rises, and a pledge to use local government to mobilise opposition to whatever government, Labour or Tory, would win the upcoming election.

February 1979: Livingstone starts his drive to capture the GLC in the 1981 election. He chairs the Greater London Labour Party Transport Working Party. Livingstone is defeated in the Hampstead parliamentary seat.

May 1979: the Tories win the general election and begin a full-scale drive against the labour movement, from which that movement has still, 20 years later, not recovered. In June, the government cuts the central government grant to councils by 3%.

At this point the unity of the left organised around *Socialist Organiser* falls apart. With the Tories in power, it has a choice of two perspectives: use local government as a basis for a fight, or knuckle under, making face-saving gestures and noises. The left flakes apart on the question of rate rises. Livingstone argues that rate rises are a progressive redistributive tax. In fact, the issue is whether the local government left will defy the Tories or duck out by evasive action such as passing on the Tory cuts to the electorate in the form of higher local taxes ("rates").

July 1979: the open division, a decisive turning point for the left in the years of the Thatcherite onslaught on the labour movement, emerges at a conference in London called by *Socialist Organiser*. A report in *Workers' Action* explains the issues:

"On the one side, a perspective of class struggle, which uses the positions of strength already held by the labour movement on local councils and elsewhere to mobilise for a serious fightback against the Tory offensive. On the other side, a perspective which makes preserving

positions on councils the priority, by a policy of 'riding the punches' of the Tory government."

[The revolutionary left attempted to] "commit the conference to a repudiation of the role which Labour-controlled councils normally fill, that of tamely participating in the administration of bourgeois society according to the bourgeois norms and the dictates of government, against the grain of working-class interests. It called for a commitment to struggle by left Labour councillors.

"The relationship between Labour-controlled councils and the living standards-cutting Tory government is not something given once and for all. It can be modified tremendously in favour of the working class. It depends on mobilisation, on struggle.

"Even if one defiant Labour council could be dealt with easily, could a string of such councils, across London or throughout the country, backed by the power of unions and tenants? (And, in fact, the last Tory government found it far from easy to deal with one tiny council in Clay Cross.)

"The conference's responsibility was to adopt a class struggle policy that might allow *Socialist Organiser* to rearm the left politically and begin to organise it against the Tory onslaught.

"With Labour-controlled councils it is now either class struggle politics or the role of administrator of capitalist politics and therefore also propagandist for bourgeois ideas."

Early 1980: Livingstone splits with the anti-rate rise majority in *Socialist Organiser*. He continues to write for *SO*.

Livingstone writes of this period: "(left-wing Labour-controlled "Red Ted" Knight Lambeth's decision just after the 1979 General Election to impose cuts)... confused the rates versus services argument and allowed our opponents to discredit the rate increase option. It delivered control of the SCLV and *Socialist Organiser* into the hands of John O'Mahony (Sean Matgamna). With the GLC selections only ten months away and the *Socialist Organiser* firmly in the hands of O'Mahony, who opposed all I stood for, I was suddenly deprived of access to what had looked like becoming a good broad left organising network. I had no alternative but to try and interest the Chartist group in leaving *Socialist Organiser*."

February 1980: *London Labour Briefing* [now *Labour Left Briefing*] is launched as the organ of the "avoid confrontation" former wing of the SCLV. The lead article is by Livingstone on the GLC campaign.

April 1980: Ted Knight, leader of Lambeth council and Ken Livingstone's closest ally, makes a 49.4% rate rise and a £1.50 rent rise. He launches a witch hunt against *SO* for criticising him. An open letter to Ted Knight in *SO* from John O'Mahony summarised the issues:

"You denounce the no rent and no rate rise policy as a 'recipe for political disaster'. *Socialist Organiser* thinks on the contrary that your policy of rent and rate rises is a policy of disguised cuts of working class living standards, and a backdoor form of collaboration with the Tories to implement cuts.

"Far from being a policy to rally forces behind Labour councils, your policies can only give [Tory local government minister] Heseltine a weapon to split and divide local communities and alienate support from Labour councils.

"All the present struggles – including the struggle to kick the Tories out – must be focused (insofar as Marxists can affect their focus) on that perspective. It is a matter of great urgency that the Marxists within the labour movement bind themselves together to help prepare the labour movement for this fight.

"The alternative may very well be a major and historic defeat for the working class of Britain."

"To justify your rate-rise policies, you refer to powers above you – the government – that you dare not take on or challenge at a fundamental level. Isn't this in essence the sort of argument Callaghan used to justify his posture before the IMF?

"If the argument holds good for you in Lambeth, confronting the Tory government, why not for [Dennis] Healey and [ex-Prime Minister James] Callaghan and [ex-Prime Minister Harold] Wilson in the weak and isolated British state, confronted by the IMF?"

In fact, the experience of the local government left and its talk-don't-fight logic did make its way through, first into Labour's Kinnockite "centre" and all the way through to Blair's New Labour (for example, David Blunkett was the Ken Livingstone of Sheffield council and Margaret Hodge of Islington). The experience was decisive in the taming of the left of that period.

May 1981: Labour wins the GLC election. Livingstone immediately ousts the right-wing leader in a left-wing coup. *Briefing's* headline says "London's Ours". Livingstone signs the lead/front page article which says:

"No-one will be left in any doubt that the GLC is now a campaigning organ and a bastion of power for the labour movement within a national context... Part of our task will be to sustain a holding operation until such time as the Tory government can be brought down and replaced by a left-wing Labour Government..." In the same period he wrote: "There can be no doubt that we are now entering the final phase of the struggle against the Tories."

The GLC Labour group refuses an invitation for the Leader to go to the [Charles and Diana] Royal wedding. Livingstone makes an anti-royalist speech. He will change his view on this question, as on so many others, in his move to the right.

The GLC gives public support to the IRA hunger strikers and their families. It backs gay rights.

At the same time the Inner London Education Authority backs down under threat of surcharge on its manifesto commitment to reduce the price of school meals. Livingstone justifies offering 8% to Underground workers in response to a 15% claim (inflation is 12%).

September 1981: Livingstone launches *Labour Herald* with Ted Knight and Matthew Warburton as joint editors. A Workers' Revolutionary Party full-timer, Stephen Miller, is installed as editor. *Labour Herald* is financed by the WRP (an extremely crazy kitsch-Trotskyist sect), which is being financed by Libya, Iraq and other Arab benefactors in return for uncritically supporting them in its press and for providing Arab governments with spy-reports on Arab dissidents and on Jews prominent in British life. (What *SO* had commented on from the beginning, was "revealed" when the WRP imploded in 1985.)

Late 1981: the WRP attempts to bankrupt *SO* when Vanessa Redgrave sues Sean Matgamna and John Bloxam for libel. It is in part an attempt to clear the way for the establishment of the new paper, *Labour Herald*. Livingstone originally signs a petition circulated in the labour movement protesting at the attempt to drive *SO* out of existence but he continues to benefit from the WRP's financial backing of *Labour Herald*, and speaks at WRP meetings from which *Socialist Organiser* people are banned.

October 1981: the GLC Fares Fair policy is introduced – a 32% Tube and bus fare reduction and a new zonal system. It is immediately subjected to a legal challenge by Bromley Council. The legal challenge is upheld by Lord Denning in November and by the Law Lords in December. It raises the same question as in the dispute on rate rises: defy or comply?

In 1982 Livingstone says he supports defiance of the courts, and votes for this in the GLC Labour Group. At the time, he was writing: "Just imagine the largest council in the country refusing to comply with the law as laid down by Denning. It would have meant an immediate constitutional crisis. It would have been the biggest act of defiance against central government by a local authority yet."

However, he also argues for a free vote on it in the Council, knowing that defiance will lose there. He votes for defiance, but it is predictably defeated by the Tories, the SDP and right-wing Labour. Then despite his prior commitment not to, Livingstone votes for the budget with the fare increases.

Deputy leader Harrington brands Livingstone as "opportunistic... because he knew that the law would have to be obeyed, but he knew that other people would see to it that it would be done..."

But Livingstone is still defended by the Pollyanna left such as *Briefing*. His biographer John Carvel describes the vote as the start of "what may be called the second Livingstone administration. The Labour group got down to the art of the possible".

In fact, Livingstone now pioneers what will become known as "Rainbow Coalition" politics when advocated by the right-wing Stalinists of *Marxism Today*.

9 April 1983: Livingstone is interviewed in the WRP daily *Newsline*. The interview appears opposite an editorial denouncing *Socialist Organiser* as agents of imperialism and "Zionism" – "From *Socialist Organiser* to Thatcher and Reagan, the Zionist connection", went the headline. He agrees with his interviewer that, yes, a recent item on a BBC financial programme about the WRP's financial links to Libya was the work of "Zionists" at the BBC out to get the WRP. Livingstone afterwards ignores public invitations to repudiate the crazy *Newsline* editorial and continues to work closely with the WRP.

June 1983: the Tories win the general election. Their manifesto includes abolition of the GLC (and other metropolitan councils) and "rate capping" to limit local government spending.

March 1984: the great miners' strike begins.

The GLC launches a "Say No to No Say" campaign to prevent the abolition of the GLC. It is a professional, well-funded campaign, aimed principally at convincing Tory supporters, the House of Lords, etc. Livingstone is promoted as a domesticated "cuddly left" figure, who is a threat to no-one.

May 1984: The Thames Barrier is opened. The Queen is invited to open it; erstwhile republican Livingstone in public bows low before her gracious Majesty.

Summer 1984: Militant-led Liverpool Council does a deal with the Tories: it is the same sort of "avoid confrontation" strategy that Livingstone had pioneered in the GLC – only now it involves pointedly leaving the miners to fight alone. [A year later, the miners defeated, the Tories will confront Liverpool Council.]

LIVINGSTONE now swings verbally left again and argues for defiance on "rate-capping". "We will effectively operate within the state in defiance of the state. That will provide the most dramatic challenge, apart from the challenge of the miners' strike, that this government has faced since 1979." Joint action by London councils would present ministers with "the prospect of a city in revolt"; it was a chance to inflict "the most savage defeat" on the government.

February 1985: Livingstone argues for defi-

antly not setting a rate in the GLC Labour Group and once again he also argues for a free vote in the Council. Expecting defiance to be defeated a free vote would allow the Leader (Livingstone) to retain his position. At the same time Livingstone is organising for a legal rate setting budget.

March 1985: The miners vote to return. In Council the left continues to vote against setting a rate; at the last minute Livingstone switches and votes for. He is "disarmingly" cynical about it. In *Tribune* during the summer he explains his politics: "I'm for manipulative politics... the cynical soft-sell."

For the first time there is open rupture between Ken Livingstone and a harder left both in the GLC (John McDonnell) and outside. Livingstone shifts openly right. He starts working with the soft left Labour Co-ordinating Committee. He calls for peace with Labour leader Neil Kinnock, who is applying the logic of Livingstone's Labour Government policy since 1979 to the national Labour Party.

End 1985: Livingstone's paper, the *Labour Herald*, folds after the WRP disintegrates.

March 1986: The GLC is abolished.

1986: Livingstone openly supports the right-wing Labour candidate in NUS against the hard left *Socialist Organiser* candidate.

Livingstone wins selection as parliamentary candidate in Brent East with the support of the right wing. The left supports Diane Abbott.

Livingstone publishes his first book, *If Voting Changed Anything They'd Abolish It*. The title of the book, a pseudo-anarchist slogan on a book of memoirs by a man who had shown himself willing to do virtually anything for "votes", was widely taken to be a neat bit of inadvertent self-satirising by Livingstone.

June 1987: The Tories win the general election. Livingstone wins Brent East.

September 1987: Livingstone is elected to the Labour Party NEC.

September 1988: Tony Benn and Eric Heffer challenge for leadership of the Labour Party. Livingstone makes private approaches to John Smith, offering to support him in the second round.

Livingstone later would say that he would have accepted a job if Kinnock had offered him one. But he is now widely distrusted as well as discredited.

September 1989: he loses his seat on the Labour Party NEC. "That was the end of my ambition to lead the Party. It died quite specifically as they announced I'd been kicked off the NEC. I realised then that my strategy of trying to reunite the left was going nowhere because the soft left was losing its confidence.

1990: Livingstone is fined for not paying the poll tax. He starts to write a column for the *Sun* which had engaged in savage union-busting in

1986-7, when it moved from Fleet Street to Wapping. There is a widespread labour movement boycott of the *Sun*. Livingstone uses his column to attack sections of the left – the Socialist Workers Party – denied the right to reply.

June 1992: The fourth successive Tory election victory. Livingstone is re-elected in Brent East.

When Kinnock stands down as Labour leader, Livingstone tries to get nominations to stand (he gets 13 out of the required 55 MPs). He runs a spoiling pseudo-campaign supported publicly by the *Sun* ("Vote Ken, a real man of the people"). The scab-herding Tory-supporting *Sun* uses "its" candidate, Ken Livingstone, to mock and jeer at the left, the Labour Party and the labour movement. Livingstone plays along. His "candidacy" blocks any prospect of a campaign to draft the serious left candidate, Tony Benn. Nonetheless, his joke candidacy wins the support of sections of the left – *Briefing* and *Socialist Outlook*.

1994: John Smith dies. Livingstone had expected to be offered a ministerial position if Smith had won the election. "He [Smith] would undoubtedly have sought to govern by bringing the left in... he had no problem with left-wingers who were pro-Europe." He tries and fails to get sufficient nominations in the new leadership election.

Livingstone helps establish the "Campaign to Defend the Welfare State" against the Welfare State Network, set up by his old opponents in *Socialist Organiser* and the SCLV. It does nothing and is entirely a spoiling operation.

June 1997: Labour wins the General Election.

When Blair had pushed the proposal for a directly elected Mayor into the manifesto, Livingstone described the idea as "barmy".

September 1997: Livingstone is elected to the Labour Party NEC.

1998: Livingstone submits a Commons motion supporting the sacking of John Haylett as *Morning Star* editor (withdrawn after pressure from other left MPs). Livingstone publicly denounces Sean Matgamna and by implication the Alliance for Workers' Liberty as "MI5 agents".

1999-2000: Campaigning to win Labour nomination for London Mayor, Livingstone professes loyalty to Blair. Declares that he is "95% Blairite". "...I would work with your Government, not against it... I am convinced that your administration has the potential to be a great reforming government on a par with those of 1906 and 1945". After he is "stitched up" and with a clear lead in the polls, Livingstone stands as an independent candidate for Mayor. He runs a right-wing media-based campaign.

2000: Ken Livingstone is elected Mayor and he sets up a cross-class Popular Front administration (Labour right-winger as deputy; Liberal for Transport); he appoints, at a salary of £1 million a year, imported New York union-buster transport expert Bob Kiley.

May 2001: he denounces anti-globalisation demonstrators in London, joining in the demonisation that preceded the illegal detention of 1,000 people for nine hours in Oxford Circus, surrounded by heavily armed police. Livingstone founds a pro-euro campaign jointly with the City of London capitalists.

THE STYLE is the man, and the man is the style. Livingstone wrote: "As my constantly shifting political relationship with Ted Knight and various left-wing factions reveals, it is the pressures of political and economic forces which determine the alliances that are made between politicians, not whether or not they like each other. I have often thought that Mario Puzo's *The Godfather* is a much more honest account of how politicians operate than any of the self-justifying rubbish spewed out in political biographies and repeated in academic textbooks. One sentence in that book typifies the way most politicians deal with each other. Tessio, the longest-serving of the Corleone mob, has switched his allegiance and betrayed the family by setting up Michael Corleone for assassination. His treachery is uncovered, he is led away to his death, and as he goes he sends Michael Corleone a final message. 'Tell Mike it was only business,' he says, 'I always liked him.' Fortunately for politicians, if not the general public, politics are conducted by ballots rather than bullets in most of the United Kingdom." (*If Voting Changed Anything, They'd Abolish It*, p.115)

Livingstone does not live up to these words, either. He has pursued a vendetta against his opponents in *Socialist Organiser*/SCLV in 1979-81 down two decades – sometimes obsession turning to lunacy as when he denounces some of us as "MI5 agents".

But as an approach to principled politics, serious politics honestly adhered to, this would be admirable: pursue your goals, minimise the personal antagonism, be objective, businesslike and in the name of progress to your goal ally where necessary with those you dislike, and oppose those you like.

But this approach in Livingstone is used in pursuit of a grubby personal "me-über-alles" career! As Ken Livingstone seems to recognise, it is in principle no different from what the gangsters do. Just business? The "business" of socialist politics does not belong to the same order of things as the business of those for whom politics is "just business". The "business" of Ken Livingstone" is... Ken Livingstone.

BRIEFING

Who are the anti-capitalists?
By Nick Holden

THE anti-capitalist movement exploded onto the world political scene in Seattle two years ago. There is very little material available on the development of the constituent parts of the anti-capitalist movement. Many commentators say Seattle "just happened".

In fact the movement seems to have different roots in different parts of the world. In the USA three streams converged at Seattle.

● Direct action groups, many with anarchist-inspired politics, had grown steadily through the 1990s; many had already staged effective local protests.

● Anti-globalisation NGOs, with significant staff, and pulling power, especially amongst students, also built for Seattle.

● US trade unions that had found themselves no longer as one with the Democrats on economic globalisation turned out to protest at the Seattle conference.

Some direct action groups in the USA had had links with the Mexican Zapatistas. Many NGO supporters had worked in elections and in trade union recruitment in central American countries, or with attempts to break the US blockade of Cuba. Activists who had a history of confrontation with state law enforcement were numerous. Because there is no Labour Party in the USA, and no significant Trotskyist organisation, young people developing a political consciousness were attracted to "direct action", "reject ideology" ideology and to neo-anarchism.

Similar trends influence the anti-capitalist movement in mainland Europe. Ya Basta! – originally Italian, and now with groups in other European countries and the USA – say that they were inspired by the Zapatista rising. They define their difference with the rest of the Italian left as "we chose to abandon ideology, they didn't."

In much of Europe there was, through the 80s and 90s, a disintegrating Communist Party, which shed militants in many directions. Some of them wished to "abandon ideology" without abandoning the idea of confronting the state. Groups like Ya Basta! and the White Overalls have a cadre that have consciously broken with some form of Communism. They also have a wide layer of youth attracted to anarchist direct action in the absence of competing strategies. Almost without exception the Trotskyist left, where it exists, has been slow to relate to the developing direct action, confront-the-state movements. Even where the Trotskyists have attempted to relate to this movement, for example the SWP and its "children groups", they have done it with the more conservative wings of the movement, such as ATTAC (the French NGO campaigning for the Tobin Tax), not with the anarchists. In the eyes of the militant youth of Europe and the USA, the stock of the revolutionary left is probably at an all-time low.

Anarchist groups in the UK don't seem to have gained from the rise of the anti-capitalist movement elsewhere. The websites of the "established" anarchist groups are "business-as-usual" propaganda vehicles and hardly mention the protests. The direct action movement in the UK, although ideologically "anarchist", is more likely to be partying than polemicising. Young people who want to challenge the system tend to do it by having "illegal" street parties. For example, the *Urban75* website is very cool, very hip, very rave and party orientated, but it contains serious discussion and organising for various protests world-wide. *Urban75* carried news updates from Genoa before almost any other UK website.

The revolutionary left has missed all this. The map of the international working class has changed – and we need to recognise the changes.

The kind of workplaces that young people work in often do not have unions.

Politically-conscious youth are expressing their politics outside of work, through anti-fascism, through defending their right to party, through involvement in a counter-culture (in which the internet plays a large part). The internet gives young people contact with the world. They form ideas about their place in the world, without attending meetings. The internet makes it possible for young people in the UK to define themselves in relation to struggles for emancipation in Korea or Mexico, without the mediating role of an organisation in their home town or even home country. Lots of internet kiddies know more about the politics of the Zapatistas than they do about the political systems they live under. The Zapatistas are exciting rebels, even the best of the politicians available at home are either dreary careerists or patently unserious r-r-r-revolutionaries.

Many of the people who turned up to Seattle, or Quebec, or Genoa, did so under their own initiative. They didn't know who they would be marching with until they arrived at the "convergence centre". Seattle could, easily, have been a disaster, with only tiny numbers of participants and then we'd all have known nothing about it.

Rough figures for Seattle suggest that something like 10,000 people were there with direct action in mind, and a further 50,000 there from NGOs and trade unions intent on "non-confrontational" protest. The protesters didn't even have an agreement about their objectives.

Seattle made it onto TV screens in the USA and, via the Internet, into homes around the world. We all saw the police brutality, and the fact that the protesters, all different, appeared united. What could have been a one-off protest became the spark for something more.

A defining feature of the new protesters is that they haven't waited for the corporate media to decide whether they are news or not. Seattle set up bicycle-powered laptops in the streets so that people could write up their reports of events as they happened. They created *Seattle IndyMedia* – a collective dedicated to open-publishing of activist news. The *IndyMedia* site quickly became the focal point for learning about Seattle.

There are now fifty *IndyMedia* websites around the world. The Italian *IndyMedia* site carried photos of the protester killed in Genoa before any mainstream media. It carried reports from the barricades on regular intervals. For the activists not at Genoa,

IndyMedia, not CNN or the BBC, was the means to finding out what was going on.

The anti-capitalist movement is growing. Genoa was a larger protest than those which had gone before, yet a larger proportion of the participants seemed willing to engage the police in direct confrontation, too. There is an enormous gap between the developed methods of protest being employed at the set-piece protests, and need for a movement that unites the whole working class in a day-to-day battle against capitalism itself.

The revolutionary left must learn how to engage with this movement and discuss with it. Our ideas, on the centrality of working-class self-emancipation, on the role of political struggle and industrial struggle aligned with the ideological struggle, and on the necessity for work in the trade unions, are irreplaceable in the class struggle – they are not very evident in the new anti-capitalism. Without them, the "anti-capitalism" of most of the protestors will be short-lived, sound and fury, and only an ephemeral small problem for the bourgeoisie.

Dialogue will not be easy. Repeatedly you encounter hostile reports of meetings and conversations with Trotskyists and Communists. To the new militants, the Trotskyists are authoritarian cults, desperate for new recruits but contributing nothing to the movement apart from sterile dogma and authoritarian organising methods. If we are to get an audience for Marxist ideas then we need to approach the movement with respect and openness and with a desire for genuine dialogue about the issues that concern its members.

A century of Satch

By Jim Denham

SOMEONE who'd watched the recent Ken Burns *Jazz* documentary series said to me: "I can't understand why Louis Armstrong is held in such high esteem in jazz circles. He always struck me as an Uncle Tom." That view is quite widely held, particularly by the more recent generation of jazz musicians, who find Armstrong's "mugging" for white audiences simply embarrassing. But there was a reason and a background for why Armstrong acted as he did: don't leap to judgement before you know the full story.

Louis Armstrong was born in New Orleans on 4 August 1901, at the absolute bottom of the pile. He was black, his mother was an alcoholic prostitute and his father deserted the family before he was born. He was destined for a life of poverty and petty crime until a Jewish family, the Karnoffskys, took him under their wing and encouraged his musical talent (including lending him the money for his first cornet). Louis never forgot them and wore a Star of David for the rest of his life. That early experience also conditioned his approach to the race question. He was proud of his Afro-American roots but never a separatist. He almost always had one or two whites in his band – a policy that his manager, Joe Glaser, encouraged for commercial reasons but that Armstrong believed in as a matter of principle. His best musical friend was the white trombonist Jack Teagarden, to whom he (allegedly) said: "I'm a spade and you're an ofay. We got the same soul – so let's blow."

Louis is, simultaneously, by far the best known figure in jazz and one of the most underrated. The reasons for this have little to do with music and everything to do with "style". Most of today's jazz fans, insofar as they know him at all, think of Armstrong as an avuncular buffoon singing lightweight pop songs in a gravel voice. He's not considered a "real" jazz musician like John Coltrane or the oh-so-cool Miles Davis. And then there's the "Uncle Tom" smear. We'll come to that later.

What is all too easily forgotten in any discussion about Armstrong, is the simple fact that he was the single most revolutionary musician of the 20th century. Long before he became the jovial entertainer that the world remembers, he almost single-handedly created jazz as we know it today.

Anyone who doubts this should listen to Armstrong's first recordings, with his mentor Joe "King" Oliver's band in 1923: Oliver and the rest chug along in the staccato, two-beat, ragtime rhythm that characterised all the jazz of that time. Armstrong (playing second cornet to Oliver) uses triplet-based quarter and eighth notes, riding on a 4/4 beat that only existed in his head. It was the rhythm that twelve or fifteen years later would be called "swing" and make Benny Goodman, Jimmy and Tommy Dorsey, Artie Shaw, Glenn Miller and a lot of other (mainly white) bandleaders rich and famous. That rhythm, together with the concept of the jazz soloist, which Armstrong also pioneered, was also the springboard for Charlie Parker and all that has followed in jazz, up until this very day.

It is true that had Armstrong never been born, someone else would have made this breakthrough sooner or later – it was a musical necessity waiting to happen. We know that Armstrong's New Orleans contemporary, the clarinet and soprano sax virtuoso Sidney Bechet, was also playing along similar lines in the early twenties. But Bechet was a (literally) wayward character, who didn't stay in the US to record very much and never achieved any serious recognition until he settled in France in the 1950s (where he became something of a folk-hero).

To understand Armstrong, the man and and the musician, you have to understand the society he was born into. New Orleans at the turn of the century was a hotbed of vice and violence. It was also, by comparison to the rest of the USA, tolerant in racial, social and cultural matters. The French had founded the city and brought a tradition of opera, symphony, dances and parties. This had meshed with musical traditions of the black slaves: work-songs and "shouts". New Orleans was the birthplace of jazz as we know it. But that was mainly due to the mixed-race "creoles", who constituted the vast majority of the early jazz musicians. It

is a myth that early jazz was the domain of Afro-American "negroes". In fact, creole musicians emphasised their French and/or Spanish heritage and tended to be quite disparaging towards negroes like Armstrong and Oliver.

On New Year's Eve of 1912 or 1913, Armstrong got arrested for some high-jinks with a pistol and was sent to the "Colored Waifs' Home" – a borstal. This place had a band and Louis soon became the lead cornet player in it. It was the best thing that ever happened to him. Years later, in the 1930s, Louis revisited the place, found his old room and snuggled down on the bunk: a man looking for security.

From the waifs' home Armstrong went on to become second cornet with "King" Oliver in Chicago (following the black migration to the new industries up there), "hot" trumpet soloist with Fletcher Henderson in New York and then to make the ground-breaking "Hot Five" and "Hot Seven" studio recordings with his old New Orleans pals Kid Ory (trombone) and Johnny Dodds (clarinet). Listening to those records is an education in personal development: Armstrong soon outstrips and overwhelms his old comrades, to such an extent that their contributions become anachronistic embarrassments.

By the early 1930s Armstrong was an international star, one of the first black American entertainers to tour Europe. Paul Robeson and Bill "Bojangles" Robinson (a big influence on Armstrong) were the only others. At this point a big contradiction becomes apparent: Louis' stage persona was the jovial, slightly wild, black trumpet virtuoso. Personally, he was completely insecure. He always needed a tough guy (like his long-term manager, the ex-gangster Joe Glaser) to look after him. Even after all the plaudits and awards, he needed the approval of an audience. After the last performance of his life (undertaken against medical advice), he watched a TV review of the show and was devastated by the slating he received ("You'll still book me, Joe?" he said, pitifully, to Glaser).

Louis "mugged" and played the harmless black minstrel to white audiences throughout his life. Younger black musicians accused him of being an "Uncle Tom". There was a grain of truth to the charge (Billie Holiday said "Louis Toms from the heart"). But they hadn't been through what he'd been through. Black entertainers like Sammy Davis Jnr., who attacked him, had never faced the full force of Jim Crow like Louis had. His choice had been to accept the system or not to perform at all. And, for Louis, performing was all that gave life any meaning.

There was one occasion, seized upon by the politically correct who want to claim him, when Armstrong entered the political arena: in 1957, segregated schools were ordered by the Federal Government to integrate. In Little Rock, Arkansas, black parents arrived with their kids at a school and were met by a mob of howling bigots. State Governor Faubus backed the racists and vowed to keep schools segregated, whatever the Federal Government said. Armstrong, on tour as usual, happened to be watching TV in his dressing room when pictures of a mob intimidating black children came on the screen. In front of the press he exploded with rage, denouncing Faubus and Eisenhower ("two-faced and no guts"). He said: "The way they are treating my people down South, the Government can go to hell." Joe Glaser pleaded with him to retract, but Louis refused and, indeed, went further, cancelling a State Department tour of the USSR.

Apologists tend to present this incident as proof that Armstrong was really a highly political person and/or a black militant: that's not true. His background, as we have seen, made him an instinctive integrationist. He admired Martin Luther King, but not the black seperatists.

Louis' attitude towards humanity is best summed up by the New Orleans guitarist Danny Barker, describing him on tour, in the dressing room: "... He be sitting down in his underwear with a towel around his lap, one around his shoulders an' that white handkerchief on his head and he'd put that grease around his lips. Look like a minstrel man, ya know...

"An' laughing you know natural the way he is. And in the room you see maybe two nuns. You see a street walker all dressed up in flaming clothes. You see a guy come out of the penitentiary. You see maybe a blind man sitting there. You see a rabbi, ya see a priest, see. Liable to see maybe two policemen or detectives, see. You see a judge. All of 'em different levels of society in the dressin' room and he's talkin' to all of 'em. 'Sister So and So, do you know Slick Sam over there? This is Slick Sam, an ole friend of mine'. Now the nun's going to meet Slick Sam. Ole Notorious, been in nine penitentiaries. 'Slick Sam, meet Rabbi Goldstein over there, he's a friend of mine, rabbi good man, religious man. Sister Margaret, do you know Rabbi Goldstein? Amelia, this is Rosie, girl used to work in a show with me years ago. Good girl, she's a great performer. Never got the breaks.' Always a word of encouragement, see. And there'd be some kids there, white and colored. All the diverse people of different social levels... an' everybody's looking. Got their eyes dead on him, jus' like they was lookin' at a diamond."

Pamphlets from Workers' Liberty

Our demands are very moderate: we only want the earth. Global capitalism and the environmental crisis. £1.50

The fight for a workers' government 60p

Radical chains: sexuality and class politics £1

Socialism and feminism £1

Why you should be a socialist 50p

Socialists answer the New Right £1.50

Globalisation: special issue of Workers' Liberty (no.63) £1.95

How do we get left unity?

Special issue of Workers' Liberty (no.52) £1.95

Lenin and the October Revolution 50p

New problems, new struggles: a handbook for trade unionists 95p

Index to back issues of Workers' Liberty £1

Education bulletins

Study notes on Capital £3.00

What is dialectics? £1.50

Send cheques, payable to "Alliance for Workers' Liberty", to AWL, PO Box 823, London SE15 4NA. Postage is free on orders above £10; others, please send 20% extra (minimum 20p).

China and independent working class politics

By Paul Hampton

THIS article argues that a renewed socialism for the 21st century will be based on independent working class politics. It uses the "Third Camp" as a formula for summing up this essential element for Marxist history and for current intervention in the class struggle. China represents a fertile example in both these respects. In 1925-27 the working class lost a revolutionary opportunity because it was subordinated to bourgeois nationalism by Stalin's Comintern; in 1949 the working class was absent because of the terrible defeat it suffered at the hands of Chiang Kai-shek. Mao's Communists were able to establish a Stalinist state and brutally exploit the working class in the aftermath of their bureaucratic revolution, and more recently to turn China towards capitalism. However, Chinese workers have consistently fought for their interests, and, despite some disastrous defeats, now have an unprecedented social weight in the country. The conclusion is that great class battles lie ahead, and that the Chinese working class will become the decisive social force in these struggles if it learns the lessons of its own history.

There is a huge task ahead of renewing socialism, cleansing it of Stalinist excrescences and sharpening its meaning in the context of 21st century global capitalism. Yet previous decades are not without their signposts, nor are the seeds of hope absent from the present. The world we live in is still defined by the existence of classes, grounded in exploitation, and contested through class struggle. This basic analysis of reality not only provides the motivation to change the world, but also implies the social agent with both the power and the interest to carry out such a wholesale transformation: the working class. For the renewal of socialism, we can do little better than to start with Marx's famous dictum that "the emancipation of the working class must be the act of the working class itself".

Implicit in the definition of socialism as the self-emancipation of the working class is the fight on all three fronts of the class struggle. It requires the working class to organise collectively at the point of production, where it has potential economic power, through its own trade unions and stewards' committees. It requires a political fight for working class representation, through the formation of a political party which intervenes in all kinds of campaigns and against all kinds of oppression, and in bourgeois-democratic politics. And it requires an unceasing struggle on the "ideological front", to combat the "ruling ideas of the epoch" and to carve out the programme, strategy and tactics to take this organised working class movement from its present state to the point where it can make its own revolution and take power into its own hands. On all fronts it implies democratic forms of organisation, the free exchange of ideas, and the means to thrash out alternative perspectives in order to take the next practical steps towards liberation.

One of the most fertile approaches to this conception of socialism is the idea of the "third camp". I take the third camp to mean consistently independent working class politics, the necessary line of march which the working class must take if it is to free itself. The third camp provides a convenient lens through which to understand earlier working class struggles: socialism from below implies the necessity of a history from below. But this is not merely virtual history from a working-class point of view, it is a history of the actual possibilities inherent in past struggles and the alternatives which workers actually faced as they fought for their interests. Similarly the third camp is not idle speculation in the present. Current politics demand to know which side are you on, and the third camp is a warning of the dangers of the lesser evil and an immediate reminder that "my enemy's enemy is not necessarily my friend". Ultimately it is a perspective of transforming the existing labour movement, but the third camp does not have to wait forlornly until the socialist forces are neatly assembled. As some protagonists put it in 1939:

> "The forces of the third camp are already at hand – scattered, demoralised, without program or perspective. The problem is to bring them together, to infuse them with

morale, to supply them with a program and perspective. To argue that these forces are small and insignificant has no political meaning, for the argument could apply both ways (if they are insignificant, they can no more 'defend' than they can 'defeat'). Political meaning is contained only in the line upon which we expect the vanguard to come together and along which we urge them to act." (Abern et al, quoted in Matgamna, 1998: 557).[1]

The past 80 years of Chinese history provide one of the best examples of the meaning of the third camp. Trotsky used the term to define his outlook during the great Chinese revolution (1925-27), when the emerging working class had the possibility of seizing power in it own interests, only to suffer a catastrophic defeat. The third camp was also a tool for understanding why the working class was absent during the 1949 revolution, and how the Maoist party-army created a Stalinist state which persists to this day. Finally the third camp helps us to understand the class struggles during the Maoist period, and following the immense economic transformation since 1978, the potential which the huge Chinese working class now has to finally consummate its own revolution.

How did the independent working class movement develop?

CHINA in 1919 was ripe for revolution. For two thousand years it was ruled by successive dynasties organised around a state bureaucracy. Still overwhelmingly a peasant country, it had stagnated for centuries until its last emperor, the five year old Pu Yi, was displaced and a republic created in 1911. After 1840 China suffered the indignity of ceding tracts of land such as Hong Kong to the European powers as "foreign concessions", and having opium foisted on its population, so that the British could better procure their tea. Imperial domination was summed up by the sign in the Shanghai municipal park which read, "No dogs or Chinese allowed".

The European overlords brought with them the misery of capitalist development. The process of industrialisation was heralded by the spread of modern rice processing factories and by the cotton mills. The working class grew rapidly – from 650,000 in 1915 to 1.5 million in the early 1920s. It was concentrated in the major cities: for example, in Shanghai in 1923, 57 factories employed between 500 and 1000 workers and another 49 employed over 1000 workers. Nevertheless the working class remained a small minority in the country as a whole. Its conditions of work were barbaric. As one observer described it:

"Some of the match factories and carpet factories, the ceramics and glass works, and the old-style silk and cotton factories could well have served an inspiration for even Dante's description of the infernal regions. Pale, sickly creatures move around there in almost total darkness, amidst indescribable filth, and breathing an atmosphere that is insupportable to anyone coming in from outside. At ten o'clock at night, or sometimes even later, they are still at work, and the feeble light of a few oil lamps lends the factories a still more sinister aspect. A few breaks are taken to snatch some food while still at work, or to eat a meal in a courtyard covered with excrement and filth of all kinds. When the time to stop work finally comes, these miserable creatures doss down in any place they can find – the lucky ones on bales of waste material or in the attics if there are any, and the rest on the workshop floor, like chained dogs." (Chesneaux, 1968: 86).

The revolution of 1911 had briefly brought Sun Yat-sen, leader of the Guomindang (Nationalist Party) to the presidency, but he was deposed by warlords and China carved up still further by civil war. However this ferment found an echo within a layer of intellectuals, who looked to western ideas such as science and democracy as the answer to China's problems. Most prominent was the May Fourth Movement, a kind of Chinese Enlightenment, which was sparked off by student demonstrations in Beijing in 1919 against the decision to transfer Germany's concessionary rights to Japan at the Paris Peace Conference. New periodicals sprouted up, the best being *New Youth*, edited by Chen Duxiu, then professor at Beijing University.

Out of this upsurge developed a labour movement, and a vanguard party. Inspired by the Russian revolution, small study circles of intellectuals, including socialists, anarchists and university teachers, came together to form the new organisation. In September 1920, *New Youth* became a communist paper, and *The Communist* was launched as an educational journal. The Chinese Communist Party (CCP) was founded in July 1921; Chen Duxiu was elected General Secretary, and Henk Sneevliet (Maring) represented the Communist International

(Comintern). Although it is true that in its early years the CCP was financed almost entirely by the Comintern, it was not an artificial creation. Rather the existing movement was redirected towards forming a new party. (Saich, 1991: 61-62), (Dirlik, 1989: 193-195).

What could the CCP do? The communists helped to build the trade unions, modelled on the Shanghai Mechanical Workers Union, which they had established in 1920, and militants inspired a strike against the British-American Tobacco company in Shanghai in 1921. However there remained the burning questions of China's situation – the absence of a democratic republic, the weight of imperial oppression, and the necessity of land reform. In 1920 Lenin counselled that, "The Communist International must enter into a temporary alliance with the bourgeois democracy in the colonial and backward countries, but should not merge with it, and should under all circumstances uphold the independence of the proletarian movement, even if it is in its most embryonic form." (1966: 149-150).

Where was this bourgeois-nationalist movement in China? Sneevliet put his faith with the Guomindang, characterising it as an amalgam of four different groups – the intelligentsia, emigrants, soldiers and workers, and therefore argued that the CCP should join it without becoming completely submerged. The Guomindang had been central to the Hong Kong seamen's strike in January-March 1922, in which 120,000 workers came out, winning a great victory. According to Sneevliet it had led the strike and recruited hundreds of militants, whereas the CCP had done very little. (Saich, 1991: 100, 106). Sun Yat-sen would only allow Chinese communists to join as individual members, but the new tactic was pushed through in August 1922. The CCP had just 123 members. Its leadership, including Chen Duxiu, voiced their unhappiness, but Sneevliet evoked Comintern discipline to pressurise them to agree. In fact asking CCP members to join the Guomindang as individuals was something of a dead issue at this point, as the Guomindang was then in a state of disarray because a warlord had just driven Sun Yat-sen out of Guangzhou. (Feigon, 1983: 172-173).

Events in China reinforced the new policy. By January 1923 Sun Yat-sen had retaken Guangzhou and returned to the city in triumph to re-establish his government there. However the most telling event was the repression of the Beijing-Hankou railworkers strike in February 1923. At Jiangan, the chair of the branch – Lin Xiangqian – was told three times to order a return to work and, when he refused, was beheaded and his head displayed on a bamboo pole. (Chesneaux, 1968: 209). The positions of the Communist Party and the Guomindang were reversed, with the Guomindang now in the ascendant. This finally persuaded Chen Duxiu and most of the other Chinese communists that the working class movement was too weak and that they should enter the Guomindang. Following the line of the Comintern, the CCP resolved that, "The Guomindang should be the central force of the national revolution and should assume its leadership". Leading members of the Communist Party were initiated into the Guomindang and they held a minority of places on its executive. The Russians helped to rebuild the Guomindang, with Borodin arriving as an adviser to Sun Yat-sen in 1923, and the Whampoa Military Academy was established to train its officers with Russian help.

Why was the working class defeated in the revolution 1925–27?

AFTER the victorious Hong Kong strike in January-March 1922 the Chinese labour movement grew rapidly. The CCP helped organise unions and played a major role in the founding of the first National Congress of Labour which met on 1 May 1922 with delegates representing 300,000 workers. Despite the murderous repression, the workers remained unbowed. On May Day 1924, 200,000 workers in Guangzhou and 100,000 in Shanghai marched for an eight-hour day. By May 1925, at the second National Congress of Labour, the trade unions announced a membership of 540,000. (Rousset, 1987: 8, 10). At this point strikes over wages spread through Japanese textile mills in Shanghai. Strikers were killed on the picket line, and thousands marched in protest. At a demonstration on 30 May, 1925, British police fired into a demonstration, killing 10 and wounding countless others. The Shanghai General Union, led by the CCP, organised a general strike two days later in all foreign owned companies. Over 160,000 workers were out by mid-June, and the strike began to spread to Chinese owned businesses. On 23 June, British and French troops shot at a demonstration in Guangzhou, killing 52 and injuring over a hundred. A general strike was called in Hong Kong, run by a Strikers Delegate Congress of over 800 delegates (out of around 50,000 strikers).

As Chesneaux put it, "The responsibilities of the strike committee went far beyond the normal field of activities dealing with a work stoppage. During the summer of 1925 the committee became, in fact, a kind of workers' government – and indeed the name applied to it by both its friends and its enemies was 'Government No. 2'" (1968: 292-293). The strike committee extended its activities to Guangzhou, and the strike lasted nearly 16 months. During that time, British power in China was virtually paralysed and the Guomindang was able to declare itself the national government. Plainly the situation had changed. In 1923 the CCP had 300 members and reached only 1000 in the spring 1925. Yet by November 1925 it had grown to 10,000 members. When the third National Congress of Labour met in May 1926 the trade unions announced a membership of 1,240,000 – by April 1927 the figure was 2.8 million. (Rousset, 1987: 11). Although the combined activity of the Comintern and Soviet diplomacy had contributed to the parallel growth of the CCP and Guomindang, they were now on a collision course.

What was the outcome of this revolutionary situation? On 20 March 1926 Chiang Kai-shek, who became leader of the Guomindang after Sun Yat-sen's death, ordered a surprise attack on a revolutionary naval unit headed by Communists in Guangzhou. The political advisers attached to this unit were arrested, along with the Soviet advisers. Chiang became master of the city, eliminating his opponents within the Guomindang. He fixed limits on CCP influence within the party. The CCP responded with timidity, accepting Chiang's conditions. In July 1926 Chiang launched the Northern expedition, aiming to drive out the warlords and unify the country under his command. Meanwhile the peasant war reached an apex. In 1926, the first National Congress of the Peasant Movement met, claiming one million members. In July 1926 the CCP set up a Peasant Department, with Mao Zedong as its head; by 1927 the party influenced approximately ten million peasants. Yet the CCP continued to denounce and hold back the peasants in Central China from rioting, pillaging and massacring landlords. In October 1926 Chiang's army ended the Guangzhou-Hong Kong strike and boycott. Only after Wang Jingwei set up an alternative Guomindang government in Wuhan did the Communists break with Chiang and instead supported the "left-wing" of the Guomindang.

The revolution was still in the ascendant. In November 1926 the Guomindang government moved from Guangzhou to Wuhan. The British were forced to abandon their concessions in this region. Chesneaux explained that, "the unions of Hubei and Hunan were, in fact, becoming a 'workers' government' to an even greater extent than those of Guangzhou had been during the Hong Kong strike and boycott." (1968: 325). They controlled large amounts of money, organised armed pickets – effectively a workers' militia paid for by the factories through the unions. The CCP grew to 30,000 members in July 1926 and 58,000 by the spring of 1927. At the time of the Northern Expedition the CCP organised 1.2 million workers and 800,000 peasants, especially through its influence in the nationalist Fourth Army. (Bianco, 1971: 55-56). In Shanghai in March 1927, workers greeted the incoming armies of the Guomindang as liberating heroes, rising magnificently with nearly 800,000 out on strike. Workers militias effectively controlled the city, and new trade unions sprang up. An insurrection in Shanghai handed over power to the general trade union and the Communists. Chiang's response on 12 April, 1927 was to orchestrate the massacre of the Shanghai working class, crush the trade unions, the peasant associations and the Communist Party. Victor Serge summed up the cataclysm:

"What has happened? This: on March 21-22, a working class insurrection, headed by the trade unions and few handfuls of courageous Communist militants, took Shanghai, China's real industrial and commercial capital, after a bitter street battle against the troops of the northern reaction. The proletariat carried out this exploit under the muzzles of English, French, American, Japanese and Italian cannon (not to mention the rest). Less than a month later, on April 13-14, the Generalissimo commanding the revolutionary-nationalist armies of the Guomindang had this proletariat treacherously disarmed and machine-gunned, defeated and strangled in a single night by his official allies. And this grievous blow –foreseen and announced for many weeks by the bourgeois press of every country – was a sad, frightful surprise for the working class militants and Communists of all countries."(1994: 63).

In April-May 1927 the CCP held its fifth congress in Wuhan. Chen Duxiu's supporters were largely removed from the central committee and the CCP further assimilated into the

Guomindang. After Chiang's massacre, the CCP, on the orders of Borodin, switched its allegiance to the "Left Guomindang" led by Wang Jingwei. Two Communists joined the Wuhan government, as ministers for labour and for agriculture, and were promptly sent into the countryside to suppress the insurrectionary peasants. Chen Duxiu resigned as General Secretary of the CCP, scapegoated for the defeats of the party. On 19 July 1927 the so-called left-wing of the Guomindang expelled the CCP and reunited with Chiang. Borodin fled China, just as the party he had so successfully reorganised along "Bolshevik" (in reality Stalinist) lines, finally triumphed. The CCP called for a general strike, but hardly a factory came out in support. Even for Zheng Chaolin, the workers by now looked on the CCP as a second Guomindang rather than their own party. (Benton, 1997: 130).

But the Chinese revolution had a final, cruel epilogue. The strategy of subordination to the Guomindang had obviously failed and the workers' had lost the initiative. Instead the Communists were ordered to organise a series of urban and rural insurrections, known as the Autumn Harvest risings. This culminated in the disastrous 'Canton insurrection', in which the CCP were ordered to take over Guangzhou by military force. Although Communist leaders in the city warned that an uprising was out of the question, the order was enforced by two of Comintern emissaries, who organised the uprising and used the Russian consulate as the insurgents' headquarters. (Bianco, 1971: 69). Not surprisingly, the putsch was isolated from the working class and easily put down. But it finally severed the link between the Communists and the working class. An estimated 38,000 Communists were liquidated. (Rousset, 1987: 12).

What conclusions can be drawn from this defeat?

"**B**UT it is precisely why I believe you have made an error... where you say that in China, 'two camps that are bitterly hostile to one another have come into being: in one are the imperialists and militarists and certain layers of the Chinese bourgeoisie; and on the other are the workers, artisans, petty bourgeoisie, students, intelligentsia and certain groups from the middle bourgeoisie with a nationalist orientation...' In fact, there are three camps in China – the reactionaries, the liberal bourgeoisie and the proletariat – fighting for hegemony over the lower strata of the petty bourgeoisie and peasantry. We know how complex and contradictory the course of the revolution is, especially in such a huge and – to an overwhelming extent – backward country like China. The revolution can still pass through a series of ebbs and flows. What we must safeguard in the course of the revolution is above all the independent party of the proletariat that is constantly evaluating the revolution from the point of view of three camps, and is capable of fighting for the hegemony in the third camp and, by so doing, in the entire revolution." Leon Trotsky, [1927].[2] (My emphasis)

The betrayal of the Chinese revolution was a major issue of disagreement between Stalin, who after 1923 consolidated his leadership of the USSR and over the Comintern, and the Left Opposition led by Trotsky. At its root were different conceptions of the revolutionary potential of the Chinese working class, with Stalin subordinating the Communist Party to the needs of Soviet diplomacy, whereas Trotsky perceived the need for further socialist revolutions, as part of his celebrated theory of permanent revolution.

The first disagreement concerned the nature of the Guomindang. Stalin, interpreting Sneevliet, argued the Guomindang was a "bloc of four classes", or a workers and peasants' party, whereas Trotsky saw it as a straightforward bourgeois formation.[3] While Trotsky did not reject an alliance between the Chinese Communists and the Guomindang, he was alarmed at the form it took. However Stalin enforced his analysis within the Comintern, which meant the vanguard of the Chinese proletariat was not merely allied, but actively subordinated to the nationalists. This was well summed up by Comintern representatives in March 1926: "The present period is one in which the Communists should do coolie service for the Guomindang." (Duxiu, 1976: 601). In fact, following Stalin's policy during this period, the Comintern seemed to replace the working class with the peasantry as the main revolutionary protagonist in backward countries.

Yet within the Comintern, and the Chinese Communist Party, there were early voices who concurred with Trotsky rather than Stalin. As Zheng Chaolin explained, "[In 1924] Peng Shuzhi brought back an article from Moscow titled *Who Leads the Chinese National Revolution?* He said that after the achievement of the national revolution, we would still

47

need to carry out 'our own' revolution. But he also said that the revolution that is 'not our own' would 'automatically' come under the leadership of the proletariat. This theory of the proletariat constituting the natural leadership of the national revolution was to the exact taste of the Chinese comrades and became the guiding theory in the Party during those few years." (Benton, 1997: 110). In fact on at least five occasions Chen Duxiu advocated a change of policy instead of the "united front from within". (Feigon 1983: 176). The root of Stalin's errors was his analysis of events in China as a struggle between two camps, essentially the imperialist powers and warlords on one side, and the nationalists on the other, with the socialist revolution put off to some distant point in the future. This was particularly damaging when a revolutionary situation developed in 1925, and the forces of counter-revolution gathered around the Guomindang. The centrality of the working class – the third camp perspective which Trotsky articulated in 1927 was well explained at the time by Victor Serge:

"China has almost five million industrial or craft workers (120,000 railway men, 420,000 miners, 300,000 textile workers and 200,000 metal workers). Working class centres such as Shanghai, Hankou and the mines of Hainan are strong strategic positions for the proletariat. All the recent epoch-making events of the Chinese Revolution are those of working class action. The boycott of Hongkong kept up for 16 months is the work of the Guangzhou workers (the Cantonese bourgeoisie, helped by the National government, has lifted it). The great Shanghai strikes of 1925 marked the take-off point of the revolution. The taking of the British concession in Hankou by proletarians is the greatest victory of the 'Northern Campaign'. Then followed the admirable exploit that was the seizure of Shanghai by the workers' insurrection..." (1994: 78).

In March 1926, the Guomindang was admitted to the Communist International as a sympathising party and Chiang made an honourary member, with only Trotsky voting against. When Chiang organised his coup later the same month, the news was suppressed in the USSR and the Comintern press glowed with pride at the "revolutionary government" (Isaacs, 1938: 125). In April 1926 Trotsky appealed to the Politburo for a change of line and in September he formally moved for the CCP to withdraw from the Guomindang. (Evans and Block, 1976: 116). Trotsky called for soviets in China at the Politburo in March 1927, before Chiang's bloody coup. He would seek to salvage the situation for the Chinese party at the Comintern in May 1927, his articles for the Soviet press having been rejected. He was not to know until long afterwards that Chen Duxiu and his supporters were struggling for precisely the same independent orientation, only to be thwarted by the Comintern.[4]

In October 1926 Stalin sent a telegram which urged the Chinese Communists to moderate the peasant movement in order to preserve the alliance with the Guomindang. When the CCP requested 5,000 rifles to advance the peasant struggle they were denied by Borodin. The Comintern still upheld the alliance even though the nationalist government imposed compulsory arbitration in strikes and the unions remained illegal in "liberated" areas. The Communists pledged not to criticise Sun Yat-sen – indeed its "daily" paper only appeared irregularly as a weekly. As late as April 1927, Stalin boasted that the Guomindang would be "utilised to the end, squeezed like a lemon and then thrown away". (Isaacs, 1938:185). In fact it was Chiang who tossed away the Communists. Even as he did so, Comintern agents were still ordering Shanghai and other workers to surrender their arms to him. Max Shachtman summed up the tragedy of Chinese revolution:

"Victory lay within reach of the hand for the Chinese workers and peasants, but something unprecedented in history took place: the leadership, clothed in all the formal authority of the Russian revolution and the Communist International, stood in the way like a solid wall. Stalin and Bukharin prohibited the proletariat from taking power. In the Chinese revolution the epigones played to the end, and with tragic results, the role which Lenin's struggle in the Bolshevik party in April-May 1917 prevented them from playing in the Russian revolution." (1974: 34).

Trotsky's third camp analysis upheld the independent role of the working class but was flexible enough to incorporate tactics towards both the bourgeois Guomindang and an alliance with the peasantry. (It would prove flexible enough to address the Japanese invasion in 1937 too.) Trotsky responded concretely to the reality of the situation as it developed, posing tasks for the Communist Party so that it could play its historic role as the vanguard of the working class. It is impossible to judge in hindsight whether, if the communists had followed Trotsky's directives, they would have inevitably led the working class to power. But all the objective prerequisites for a successful seizure of power were present by 1927, except for the necessary leadership to consummate the process.

Only a few hundred supporters of Trotsky, from within the CCP and from amongst the returning students from Moscow, drew the lessons from this disaster and retained a commitment to the working class in China. Among them were Chen Duxiu, Peng Shuzhi and Zheng Chaolin, leading figures from the leadership of the Communist Party. According to Wang Fanxi, by late 1927 Chen had already come into contact with some of Trotsky's ideas from students returning from Moscow. (Feigon 1983: 199). By the middle of 1929 Chen Duxiu had organised an opposition group and Liu Renjing had made direct contact with Trotsky. On 1 May 1931 the unification of the Chinese Left Opposition (CLO) took place, with 438 members. If the prospects were bright after unification, why did the Chinese Opposition fail to make an impact? Remaining in cities, they were decimated by Guomindang and later CCP repression. Benton argues that the disciplinary measures of the CCP, together with its relative affluence compared to the CLO (the CCP received $400,000 a month from the USSR) were significant, but the main reason was Guomindang repression. Chen and Peng were arrested in October 1932 (1996: 109-113). Benton also argued that they were unable to develop a strategy for the new opportunities which opened up after the Japanese invasion in 1937. Although there were some Trotskyist-led guerrillas, including some 2000 in Shandong, they were destroyed by the CCP. (Fanxi, 1991: 214). Nevertheless they held up the banner of authentic Marxism in a period of terrible defeat for the working class, and despite their size, offered a way out of this impasse for the Chinese proletariat.

Why was the working class absent in the 1949 revolution?

"YET the proletariat played a negligible role in the last and decisive phase of the revolution. Neither major strikes nor urban uprisings paved the way for the Red Army as they had 20 years earlier for Chiang Kai-shek in Shanghai. There were very few workers in the triumphant Red Army; it was composed essentially of peasants and officered by other peasants and intellectuals." Bianco (1971: 83-84).

At the end of 1926, two thirds of CCP members were workers, a quarter were intellectuals and 5% peasants. Yet by 1928 only 10% were workers, just 3% by 1929 and virtually none by 1930. In 1928 the CCP "did not have a single healthy party nucleus among industrial workers". (Isaacs, 1938: 333, 394); what remained of the vanguard was dissipated into the countryside. Mao established his first revolutionary base in October 1927 with 1,000 men. Within three years this peasant army numbered 65,000 and in November 1931, the "Chinese Soviet Republic" was founded in the south Kiangsi area, covering a population of 2.5 million by 1932. (Bianco, 1971: 64-65). When the second congress of "soviets" met in January 1934, there were only eight urban workers out of 821 delegates. During the Long March, out of 90-100,000 who set out, only 7-8,000 arrived with Mao in Shensi a year later, with perhaps with only 30,000 eventually reaching northwestern China, further separating the party from the working class centres and entrenching the peasant composition of the party-army. (Rousset, 1986: 3). In short the Chinese Communist Party was a completely different entity from the one built and smashed in the 1920s.

Nevertheless, the consolidation of the Communist party-state after 1935 under Mao's undisputed leadership proved to be a crucial turning point. The Guomindang was unable to threaten the existence of the party, and the Japanese invasion offered the opportunity to incorporate more territory under its control. (The invasion also further dispersed the working class on the eastern seaboard.) When Japan surrendered in 1945, there were 19 Communist base areas. In 1937 there were 80,000 men in the Red Army; in 1945 there were 900,000 soldiers, and Mao claimed a militia force of 2.2 million men. In 1937 the CCP governed 1.5 million peasants in desolate Shensi; in 1945 there were 90 million peasants under Communist control. In 1945 the party had 1.2 million members, controlled about 10% of Chinese territory and was a serious contender for power. (Bianco, 1971: 150). Yet in Shanghai the CCP apparently had only 800 worker-activists in 1948. It had succeeded in creating a social force capable of ruling; the tragedy was that this force had nothing to do with working class self-emancipation. However they came to power, the Chinese Communists certainly did not do so in the manner of the Russian Bolsheviks in 1917.[5]

Regarding the kind of revolution possible if the working class was unable to take power, Victor Serge offered an interesting interpretation. Quoting the Soviet sinologist Ivine, he argued that over the last 2,000 years China had experienced five great peasant rebellions, all led by vast secret associations of poor peasants against the big landowners, the usurers, the feudal lords and the state bureaucracy; all of them ending in the more or less complete expropriation of the rich classes; after which the process of concentration of wealth and the pauperisation of the small cultivator began again, until the next peasant uprising. He believed that the "history of China provided a spectacle of the tragic repetition of an economic process that for 20 centuries until our own day has only undergone minor modifications... Precise information seems to indicate that we are on the eve of a peasant movement comparable with the greatest ones of the past. Will the former cycle of revolutions be repeated once again? That is the question." (Serge, 1994: 85-86). This was an important insight, but I think it overlooks the fundamentally modern character of the Chinese revolution, and the unique role of the Communists in crafting their own path to power (which Serge could not have foreseen in 1927).

Trotsky himself drew attention to these possibilities in his article *The Peasant War in China*, (1932), but he also posed the question of what would occur when the "Red Armies" encountered the working class, suggesting the likelihood of conflict. Comparing them with the Social Revolutionary armies during the civil war he foresaw disaster for the working class if the peasantry became the foot-soldiers of another social force. He wrote: "In old China every victorious peasant revolution was concluded by the creation of a new dynasty... Under present conditions the peasant war by itself, without direct leadership of the proletarian vanguard, can pass only on the power to a new bourgeois clique... And this would signify in turn a new massacre of the workers with the weapons of 'democratic dictatorship'." (Evans and Block, 1976: 527-528, 530). He even speculated that the CCP and the Chinese Left Opposition might come to represent different class bases, although at this time he did not conceive of the Communist apparatus in Russia or abroad as an autonomous force. Yet Trotsky's prognosis contained more than a germ of truth, and he provided further insight on this Stalinist variant only days before his assassination in 1940:

"The predominating type among the present 'Communist' bureaucrats is the political careerist, and in consequence the polar opposite of the revolutionist. Their ideal is to attain in their own country the same position that the Kremlin oligarchy gained in the USSR. They are not the revolutionary leaders of the proletariat but aspirants to totalitarian rule. They dream of gaining success with the aid of this same Soviet bureaucracy and its GPU. They view with admiration and envy the invasion of Poland, Finland, the Baltic states, Bessarabia by the Red Army because these invasions immediately bring about the transfer of power into the hands of the local Stalinist candidates for totalitarian rule." (Breitman, 1973: 350-351). (My emphasis)

Why was the working class absent? It was not primarily due to a weak social base – 1925-27 had shown that – nor was it simply down to an economic crisis. The catastrophic defeat suffered in 1927 must be considered one of the principal causes of the workers' absence in 1949. The reasons were again essentially political – the repression by the Guomindang, the disorganisation of workers into sham unions, together with the shattering of the vanguard for a generation. Quite simply, and despite the best efforts of the Chinese Trotskyists, the third camp of the working class was crushed beneath the juggernauts of the Guomindang and the Communists.[5]

Why was a Stalinist state established in China after 1949?

"ANY political party or state apparatus which enslaves the working class is, in this day and age, from a proletarian, socialist, revolutionary point of view, fundamentally and completely reactionary. Therefore the CCP and the state apparatus which it has set up are also reactionary. Yet at the same time we must recognise the following facts: They have overthrown the Kuomintang [Guomindang] government, which represents foreign imperialism and the native bourgeoisie and landlord class; they are wiping out the anachronistic agrarian relationships in China's farming villages; they have dealt a mighty blow to the foreign imperialist powers led by the United States. All of these actions, from the point of view of Chinese nationalism and democracy, have an undeniably progressive character. The difficulty is this: how and why can a fundamentally reactionary political party and government perform objectively progressive acts?" Wang Fanxi, (1951: 102).

The only real attempts to develop and extend Trotsky's analysis at the time were the articles by Jack Rader, under the pseudonym of Jack Brad, in the pages of *Labor Action* and the *New International*, and Chinese Trotskyists like Wang Fanxi. Rader's articles were a model of clarity and accuracy in their prognoses of the situation. Unable to seriously influence workers' in China, these articles at least pointed to a different outcome than either a Guomindang or Communist Party victory, and thus upheld the third camp banner of Marxism, which championed the independence of the working class.

Rader acknowledged that the CCP had established a peasant base, but given its separation from the working class it had become in composition and outlook a rural party. It had even developed an ideology in which the peasantry was given leadership in the Chinese revolution, acting through the organisation of the Communist Party. But from a Marxist perspective, "Nowhere in modern history has a national revolution been led by a party based on the peasantry. The unique Chinese experience is possible because of that unifying ingredient which is absent in the peasantry as a class [i.e., the Communist Party]. With its discipline, ideology, leadership and indefatigable organisational labors it creates cohesion and gives unified direction." (1949a: 50).

The answer lay in the transformation of the party. Echoing Trotsky's final verdict on other communist parties, Rader argued that, "Since 1927 Stalinism has not been a political party in China but an armed camp, an embryo state. Party members and leaders were equivalent to state officials. Sometimes the fortunes of the state party were low indeed, as after the Long March when it was reduced to 40,000. In those days, and even today, not only were and are party and state identical, but the two are coefficients of the army's power and are identical with it too." (1949a: 50) Since the founding of the Chinese "Soviets" in the South, there has existed a special GPU or political police. (1949b: 4). As such the Chinese Communist Party was a Stalinist party, with identical aims to its Russian parent and would seek power in order to create its own system of class exploitation:

"The Chinese Communist Party is aiming at a monopoly of political power. All compromises with coalitions, with propertied classes in city and village will not alter this basic fact. They will permit the city bourgeoisie to retain their factories and mercantile establishments (provided they do not encroach on big industry and big commerce which will be nationalised). But they will not permit then to organise political parties to represent these interests. They will support the village tukhoa (kulak), but at the same time insist that he accept the party as his sole defender. They will form unions and workers will be forced to join, but any party that arises to speak for the workers outside of officially created organisations will be dealt with as counter-revolutionary." (1949b: 4)

Rader defined the seizure of power by the CCP as a "bureaucratic revolution", in which the working class did not play an active role. He contrasted this revolution with others in modern history, in which, "a rainbow variety of ideologies has had to struggle for support and position of hegemony... This was the source of the enormous release of energy and the dramatically democratic nature of the revolutionary process. Millions, emerging on the stage of history, become politically literate overnight, developing unforeseen talents, assuming new roles and carving out a new historic path." In China he argued that the opposite had occurred: "The CP is marching to victory over a road which is a political desert. No contenders are in the field against it and no other political movement allied with it. The military character of its conquest is a consequence of this reality. We are witnessing the classical form of bureaucratic-collectivist revolution, the pre-condition for which is the prostration of the great urban social classes which have been the prime movers of history since the Renaissance." (1949c).

He cited examples of CCP directives for the newly conquered cities requesting that: "'All law-abiding enemy functionaries, personnel of economic and educational organs and policemen should not be taken prisoner or arrested. They must be given duties and remain at their original posts under orders of definite organs and personnel, to watch over their original organs." (*China Digest*, August 13, 1948, 1949a: 52). At the outset of the conquest of the Yangtze valley, an eight point proclamation, "hoped that workers and employers in all trades will continue work and that businesses will operate as usual". Even in Shanghai, where great unrest was caused by the inflation, where a great strike wave had occurred and the Guomindang's power had ebbed, the workers remained non-political, not even organised as a class grouping." (1949c).

But he did not fail to note the significance of what was occurring, even if the revolution was being led by the mortal enemies of the working class. For the first time a Stalinist state of continental proportions had been established outside of Russia and on the basis of its own conquest of power. An historic event had occurred:

"The conquest of all China by Stalinism is an event of world history whose full significance will unfold with time. If Stalinism can organise effectively this continent and begin its industrialisation, it may well be one of the turning points of history. A powerful social force, albeit a force of counter-revolutionary Stalinism, is sweeping aside the three millennia-old incubus of decay and stagnation. China is being torn from her antiquated roots and thrust into the modern world maelstrom. The tragedy of the Stalinist victory lies in this: that this gigantic event takes place under the aegis of a totalitarian rather than liberating leadership, one which will tie China to the Russian despotism in world politics as in domestic economic construction." (1949c).

What could working class socialists do in this situation? Rader argued that the working class was not yet completely permeated by Stalinism and could still be imbued with political independence. The CP was primarily an agrarian party and an independent proletariat could eventually organise its own organs, take power in the rich coastal cities, and organise an independent democratic movement which could call the peasants to revolutionary action. He thought workers should call for immediate arming of all the people in fighting units of their own, with their own elected officers. They could organise under the programme of ousting the capitalists regardless of party; for social and political democracy, not a new one-party regime; for maximum freedom to organise, without CP direction; against the CP doctrine of revolution by "stages"; for the restoration of revolutionary leadership of the workers; and for full freedom of speech and press. (1949a: 54).

The major problem for the CCP was how to create a new national ruling class around the party as a core by recruiting from many sections of the population, especially the young intellectuals. Rader denounced the Consultative Conference they set up, counterposing to it "democratic assemblies of freely elected delegates". He also defended the right of Formosans to self-determination, noting that Chiang had massacred 20,000 in 1947, and that if the CCP were victorious, they would establish a new tyranny. He called on the Chinese masses to fight against all imperialism and its agents, American and Russian. Most of all, "The workers of China need a party of their own. That is the beginning of a program." (1949a: 54) [6]

A similar balance sheet was offered by Wang Fanxi inside China at the time. He showed that a third camp perspective, if not the forces to coalesce around it, was still alive in China, when he wrote: "In judging and estimating the nature of a movement, a political party, or a state, for the proletarian revolutionist there is one unchanging standard: What is its relation to the working class, that is, to the only revolutionary class in the modern world? For us there can be no more decisive standard than that, nor can there be any other point of departure." (1951: 100). Wang argued that the CCP had not improved the position of the working class, while economically it had lowered their standard of living. In reality, like the Guomindang, the Communists enslaved the Chinese working class. For Wang it was the 20 year absence of the working class from the political stage which determined what he called "the peasant aspect, the capitalist nature and the bureaucratic-collectivist direction of Chinese Stalinism". Although Wang's views did not completely coincide with Rader, and he later revised his analysis, his early assessment still has great merit. The tragedy was that he found it increasingly difficult to correspond from his virtual prison on Macau, and of his few hundred co-thinkers on the mainland, almost all were imprisoned after 1952. [7]

What was the social nature of China after 1949?

ONE of the yawning gaps in the development of a third camp perspective is an extension of the analysis pioneered by Rader and Wang to the whole Maoist period, and to the ruling Stalinist bureaucracy's subsequent turn towards capitalism under Deng. The rightful starting point is Marx's method for differentiating class societies, "the specific economic form in which surplus labour is pumped out of the direct producers determines the relationship of rulers and ruled". (Marx, 1977: 791). After 1949, the Communist party-army used its military victory to smash what remained of the old bourgeois state, organised around the Bonapartist Guomindang, and its monopoly of violence to create a new state. In essence this was an expansion of the "Soviet" established in 1931, over a larger territory, although the CCP sought to incorporate others who had allied with it in the so-called "united front" against the Japanese and the Guomindang.

This new state proceeded to expropriate the landlords and the capitalists, to nationalise the means of production and to establish a new form of exploitation, on the blueprint of the USSR, creating a new ruling class around the Communist Party. The mode of surplus extraction was direct and collective. Through the nationalisation of industry and the collectivisation of agriculture, the new ruling class could control the means of production, and set the tempo for industrial expansion through its five year plans, first instituted in 1953. The amount of necessary labour workers and peasants had to perform to reproduce themselves (i.e. to produce the means of consumption) was directly managed through a system of subsidies and rationing, whilst the state could appropriate their surplus labour essentially as tribute directly from the factories and farms. That such a bureaucratic-command system was bound to malfunction does not negate the fact that the CCP was the "sole master of the surplus product".

By 1956, 97% of rural households worked in co-operatives and 88% on collective farms; in the same year 68% of factories had been nationalised and the remainder transformed into joint state-private enterprises. According to Mao, China had 12 million industrial workers out of a population of 600 million in 1957. As Cheng and Selden argue, the hukou system of population registration was crucial to the social relations established by the party-state, in particular the restrictions on labour migration and the channelling of the agricultural surplus product to the cities. Hukou registration determined their identity, citizenship and proof of official status. (1997: 24, 32). Although it had antecedents in the ancient baojia system of mutual surveillance and the Soviet passbook system, the hukou was a unique, contemporary phenomenon. It divided the cities from the countryside, where peasants were expected to live self-sufficiently, and regulated the supply of labour to the cities. Introduced after 1953, the hukou privileged those who lived in urban areas, with the state taking on direct responsibility for their well being and exploitation. This was carried out principally by the danwei (work units) system; without it workers lost their eligibility for food, clothing, housing, employment, education, marriage and army enlistment.

In the cities, the mechanism for regulating workers' means of consumption (the so-called "iron rice-bowl") was the danwei. After 1958 work units took responsibility for the provision of housing, food, healthcare and pensions, replacing the earlier form of registration based on the family unit. Between 1953-56 private home ownership was largely eliminated in urban areas and the state established a monopoly over urban housing. At the same time, state control over food was established, and food rationing introduced for grain and clothing in 1955, features which were to remain for over thirty years. Stalinism with Chinese characteristics lacked capitalist markets: its symbolic rents, low prices and notional wages did not correspond with the proportions of social labour employed. The outward appearance of this system were the coupons for sugar, rice, soup and cigarettes and the queues in the cities which were still a visible part of life a decade ago.

The Great Leap Forward sparked rapid urbanisation between 1958-60. Some 38 million people left their villages; even in the state sector employment rose by 21 million in 1958 alone. The urban population rocketed from 15% to 20% of the population, as rural Chinese temporarily burst the fetters of the hukou system. But as Michael Harrington observed astutely at the time, "Yes, Chinese Communism industrializes – but at enormous cost and through enormous waste". (1958: 100). The principal cause was the terrible starvation unleashed by the forced collectivisation of agriculture, the forced extraction of the agricultural surplus by the state, now known as the "great leap famine", responsible for perhaps 20 million deaths in the space of four years. Grouping peasants into large agricultural communes, and into production brigades, creating mess halls for food and indoctrination, the regime did away with the old relations in the countryside, and resisted the creation of household responsibility which peasants developed to avoid the crisis. (Yang; 1997: 282-4). Yet within the space of two years, some 20 million workers were laid off and sent back to the countryside. (Cheng and Selden, 1997: 44). Thereafter people were forced to reside in the place of their birth, except for women who might live at their husband's domicile. It is not surprising that Mao is remembered by ordinary Chinese for his slogan, "in order to have construction, you must first have destruction".

China's limited industrialisation for 30 years after the revolution was hardly analogous to the primitive accumulation of capital which ushered in the modern epoch in Europe. The system bound workers and peasants to the means of production, indeed millions simply lived and died in their place of birth and with their tools. It did not create a capitalist class but rather a Behemoth state which arbitrarily drove the exploitation of the direct producers with only limited success. By the 1970s, the system was simply unable to generate the surplus necessary to carry out the transformation of the Chinese economy. The chronic malfunctioning of the system was built into its very nature; in competition with capitalism it was bound to fail.

As if to illustrate its perversity, the Chinese bureaucracy had recourse to the most primitive forms of exploitation, just as Stalin did in the thirties. A huge pool of slave labour, encarcerated in over a thousand labour camps by the 1970s, served both as an economic resource for the state and a chilling reminder of the costs of opposition. China lurched from the great leap famine through the cultural revolution with its barely formed system unable to satisfy its ruling class, let alone the needs of workers and peasants. And with workers' democracy ruled out by the nature of their rule, the only place for the CCP to go was the market.[8]

How has China developed towards capitalism since 1978?

WITHIN two years of Mao's death, China under Deng Xioping began to lurch towards capitalism under the guise of a "socialist market economy". Deng's change of direction with slogans like "it doesn't matter what colour the cat is, as long as it catches mice", might be rationalised as gradualism, but in fact the aperture unleashed a wave of class struggle in the countryside. Believing they now had the chance to make money, peasants broke out of their "communes" to produce for profit, going beyond the intentions of the CCP in embracing household responsibility. This process has transformed the countryside, with 200 million clambering out of absolute poverty (defined as $1000 per year) releasing labour for the township enterprises which now generate 40% of China's industrial output. Signalling the collapse of the old communes, 800 million now effectively stand outside of the old system of exploitation, but only to exchange it for the bondage of the market place.

Over the past twenty years China has undergone the most rapid industrialisation yet seen in human history. In the words of Paul Theroux, "Yesterday's paddy field is tomorrows high rise, and a thousand factories bloom". Twenty years ago Shenzhen near Hong Kong was merely a rural hamlet; today it is a super-city with four harbours. Suzhou Industrial Park near Shanghai, known as 'Little Singapore', is currently under construction after foreign investment of $20bn and will soon house 600,000 people. Shanghai itself is once more Asia's largest city, its polluted skyline dotted with high-rise towers, its rivers spanned by new bridges and its new roads teetering on top of the old, all built with the new money. While there is still a red star over China, capitalism is rapidly engulfing the firmament.

The Chinese government boasts of its virility in the language of economic growth statistics. The United States took 47 years between 1839-86 to double its per capita income, whereas China has managed the same feat between 1978-87, and again from 1987-96. China is now the world's largest producer of grain, meat, cotton and peanuts, as well as steel, coal, cement, fertiliser and TV sets. Already one of the largest economies in the world, it is expected to rival the US as the largest on the planet within two generations. The harbinger of capitalism has been the foreign investment of the Chinese diaspora, especially from Taiwan and the newly integrated Hong Kong. The prosperity of the eastern seaboard has created a labour market and thus undermined the danwei; market wage rates and prices have replaced state rationing and new housing is either sold or rented at exorbitant cost to tenants.

According to Sargeson, terms such as exploited (boxue) and class (jieji) and wage labourer (dagong) are now commonplace in workers discourse about their working lives. Presently, millions of Chinese workers fit Marx's description of the proletariat which was formed in Europe in the early stages of industrialisation. In 1979 there were 49 million workers employed in industry, commerce, transport and services which were not state-owned; by 1995 this figure had increased to 167 million, or 60% of China's non-agricultural workforce. (1999: 3-4). On this broad definition, the Chinese working class now numbers over 270 million people.

One of the signs of the development of capitalism in China is the dramatic decline of state-owned firms. In 1978, state-owned enterprises produced three-quarters of China's total output. In 1995 this had fallen to approximately one-third, less than was produced by collectively owned rural firms. Overseas investment, ostensibly from companies registered in Hong Kong and Macau, means that over 20% of China's exports earnings now come from foreign-invested enterprises, and private firms employ approximately 56 million people. (Sargeson, 1999: 27-29). Another is this huge increase in the number of contract and temporary workers. The party-state has simplified hiring and firing practices, eliminated life-long employment in state firms and supported performance-related pay. Because of continued political domination by the CCP, these reforms have resulted in a proliferation of rent-seeking and entrepreneurial activity on the part of government officials. In this bastard-capitalism, connections to the bureaucracy facilitate business activity, with all the implied corruption and nepotism.

To facilitate labour mobility and the operation of a labour market, the government has approved temporary residence permits and the transfer of personnel dossiers. In 1990 only 12% of the urban workforce were on temporary contracts; within six years this figure rose to 41%. Some estimates indicate that one-third of the adult work-force, or approximately 200 million people, were surplus to agricultural requirements and were underemployed or unemployed. Even a decade ago there were 70-80 million migrant rural workers in China's towns and cities. (Sargeson, 1999:31-34) Youth, mainly women, work in the new factories as little more than modern indentured labour. Two-thirds of the population still live in the countryside, and 300 million people still subsist on less than $1 a day. Last year 20 million workers were sacked or indefinitely sent home, yet the government quotes a figure of 3% for unemployment.

Conditions in the new economic zones recall the description of factories nearly a century ago. One survey found a factory in Shenzhen with 521 separate punishments for workers' infringement of workplace regulations. Prohibitions on using the toilet, drinking and talking during working hours, go together with draconian piece-rate systems and the use of electronic prods by supervisors. Even in state-owned firms, where workers had been relatively privileged, authoritarian management, long working days, productivity pay and harsh discipline have become the norm. Workers do not have the right to strike, unless their workplace is unsafe. Independent unions are prohibited, and leaders liable to imprisonment. Even official union membership is rare among workers in private business. Despite the 1995 national labour law, which was supposed to regulate conditions for the (40 hour) working week, minimum wages and safety are ignored with impunity. (Sargeson, 1999: 40-41).

The period since 1978 is far closer to the era of the primitive accumulation of capital, in the manner as Marx described it: the creation of a class of capitalists and a class of proletarians. (Holmstrom and Smith, 2000: 2, 15). Allowing for the obvious differences between feudalism and Stalinist collectivism, what has happened over the past twenty years in China does look uncannily like the process of separating the direct producers from the bondage of the old social relations in town and country (i.e., the hukou, danwei, etc.), and subjecting them to tyranny of the labour market. On the other hand, this period has also witnessed the emergence of a rapacious capitalist class, out of a section of the old bureaucracy that has acted in collusion with overseas capital. The incorporation of Hong Kong and the tension between China and Taiwan are significant in this respect. It also implies that huge explosions are ahead as these social forces come into conflict.

How has the working class struggled under CCP rule ?

RECENT academic research has challenged the commonly-held myth that Chinese workers basically supported the Maoist regime. Numerous times since 1949 the working class has risen up in major acts of protest, and working-class dissent over the past fifty years has been the most heavily repressed by the Communist Party. There is little doubt that the last half-century of Chinese history has been characterised by uninterrupted class struggle, sometimes open, sometimes hidden.

Sheehan's research confirms that the working class was "relatively passive" when the CCP took power. (1998: 26). The right to strike was included in the constitution, but workers were told they no longer needed to use these old methods of struggle. A sign of caution towards the new regime was that workers did not dismantle the old Guomindang "unions", preferring these organisations to nothing at all. Although workers' congresses were established in factories, they became rubber stamp bodies for factory management committees, with party cadres and factory directors making the crucial decisions. The official trade unions preached the doctrine of increasing production and labour discipline. The All China Federation of Trade Unions (ACFTU) defined their tasks as, "To ensure and consolidate labour discipline,

55

correctly organise labour, fully and rationally use working hours, raise labour productivity and turn out quality products". (Harrington, 1958: 91). The nationalisation of industry tended to reduce the democracy and participation of the workers, and former capitalists received interest payments and sometimes posts in these new joint enterprises, which was resented by workers.

The working class is often written out of accounts of the Hundred Flowers protests, yet workers talked of "creating another Hungarian incident" (Sheehan, 1998: 48). Workers' complaints included high fares and rents, sick pay and the abolition of end of year bonuses and allowances. The unofficial Guangzhou dock strike in the spring of 1957 involved half the workforce. Workers formed autonomous unions, sometimes called "redress grievance societies" and adopted a "waged-labour mentality". Workers continued to complain that party cadres had special sanatoria and canteens, and some denounced the party as a new ruling class. Research by Perry reveals that in the spring 1957, there were major labour disturbances in Shanghai, including more than two-hundred walk-outs, one hundred organised showdowns and over 700 less serious disturbances. By comparison in 1919 there were 56 strikes, 175 in 1925, and 280 strikes in 1946. Only the last six months of Guomindang rule witnessed more strikes, when the numbers rocketed to over three thousand. (Perry, 1997: 234, 254). These figures are one more illustration that far from being a golden age, this period was one of fundamental social cleavages.

Perry does not deny the role of Mao in encouraging protests during this period, but puts the causes down to economic restructuring. Some 90% of strikes took place in the newly formed joint-ownership enterprises, the majority of them in small workplaces with less than one hundred workers. These changes had affected workers' real incomes, and led to disparities in welfare assistance, housing subsidies, bonuses and job security in favour of workers in state-owned companies. They were generally not about wage differentials. (Perry, 1997: 240). Some workers resented the loss of worker supervision which had been introduced over the previous decade, and many strikes involved apprentices livid about changes to the length of their tutelage. About one-fifth of the industrial action involved the whole factory, although usually less than half the workers took part. The focus of dissent was usually factory management, but also included the official unions and party cadres. But this movement was crushed, and the official union purged of sympathetic elements.

During the Cultural Revolution (1966-69), workers took advantage of divisions within the CCP to push the movement in directions in which it was not intend to go. Some ex-Red Guards, such as Shengwulian, developed a critique of the regime using Maoist verbiage. Workers complained of the increased use of temporary and contract labour, and the keeping of dossiers on them at work. The army was sent in to restore order in some factories and rebel workers' federations were suppressed. In 1974, big character posters attacked cadres' privileges and characterised the bureaucracy as a ruling class. Workers again formed independent unions, and in Hangzhou 30,000 troops were used against strikes. Over one million demonstrated in Beijing in 1976 to oppose the Gang of Four. Although workers tended to side with Deng against the old Maoists, they soon became critical of his reforms, which removed the "iron ricebowl" of job security whilst retaining the "iron armchair" for party cadres.

The Democracy Wall movement between 1978-81 published journals and explicitly addressed the question of whether the workers really were the "leading class" and "masters of the enterprise", as official propaganda stated. Again rebels characterised the party as a new ruling class – the journal *Spray* discussed exploitation under public ownership. (Sheehan, 1998: 163). Wang Xizhe raised ideas of direct democracy, modelled on the Paris Commune and Russia in 1917. In the background was the rise of Solidarnosc in Poland, from which workers drew great inspiration, stimulating demands for independent unions at the Taiyuan steel works, and in Shanghai. The fear of a "Polish crisis" led to the suppression of the movement and a number of nominal freedoms were stripped from the constitution, including the removal of the right to strike in 1982. The new journals too were suppressed on the grounds that they had not registered with the authorities; the authorities of course had no intention of accepting a free workers' press. The CCP was quite explicit about its fear of a link up between dissident publishing efforts and the self-organisation of workers. (Sheehan, 1998: 193).

The reasons for protests in Tiananmen Square in 1989 also deserve elaboration from a third camp perspective. Workers had lost confidence in the government after a decade of reforms. A survey by the official trade unions (ACFTU) in 1988 found that less than 10% of workers thought the unions spoke up for workers or solved their problems. Around 25% said unions only collected dues and organised recreation and 70% said the workers' congress was not effective. (Sheehan, 1998: 202). The ACFTU estimated that the majority of incomes had fallen by 25-30%, with many workers reduced to subsistence. Workers resented the growth of contract labour in the state sector, worsening health and safety at work, a punitive style of management and corruption.

During the Tiananmen protests students did not generally seek working class support, confining the workers' headquarters to the far side of the square until the end of May. Students were increasingly pulled towards the internal power games of the elite, and held back general strike calls at the end of May. The Beijing Autonomous Workers' Federation began organising in April, before announcing itself on May 18. Workers' federations spread across many major cities, and although they involved perhaps 150 hard-core activists, they had registered 20,000 workers, including in state-run factories such as Shougang (Capital Iron and Steel) and Yanshan Petrochemicals. Workers denounced the regime of Deng and Li Peng as "this twentieth century Bastille, the last stronghold of Stalinism". (Sheehan, 1998: 214-215).

The working class became the major force in the democracy movement prior to its brutal suppression. The shootings in Beijing prompted great heroism on the part of the workers there, and the creation of new organisations in places like Guangzhou. The number of strikes and the dip in production figures measure the extent of workers' involvement. Whilst the regime claimed workers remained aloof, the workers' organisations suffered the fiercest attacks in the press, and workers the severest repression in the crackdown. Internal documents from the official unions admit to the political nature of the Tiananmen protests. In 1991 the Ministry of State Security investigated fourteen underground workers' organisations, with between 20 and 300 members, two modelled explicitly on Solidarnosc. In 1994 campaigns for the right to strike and the formation of independent unions were set up.

Perry concluded her study of the 1957 Shanghai strike wave by arguing that it was the fragmentation of Chinese workers that was the key to their militancy. The image of the danwei as co-opting the proletariat and thus diluting protest is only part of the picture, since these workers were only a minority of the industrial labour force. In 1957 it was those excluded from the benefits of reform who took the lead. By way of a contrast, she argues that the state-employed workers on permanent contracts, who stand to lose most by the re-introduction of capitalism after 1978, are most likely to rebel. (1997: 250-254). The heartlands of the new unemployment in the north-east have recently witnessed an increase in strikes, sit-ins, petitions and factory occupations. What is certain is that neither Stalinism nor capitalism eliminated the basic economic contradictions which drive the class struggle.

Conclusion: what are the prospects for the third camp in China today?

OUT of 50 years of economic development has mushroomed a 200-million strong working class, a force of tremendous revolutionary potential, a fact well known to the CCP leaders who have maintained it in an atomised state without the capacity to form its own legal organisations. Yet the Tiananmen demonstrations shook the totalitarian state to its foundations. As capitalism continues to seep into the pores of Chinese Stalinism, the Communist Party continues to lose its grip on the people it oppresses. What the working class lacks compared with its heroic forebears is the necessary organisation and consciousness.

The situation is highly fluid. The CCP is still in power. According to Harry Wu it still has 15-20 million people in labour camps. The army itself owns 20,000 companies and the state still controls hundreds of thousands of firms. At its last congress in 1997, the CCP rejected privatisation of the largest enterprises, whilst agreeing to sell off some of the smallest with a new shareholding arrangements (effectively forced lending). The banking system is insolvent with $600bn of loans outstanding – its economists breathed a sigh of relief when China avoided the "Asian flu" financial crisis two years ago. Also, the signs are that after playing catch-up, the phenomenal growth rates of the past two decades are now slowing down.

The Communist party-state is squeezed by the transformation of the countryside and by capitalists from within, and the pressures of the global market from without. Whether the CCP will introduce full-blown capitalism itself, or be swept away by the forces it has unleashed, remains an open question. Undoubted revolutionary possibilities are ahead. Therefore in the current situation, third camp socialists have to do everything possible to help the Chinese working class play an independent role, to exploit the loosening of the hukou and turmoil created by the introduction of the market to fight for their own interests. The death of Stalinism in China would be fitting epitaph to the recent anniversary celebrations, but not if it replaced simply by the chaotic, bastard-capitalism which Russia has endured over the past decade. Far better for the Chinese working class to rediscover the militant tradition of its youth, when it stood on the threshold of its own revolution, a tradition that has not been snuffed out despite eighty years of brutal domination.

Notes

1. Abern, Bern, Burnham and Shachtman, [1939], "What is at issue in the dispute on the Russian question? A statement of the position of the minority", in Matgamna, (1998). The term "third camp" is usually associated with the Workers' Party and its successors, but I want to argue that the concept was (and still is) relevant beyond the Cold War dichotomy of Stalinism and capitalism. Clearly there are different nuances and interpretations of the third camp, but I find Trotsky's version a most powerful analytical tool.
2. Trotsky, Leon [1927] "Letter to Alsky", in Evans and Block, (1976).
3. Trotsky described Sun Yat-sen's ideas as bourgeois as early as 1924, Trotsky (1973: 8).
4. For Trotsky's opposition to Stalin see, Lauscher, Hans (1994), 'Trotsky and the Guomindang', *Revolutionary History*, 5: 3. See also Trotsky, Leon [1926] "The Chinese Communist Party and the Kuomintang", and the rejected article, "Class Relations in the Chinese Revolution", [1927] in Evans and Block, (1976). Victor Serge played a leading role in the Left Opposition's work on China during this period.
5. Trotsky's articles on the Sino-Japanese war are also in Evans and Block, (1976). Dissent from these views, especially after 1941 are found in Fanxi, (1991: 204-245), Benton (1996: 78-90), Benton, (1997: 254) and in Shachtman (1942), 'China in the World War', *New International*.
6. A version of Rader's principal article (1949a) was reprinted in *Workers' Liberty* 58 (1999), as "Where did Chinese Stalinism come from?". Rader also predicted that a conflict between Russian and Chinese Stalinism – both nationalistic – was inevitable, although he did not believe it would occur immediately. (1949c).
7. "Appeal for Protests against Mao Terror", *Labor Action*, October 26, 1953. Wang Fanxi discusses the evolution of his own thinking in his memoirs (1991: 255-273). His views on the 1925-27 events, originally an introduction to Trotsky's writings on China published in German, were reprinted in *Workers' Liberty* 12/13 (1989), as "Trotskyism vs Stalinism in the Chinese Revolution". By the late fifties, Wang came to endorse the mainstream "Trotskyist" interpretation (albeit critically), that China had become a "deformed workers' state" after 1949. Nevertheless I believe his early analysis remains a more significant contribution to the understanding of this period in Chinese history.
8. Does this argument imply a "peaceful road" to capitalism? Only in the sense that Lenin defined the Prussian road to capitalism, i.e., that after the failure of the German bourgeoisie to make a revolution in 1848, the Junker state laid the basis for the development of German capitalism. It certainly does not imply an unwinding of the film of reformism backwards – China never had a socialist revolution, so there never was a "workers' state" to be overthrown peacefully.

References

Benton, Gregor (1996), *China's Urban Revolutionaries*, Atlantic Highlands, NJ: Humanities Press.

Benton, Gregor (ed), (1997), *An Oppositionist for Life, Memoirs of the Chinese Revolutionary Zheng Chaolin*, Atlantic Highlands, NJ: Humanities Press.

Bianco, Lucien (1971), *Origins of the Chinese Revolution, 1915-1949*, Stanford: Stanford University Press.

Breitman, George (ed), (1973), *Writings of Leon Trotsky: 1939-40*, New York: Pathfinder.

Cheek, Timothy and Saich, Tony (eds), (1997), *New Perspectives on State Socialism in China*, Armonk, NY: M.E. Sharpe Inc.

Cheng, Tiejun and Selden, Mark (1997), "The Construction of Spatial Hierarchies: China's Hukou and Danwei systems", in Cheek and Saich, (1997).

Chesneaux, Jean (1968), *The Chinese Labour Movement 1919-27*, Stanford: Stanford University Press.

Dirlik, Arif (1989), *The Origins of Chinese Communism*, New York: Oxford University Press.

Duxiu, Chen (1929), "Appeal to all the Comrades of the Chinese Communist Party", in Evans and Block, (1976).

Evans, Les and Block, Russell (eds), (1976), *Leon Trotsky on China*, New York: Pathfinder.

Fanxi, Wang [MY Wang], (1951), "The Stalinist State in China", *New International*, March-April.

Fanxi, Wang [Wang Fan-hsi], (1991), *Memoirs of a Chinese Revolutionary*, New York: Colombia University Press.

Feigon, Lee (1983), *Chen Duxiu: Founder of the Chinese Communist Party*, Princeton: Princeton University Press.

Harrington, Michael (1958), "Despotism's fortress in Asia", *New International*, Spring-Summer.

Holmstrom, Nancy and Smith, Richard, (2000), "The Necessity of Gangster Capitalism: Primitive Accumulation in Russia and China", *Monthly Review*, 51: 9.

Isaacs, Harold (1938), *The Tragedy of the Chinese Revolution*, London: Seeker & Warburg.

Lenin, Vladimir (1966), [1920] "Draft Theses on National and Colonial Questions", *Collected Works, Vol 31*, Moscow: Progress Publishers.

Marx, Karl (1977), *Capital, Volume III*, London: Lawrence and Wishart.

Matgamna, Sean (ed), (1998), *The Fate of the Russian Revolution*, London: Phoenix Press.

Perry, Elizabeth (1997), "Shanghai's Strike Wave of 1957", in Cheek and Saich, (1997).

Rader, Jack [Jack Brad], (1949a), "What is Chinese Stalinism?", *New International*, February.

Rader, Jack [Jack Brad], (1949b), "Are the Chinese Stalinists different?", *Labor Action*, February 7.

Rader, Jack [Jack Brad], (1949c), "Bureaucratic Revolution Rolls over a Passive China", *Labor Action*, May 23.

Rousset, Pierre (1986), *The Chinese Revolution – Part II: The Maoist Project Tested in the Struggle for Power*, Amsterdam: IIRE.

Rousset, Pierre (1987), *The Chinese Revolution – Part I: The Second Chinese Revolution and the Shaping of the Maoist World Outlook*, Amsterdam: IIRE.

Saich, Tony (1991), *The Origins of the First United Front in China: the Role of Sneevliet*, Leiden: Brill.

Sargeson, Sally (1999), *Reworking China's Proletariat*, London: MacMillan.

Serge, Victor (1994), [1927] "The Class Struggle in the Chinese Revolution", *Revolutionary History*, 5: 3.

Shachtman, Max (1974), [1933] *First Ten Years of the Left Opposition*, London: New Park.

Sheehan, Jackie (1998), *Chinese Workers': A New History*, London: Routledge, (1998).

Trotsky, Leon (1973), [1924] *Perspectives and Tasks in the East*, London: New Park.

Trotsky, Leon [1927] "Letter to Alsky", in Evans, Les and Block, Russell, (1976).

Trotsky, Leon [1940], "The Comintern and the GPU", in Breitman, George (1973).

Yang, Dali L. (1997), "Surviving the Great Leap Famine: The Struggle over Rural Policy, 1958-62", in Cheek and Saich, (1997).

Ziegler, Dominic (1997), "Ready to face the world? A Survey of China", *The Economist*, March 8.

Ziegler, Dominic (2000), "Now comes the hard part: A Survey of China", *The Economist*, April 8.

Sylvia Pankhurst and democracy

By Susan Carlyle and Sean Matgamna

Women in capitalist society

THE development of industrial society threw masses of women into the factories. Whole industries, like the cotton industry, had a majority of women and children workers, existing in terrible conditions of super exploitation; as Marx put it in *Capital*, "Robbed of all that had previously been considered necessary for life".[1]

Middle-class women, on the other hand, were thrown into the home. Whereas previously such women, wives of artisans and so on, had taken part together with their husbands and children in production, now they became ladies of leisure, locked into the home, deprived of education – that is, deprived of the possibility of acquiring the professional qualifications necessary to break out of the home.

The political and legal position of women was basically one of a denial of citizenship. Women were shut out from most of "the rights of man and the citizen" won by men over hundreds of years in great historical events like the English (mid-17th century) and the French (end of the 18th century) revolutions. The bourgeois revolution largely passed even bourgeois women by. Bourgeois women had far fewer formal rights than proletarian men.

Not only were women denied the vote; their general legal situation until the end of the 19th century must seem scarcely believable today.

Married women had almost no legal existence. On marrying, the woman passed from being her father's property to fall under her husband's authority, her property and earnings automatically passing to him. She could not enter into contracts, sue or be sued. This system was called "coverture"; essentially, it was the absorption of the woman's identity into her husband's citizenship rights, as a subordinate part of them and of him.

Until an Act in 1857 removed that right, a husband could get a writ of *habeas corpus* to compel anyone sheltering his runaway wife to deliver her up to him, and he could unleash the full vengeance of the law against a refusal to comply. It was not until the Married Women's Property Act of 1882 that a woman gained possession of her own earnings. Until 1891 a husband had the right to kidnap and imprison his wife.

Until 1857, divorce was only possible through a very expensive private Act of Parliament. The Act of 1857 allowed the husband divorce on grounds of adultery; the woman was required to prove him guilty of the rape of another, of sodomy, of bestiality, or of adultery in conjunction with incest, bigamy, cruelty or desertion.

In the early industrial period, proletarian women as well as all other proletarians were deprived of the vote. Bourgeois and aristocratic women, members of the classes that did have full citizenship, were pointedly and brutally discriminated against compared to the men of their class, and many felt and resented it.

To a very considerable extent, the struggle of women throughout the 19th and into the 20th century (it was not until 1944 that women in France achieved the vote, and in Switzerland not until 1971!) was a struggle to catch up with the citizenship rights achieved by the men of the ruling class and with those elements of citizenship won by men in the great bourgeois revolutions.

To alleviate and to change the condition of gross inequality, the vote became a focus for action – a tool to be grasped, a lever to open up other changes. For proletarian women, as we shall see, the vote was also seen as a lever to achieve general social legislation in the interests of the working class.

---

1. The cheapening of labour power was achieved by "sheer abuse of the labour of women and children, by sheer robbery of every normal condition requisite for working and living, and by sheer brutality of overwork and night-work".

Sylvia speaking to an East End audience outside the newly opened suffragette headquarters in Bow, c. 1912

The vote was extended piecemeal to broader layers of the population, radiating from the bourgeoisie outwards. Very few countries in Europe could be described as representative democracies, in terms even of a purely male electorate, until after World War I. In Germany, for example, the Reichstag was elected on an unequal suffrage – the vote of a worker had less weight than other votes – and, anyway, did not have real power.

In England, the first mass working class movement in history, Chartism, was organised in the 1830s and 40s around demands for the vote. Even after the end of Chartism, suffrage agitation continued to be a major part of the concern of the labour movement, of the radical wing of the Liberal Party, and of the trades unions associated with it. In the last third of the 19th century, the political labour movement in countries such as Germany, Austria and Belgium took shape to a serious degree around a struggle for the vote.

In Britain, bourgeois democracy was far from fully developed. Not only did the House of Lords, an unrepresentative, hereditary, caste institution, have a veto over the elected House of Commons, but the electorate for the Commons itself was limited. As late as 1911 only 59% of Britain's adult male population had the vote (that is, some eight million out of a total population of 41 million), and there were seven different types of franchise in operation. Adult sons living with families, male lodgers, fathers of families living in lodgings − all these were disenfranchised. The demand that all adult men should have the vote was important until after World War I.

The labour movement, under the influence of Millite liberalism, was generally in favour of adult suffrage, advocating a vote for all males and females over 21. But it was not usually willing to fight very seriously for the rights of women.

In this situation, a recurring issue in the women's rights movement was one of the relationship between non-working-class women struggling for citizenship and proletarians of both sexes also struggling for citizenship. For women demanding the vote, the question was continually posed of how to relate to the demand for adult suffrage. Should suffragists strive to attain citizenship rights for *all* disenfranchised women and in alliance with disenfranchised men? Or would they demand only the inclusion of women possessing the required property qualifications in the existing differential suffrage?

This issue became the focus of a sharp class differentiation within the women's suffrage movement.

The early women's suffrage movement

IN 1867 John Stuart Mill attempted in the House of Commons to move an amendment to the Second Reform Act which gave the vote to large numbers of non-bourgeois men living in towns − to include women in its provisions. It was defeated. Thereafter, from 1870 to 1878, and from 1884 onwards − save 1899 and 1901 − there were Private Members' Bills to grant women suffrage on the same basis as men.

In 1884 Gladstone threatened to abandon the County Franchise Bill − which did for the rural electorate what the Reform Act of 1867 had done for the cities and towns − if an amendment granting votes to women was carried: 104 Liberal MPs pledged to women's suffrage turned tail. In 1897, a Bill was passed by 71 votes; in 1904, by 114; in 1908, by 179. These votes, usually on first readings, came to nothing because the government would not provide time in the House of Commons to get the Bills through. In addition, from 1886 to 1905, the Tories, with one short break in the 1890s, were continually in office.

The suffrage movement had a continuous existence from the 1860s, being particularly strong amongst the advanced Liberals of Manchester. The National Society for Women's Suffrage was led by Lydia Becker, a Manchester Liberal. In 1888 there was a secession which created the Central National Society for Women's Suffrage, consisting of those who did not stand politically neutral and were willing to admit women's suffrage groups linked to the Liberal Party. In 1889 a Women's Franchise League emerged, also linked with the radical wing of the Liberal Party. Richard and Emmeline Pankhurst hived off in response to a decision by Lydia Becker in alliance with a Tory MP, Forsythe, who moved a Private Member's Bill, to include a clause in that Bill which read "...providing that nothing in this Act shall enable women under coverture to register or to vote", thus excluding married women. In 1890 Lydia Becker died and was succeeded by Millicent Garrett Fawcett, who was more "advanced" and more militant. In 1897, 16 suffrage societies united in a National Union of Women's Suffrage Societies.

By 1909 the National Union of Women's Suffrage Societies had 70 member societies. By 1913 it had 400 affiliated organisations, making it one of the biggest women's suffrage movements in the world.

From its inception in 1868 the Trades Union Congress came out for women's suffrage as part of its demand for adult suffrage. In Lancashire, a working women's suffrage movement developed, demanding adult suffrage.

The problem with these suffrage societies, committed to extending the vote to women on the same basis as men, a basis that disenfranchised perhaps one in two working-class men and would leave the big majority of working-class women still without the vote, was expressed like this by Mary MacArthur, organiser of the Women's Trade Union League:

"We have... a tremendous suffrage movement in England, but unfortunately the sympathisers of that movement are mainly middle-class, leisured women. They are asking for the suffrage on a limited basis, a basis that would not enfranchise the women we represent. If the Bill was passed, not 5% of the women we represent... would get the vote." (*Daily Herald*, 4 November 1913; cited in Winslow.)

According to Sylvia Pankhurst (*The Suffragette Movement*, p.416), the members of the suffrage movement were always very middle-class.

The opposition to women's suffrage

TO UNDERSTAND the opposition to the vote for women, one thing needs to be grasped: people then took the vote more seriously than it is taken now. The vote and formal democracy had not yet been fully domesticated and tamed; the bourgeoisie had not yet got used to living with them. Advocates and opponents of votes for women expected that there would be social consequences to granting women the vote.

The opponents of women's suffrage were both numerous and powerful. They consisted of professional party politicians, unoccupied "men about town", naval and military officers, and the brewing interest, which was closely linked with the Conservative Party.

Not only was there a general conservative resistance to the enfranchisement of women, there were also specific fears of what women would do with the vote. It was feared that there would be drastically puritanical social reforms which would interfere with the liberties of men, especially temperance legislation and severe punishment for sex offenders – causes that were vocally very much an aspect of the women's movement both in Britain and America. It was feared that in a war-like world, the women's vote would be a vote placing peace before the interests and imperatives of the Empire. This was a consistent theme from anti-suffrage propaganda, that women, not being warriors, could not be responsible custodians of the Empire. It may indeed have influenced the future extreme chauvinism of both militant and non-militant suffragists in World War I.

There was also "radical" opposition to women having the vote, on the continent and probably amongst sections of the Liberal Party in Britain.

Where some opponents feared women's suffrage as they feared all radical demands to extend the suffrage, sections of the left feared that women, granted the vote, would be a tool in the hands of the churches and of reaction. Such attitudes infected the socialist movement or inhibited it.

This was so even in Belgium, where, to gain the suffrage, the labour movement had resorted to revolutionary tactics. A series of general strikes had in 1893 forced manhood suffrage on the ruling class (which then cheated by using a plural voting system as counter-balance). The Belgian Labour Party had a demand for adult suffrage in its programme. In 1902, during a struggle against the plural voting system for men, it abandoned the immediate demand for women's suffrage as the price of an alliance with the Liberal Party, which, above all, feared clerical power.

(Opposition to such politics was part of the work of the left wing of the European socialist movement. Rosa Luxemburg, commenting on the betrayal of women workers by the Belgian socialists, pointed out that unless the socialist movement could rouse up the women there could be no socialist transformation of society. Rosa Luxemburg, "On the Belgian General Strike", *Permanent Revolution* No.1, spring 1973.)

Such "radicals" paralleled from the other side the sort of position the Women's Social and Political Union (WSPU) – which abandoned working-class women – was to adopt on the question of adult suffrage.

The Pankhursts

RICHARD Marsden Pankhurst, a Manchester barrister of a radical liberal and then socialistic persuasion, was active in the suffrage movement as early as the 1860s. In 1870 he drafted a Bill to give women the vote on the same terms as men according to the 1867 Act. It passed a second reading in the House of Commons, after which Gladstone stopped it going further.

This Bill was the basis of the subsequent private members' initiatives until Becker and

Forsythe amended it to exclude married women in the 1880s. Together with Emmeline Goulden, whom he married in 1879, he was active on such questions as the agitation that secured the Married Women's Property Act in 1882.

In the 1880s, the Pankhursts moved to the left, until they finally broke with the Liberal Party. When the Independent Labour Party (ILP) was founded in 1893, they became prominent members. Richard Pankhurst was one of 28 candidates from the ILP who contested the 1895 General Election, standing for Gorton in Manchester. He died in 1898.

Emmeline Pankhurst continued in the same activities and was elected as a member of the National Administrative Council of the ILP. She was a close friend of Keir Hardie, the pioneer of independent (from the Liberal Party machine) working class representation in the House of Commons.

In fact, the Pankhurst family was saturated with the general socialism of the ILP and what is interesting is not so much that Sylvia Pankhurst retained, as in fact she did, these basic attitudes, and deepened and developed them, but that Emmeline and Christabel veered sharply away from the labour movement under the influence of the politics they developed in the course of the agitation for women's suffrage that they undertook after 1903.

The Women's Social and Political Union

FOUNDED on October 10 1903 by half a dozen women meeting at the Pankhursts' house in Manchester, the WSPU emerged against the background of a strong and growing suffrage movement, that included a working class based movement in Lancashire. Its militancy was a response to long pent-up frustration at decades of repeated victories for First Readings of House of Commons Bills to give women the vote that led nowhere. Its perennial slogan reflected that experience: "The vote this year." Its programme, like that of all the non-working-class suffrage societies, was for immediate extension of the suffrage to women on the existing property basis and irrespective of all considerations about adult suffrage; soon it would counterpose such demands to adult suffrage.

Christabel Pankhurst's first mentors on the question of women's suffrage were Eva Gore-Booth (sister of the Irish socialist-nationalist, Constance Markievicz) and Esther Roper, who in 1897 had founded the North of England Women's Suffrage Society. The NEWSS was distinguished from most other suffrage societies affiliated to Millicent Garrett Fawcett's National Union of Women's Suffrage Societies by a concentration on recruiting working-class women. It prefigured what Sylvia Pankhurst would do in east London. Christabel Pankhurst would turn violently away from such concerns.

The early WSPU women – the Pankhursts, Mrs Despard, Mrs Cobden-Sanderson, etc. – were all members and supporters of the Independent Labour Party. Keir Hardie, founder of the ILP, gave the WSPU encouragement and support, found it money and premises, and agitated for its demands in Parliament. Hardie found for Mrs Pankhurst the Pethick-Lawrences, rich ILPers with much resources to devote to the WSPU. According to one commentator, "Without the support of Keir Hardie the WSPU could never have flourished as it did" (Antonia Raeburn).

The essential, new, feature of the WSPU was that as a body originating in the labour movement it focused on votes for women *now* on the existing class-biased basis, as distinct from adult suffrage. *This implied from the beginning a turn away from the labour movement.*

The second new feature was militancy. The Pankhursts had been involved in militant activity as early as 1892 in their conflict over votes for married women. Sir Alfred Rellit secured a place for a Bill to enfranchise spinsters and widows, and at a St Janus Hall meeting in support of it, the National Women's Franchise League stormed the platform of the National Union of Women's Suffrage Societies. In 1904, six months after the WSPU was inaugurated, Mrs Pankhurst protested outside the House of Commons after one more Women's Suffrage Bill had been "talked out".

In the autumn of 1905, Mary Kenney and Christabel Pankhurst protested at the Free Trade Hall in Manchester at a Liberal election meeting, demanding to know what the

Liberal Party intended to do for women's votes if they won the imminent election. They were imprisoned briefly, bringing welcome notoriety and publicity to both themselves and the cause. This action inaugurated the policy of vigorous pursuit of Liberal leaders and MPs, insistent questions and demonstrations at their meetings and, in general, harassment. The membership of the WSPU grew as Liberal women became disaffected by their Party's conduct in office from January 1906.

Something over 1,000 women were jailed for militant action in the period up to World War I. But the suffragettes, as the militants became known, in distinction from the suffragists, were never more than a small minority of those women organised and active to get the vote.

The watershed in Britain and for the fortunes of the WSPU was the election of a Liberal government at the end of 1905 and the formation of the Campbell-Bannerman government. It aroused great expectations and rapidly disappointed them.

Campbell-Bannerman himself favoured votes for women but he was not prepared to fight to make this a government measure. He received a deputation of suffragists – from suffrage and co-operative societies, temperance workers, Conservatives, Liberals, socialists and trade unionists – claiming to represent 260,000 organised women, but nothing came of it. Herbert Asquith, Home Secretary and, after 1908, Prime Minister, was the main opponent inside the Cabinet of votes for women; he may have been influenced by some of the considerations influencing radical opponents, though he was no radical.

The Great Unrest

SOON after 1906 Britain entered a prolonged crisis, culminating on the eve of World War I in a serious threat of civil war over Irish Home Rule. These were the years of the "labour unrest", and of a widespread "militancy" by other groups. The WSPU was shaped by and in that situation.

The election of the Liberal government triggered a Constitution Crisis in which the Liberal Government decided to break once and for all the power of the House of Lords to veto the decisions of the elected chamber, and did so in a bitter conflict in 1909-10.

The Catholic Irish had been pressing for Home Rule, and since 1886 the Liberals had been committed to it. The 1906 government was to wait until it had lost its majority before in 1912 introducing a new Home Rule Bill. When it did so it provoked a revolt, not only from the Ulster Unionists but also among big sections of the Tory Party. They encouraged the Ulster Unionists to arm and drill, and backed their declaration that they would not be bound by the enactments of the government in London or the government it might set up in Dublin.

They encouraged officers in the army to refuse to obey orders. In fact, they behaved as "revolutionaries of the right": Lenin commented from afar that they had given a good lesson to the English workers on how to treat the constitution with revolutionary contempt.

Others, from Irish nationalists to Dublin strikers to the east London suffrage movement led by Sylvia Pankhurst, would take the militancy of the Ulster Unionists as a model and organise their own private armies.

The labour movement was disappointed with the performance of its newly independent MPs, of whom 40 were elected in 1906. They became a tail of the Liberal Party in the Commons. This experience, together with the fact that real wages were falling in this period, generated a wave of industrial militancy, the so-called "labour unrest" which was often of a revolutionary syndicalist temper. The great general workers' unions thrown up after the "match-girls'" and dockers' strikes of 1888-9 had fallen into the control of self-serving non-militant leaders.

It was against this background of crisis, militancy, extra-constitutional activity and a Liberal government that had disappointed its supporters and then had increasing difficulty in coping with its Tory opponents, losing its overall majority in 1910, that the WSPU campaign unfolded, first as militant action at meetings of opponents of votes for women and in the streets, and then as sabotage and petty terrorism.

WSPU breaks with the labour movement

O F THE existing political parties, the Labour Party was the only one committed to votes for women. The first annual conference of the Labour Representation Committee in 1901 unanimously passed a resolution for adult suffrage, that is, manhood and womanhood suffrage.[2] As we have seen, in an electoral system that discriminated against working-class men and would, with votes for women "on the same basis as men", continue to discriminate against working-class women, the middle-class suffragists had not a great deal to offer the majority of proletarian women.

The WSPU attracted a traditional working class taunt against middle-class suffragists – that what they wanted was not votes for women but "Votes for Ladies". Sylvia Pankhurst admitted: "The influence of that taunt militating against real support of the suffrage movement in working class circles was ever a strong undercurrent."

Whether or not to support extensions of the suffrage on the existing basis became an urgent issue in the labour movement.

In 1905 Emmeline Pankhurst argued within the ILP that the women who had the municipal franchise were 90% of them working women (and therefore not automatically anti-Labour). In 1905 and at the three subsequent Labour Party conferences, attempts by Keir Hardie to win support for immediate extension were defeated in favour of calls for universal suffrage: to support that, they felt, would be to compromise or betray the cause of disenfranchised working-class women and men. A linked controversy was what attitude the labour movement should take to a promised Liberal government Bill to enfranchise all men over 21 if it did not include also provisions for extending the vote to women on equal terms: to support it would be to betray working-class and other women.

The Women's Labour League was founded at about the same time as the WSPU. At its conferences it consistently passed motions in favour of universal suffrage. At the WLL annual conference in 1912, a motion was passed calling on the Parliamentary Labour Party to vote against any enfranchisement Bill which did not include women. At the Labour Party's 1912 annual conference, Arthur Henderson moved a similar motion, which was carried by 919,000 votes against 686,000 votes (of which 600,000 were miners' votes).

The immediate cause of friction between the labour movement and the WSPU, and the occasion of Mrs Pankhurst leaving it (that is, leaving the ILP), was the fact that the WSPU declared war on the Liberal government which the Labour Party was, in fact, supporting (the nascent Labour Party still had many Liberal ties).

The WSPU demanded that the government should sponsor a Franchise Bill and embarked on a campaign of disrupting meetings to coerce the government. Militant women were assaulted and jailed. As their bitter conflict with the government developed, from 1906 onwards, the WSPU demanded that all friends of women's suffrage should make war on the Liberal government and subordinate every other consideration to getting votes for some women immediately. They demanded that the Labour Party should consistently vote against the government in a spirit of sabotage.

The model here was the tactics associated with Charles Stewart Parnell. The difference was that Parnell had a phalanx of disciplined MPs and a mass movement of Irish nationalist electors behind him, whereas the WSPU had no such level of support.

Christabel Pankhurst became increasingly convinced that votes for women would come from the Tory Party. Her precedent was 1867, when Disraeli's Tories "dished" the Liberals by jumping over their heads and bringing in the Second Reform Act. Determination to oppose the government in everything, backed up by such beliefs as to who would actually give the vote to women, led the WSPU eventually to demand that their friends including supporters of the Labour Party, should vote Tory as being the strongest anti-Liberal force.

The labour movement left a great deal to be desired when it came to fighting for women's rights. Many leaders paid only lip-service to votes for women. At least one ILP leader, Philip Snowden, openly opposed giving women the vote. But the labour move-

---

2. But not all "socialists" in the Labour Party were so quick off the mark. The Fabian Society only added "the establishment of equal citizenship between men and women" to the society's list of objectives in 1906.

ment certainly did not push out Mrs Pankhurst. On the contrary, it responded initially with very great tolerance. Towards the end of 1906 the WSPU, led by members of the ILP, with Mrs Pankhurst still a member of the National Administrative Council of the party, campaigned on a negative policy and refused to declare themselves in any way in favour of a Labour vote.

They stated that so long as votes were cast against the government, they cared not to whom they went. In 1906 the WSPU broke its links with the ILP.

At the Belfast Labour Party Conference of 1907 a motion to support women's suffrage on the existing franchise was lost by 605,000 to 268,000. Conference wanted nothing short of adult suffrage. Keir Hardie only managed to keep a personal right not to have to vote in Parliament against votes for women on a limited suffrage by threatening to resign. The Easter 1907 ILP Conference, however, voted in favour of the motion defeated at Belfast.

Moves to censure Mrs Pankhurst at the ILP 1907 Conference were defeated by the ever-tolerant Keir Hardie. He told Conference that it must choose whether or not to retain some of the ILP's most valuable women members. Nevertheless, Emmeline and Christabel Pankhurst resigned from the ILP in the same year.

There was a fundamental logic to this separation, flowing from the fundamental political character of the WSPU and the type of suffrage it demanded. It was possible to conceive of a fight for the vote for all women in alliance with the labour movement and the masses of unenfranchised men. For the labour movement, many of whose men and all of whose women were without the vote, to be enthusiasts and activists for "votes for ladies" was, from a working class and a working-class woman's point of view, quixotic nonsense.

The limited suffrage to which the WSPU was committed indicated a different type of alliance: not with the working class but with aristocratic and bourgeois women.

For there were powerful and influential forces in society who, though bitterly opposed to adult suffrage, could be approached and allied with to achieve a limited suffrage. Some sections, though a minority, of the Tory Party, even though they were inveterate enemies of the adult suffrage advocated by the labour movement, supported the inclusion of women in the existing system of franchise.

Eventually, the WSPU developed a bitter animosity towards the Labour Party. In turn, some in the Labour Party, specifically Labour leader Ramsay MacDonald, attacked the militants for their militancy. The militants replied that women could not be expected to behave according to the polite rules of a democracy which for political purposes did not recognise their existence. But the most bitter WSPU attacks were directed at those, like Keir Hardie, who were wholly on the side of the WSPU.

The initiating radicals in the WSPU became so focused on the injustice to women within the existing system that their previous conception faded of the injustice of the system as a whole. Thus, the WSPU that had originated amongst ILP *women* quickly became a body of rich, middle-class and aristocratic *ladies*.

Sylvia Pankhurst and the WSPU

SYLVIA Pankhurst, born in 1882, was 15 when her father died; to remain true to his ideals seems to have been her personal driving force for much of her life. Something her father said to her remained her guiding idea: "If you do not work for others, you will not have been worth the upbringing." Her youth was passed in the ILP and in typical socialist movement activities such as the Clarion Cyclists' Clubs and free speech fights to establish the socialists' right to hold outdoor, street corner meetings – which involved conflict with the police.

She was influenced in both art – she was an artist – and politics by William Morris. Whereas Christabel Pankhurst, born in 1880, set the pace for Mrs Pankhurst in the turn away from the labour movement after 1907, Sylvia's emotional and intellectual roots were much more firmly planted in labour movement soil. Sylvia Pankhurst chose, as a recent biographer, Barbara Wimslow, puts it, to "fight not just for one political reform on behalf of a select group of women, but for full social, political and economic emancipation".

She took part in the militant activities of the WSPU from the beginning. In 1906, together with Annie Kenney, she set out to organise in London for the WSPU. For the opening of Parliament in 1906, they organised a big demonstration to the Palace of Westminster. They worked with the Marxist feminist Dora Montefiore, a member of the Social Democratic Federation, who would be a founder member of the Communist Party in 1920, who was already organising for the WSPU in London. Four to five hundred women from the East End of London turned out, mobilised by labour movement supporters of the WSPU, some of them carrying red flags. They were taunted by servant-employing bystanders. "What about the washing?" and "Why don't you darn the old man's socks?" were some of their jibes. After that Sylvia focused on her art studies at Chelsea, but she took part in propaganda stunts at meetings, was jailed, and went on hunger strike repeatedly.

Sylvia herself described one of many such occasions. In 1913, "I had been forcibly fed for five weeks and only secured release by walking up and down my cell for 28 hours, staggering, falling and fainting, a horrible ordeal I shudder even now to recall. She [Mrs Pankhurst] was shocked when she saw me emaciated in the extreme, with eyes horribly bloodshot, like cups of blood."

In 1912 the WSPU turned to what became known as "secret militancy". This was in fact small-scale terrorism. They started a campaign of bombings, window-breakings, art-gallery picture-slashings, and so on.

In consequence, hundreds were jailed and there was a very great deal of repression. WSPU headquarters declared this newly destructive militancy alone of value; the public, converted as far as it could be, must now be *terrorised* into compelling the government to give the vote.

Repression, imprisonments, breaking-up by the police of meetings followed. Most of the leaders — Christabel Pankhurst was in exile in Paris — existed under the regime of "Cat and Mouse". After a hunger strike ordeal like that which Sylvia describes above, they would be released on a short licence of perhaps a few days to recover their strength, to be arrested and incarcerated again at the government's whim, usually when they tried to continue the struggle. "The suffragette movement was being driven underground", explained Sylvia a quarter of a century later.

She herself disagreed with the terrorist turn. While fully in favour of the older militancy, she felt that, contrary to the assumptions of the WSPU HQ (that is, Christabel and Mrs Pankhurst), "propaganda was more than ever imperative; only because a wide public supported the militants and their cause was suffragette destruction embarrassing the Government. Despite all difficulties and the mood of indifference towards propaganda, I had stirred the local autonomous branches of the WSPU to organise campaigns throughout the country, and another monster meeting in Hyde Park; but that was not enough. A mass movement, manifesting urgent popular impatience, was both necessary and possible. Mass crowds must be mustered, not merely to watch the exploits of a few hundred brave women, but for vigorous hostile action. I chose the East End, that great reservoir of work and poverty from which thousands could march to Parliament, as the core of this new movement".

At that time, as part of the militant working class eruption, which took the form of self-organising and rolling waves of strikes, the hitherto unorganised women and girls in tailoring shops and food factories fought and won strikes and enrolled in the National Federation of Women Workers. "The most outstanding action was the Bermondsey Women's "Rising" during the London Dock Strike of 1911. Women of the jam, glue and pickles factories of the neighbourhood poured out into the streets, shouting and singing. Fifteen thousand of them cheered [dockers' leader] Ben Tillet at a meeting in Southwark Park, and within three weeks employers at 15 out of 20 factories had agreed to wage increases" (Sylvia Pankhurst).

Working in the East End

EAST London too was affected by the general unrest and we have already seen that hundreds of East End women were prepared to demonstrate for the suffrage in 1906. The first East End branch of the WSPU was in Canning Town. But here geography implied class; and class implied support for adult suffrage: most East End women would

THE
WOMAN'S DREADNOUGH'

GUARANTEED WEEKLY CIRCULATION—20,000 CO

Published by the East London Federation of the Suffragettes.

Edited by SYLVIA PANKHURST.

No. 14.   SATURDAY, JUNE 20TH, 1914.   PRICE ONE HALFPENNY

NO PRICE TOO GREAT TO PAY FOR FREEDOM

THIS WEEK'S MEETINGS.

Sunday, June 21st, 3 p.m.—Victoria Park.
7.30 p.m.—The Women's Hall, 400 Old Ford Rd., Bow—Dr. Mansell-Moullin, Mrs. Merivale Meyer.
Monday, June 22nd, 3 p.m.—The Women's Hall, 400 Old Ford Rd., Bow—Members' meeting.
8 p.m.—The Women's Hall, 400 Old Ford Rd.. Bow—Speakers' Class.
8.30 p.m.—Swiss Cottage, S. Hackney—Miss Holmes.
8 p.m.—Priscilla Rd., Bow.
8 p.m.—Freemason's Rd., Canning Town—Mrs. Laski.
Tuesday, June 23rd, 8 p.m.—Dock Gates, Poplar—Mr. Mewitt.
3 p.m.—Limehouse, Burdett Rd., and Coutts Rd.
Wednesday, June 24th, 8 p.m.—319 East India Dock Rd., Poplar—Miss Jacobs.
8 p.m.—Crowder's Hall, 178 Bow Rd.—Mrs. Tyson.
8 p.m.—Chrisp St. & Charles St., Bromley.
Thursday, June 25th, 3 p.m.—319 East India Dock Rd., Poplar—Miss Canning.
3 p.m.—Deacon's Vestry, Burdett Rd., Limehouse.
8 p.m.—124 Barking Rd., Canning Town.
8 p.m.—Woolstock Rd., Poplar.
Friday, June 26th, 8 p.m.—Ford Rd., Bow.
8 p.m.—Piggott St., Poplar—Mr. June.
8 p.m.—Beckton Rd., Canning Town—Mrs. Laski.
8 p.m.—The Women's Hall, 400 Old Ford Rd., Bow—Members' Meeting.
Sunday, June 28th, 5 p.m.—Trafalgar Square E.C.S.U. Demonstration.

HOW ASQUITH SHIRKS.

We print below the correspondence which passed between the members of the East London deputation and the Prime Minister who is partly supported by women's money and one of whose duties it is to listen to the grievances of His Majesty's subjects and devise a means of redressing them. The wording of Mr. Asquith's second letter is especially significant as showing that he has not grasped the fundamental duties of his position. He says that *the views of the Government* were explained at considerable length. It seems that Mr. Asquith has yet to learn that deputations do not visit him to hear his views on any subject but to lay the views of the people he is supposed to represent before him.

[COPY.]

June 13th, 1914.

Dear Sir,—As members of the deputation who came to the House to see you on Wednesday last, we must express very strongly our dissatisfaction at not being received by you. We can see no reason why you should not see us and hear what we (as working women) have to say about the franchise. You cannot possibly know what he views of the people are if you will not listen to them. You have never received a reputation of working women on this ques-

he is unable to receive a deputation, and he regrets that he is unable to reconsider this decision. As you are, doubtless, aware, deputations have been received by the Prime Minister and other Members of the Cabinet, which were representative of the constitutional organisations connected with the Women's Suffrage Movement. At nearly all these deputations working women were either present or their opinion represented. The views of the Government were explained to the members of the deputations at considerable length, and no change has taken place in the situation since then.

The Prime Minister has been compelled to refuse requests from a large number of bodies for similar deputations, and, after careful consideration of all the circum-

convince the Premier where he is wrong. Just a word from him, consenting to receive our deputation, would save that noble little woman, Sylvia Pankhurst, from death by starvation. Should she die, it will be a very serious matter, for ours is a true Socialist's spirit. "An injury to one is an injury to all." I trust you will act as soon as possible, as delay is dangerous.

The letter, to which the name and address of the writer were appended, has received an unsatisfactory and evasive reply. Others who have written to Mr. Thorne have received exactly the same answer, showing that he does not even consider his constituents' letters individually, but has supplied his secretary with a draft copy to be used to all who write on this subject.

He was followed by Mrs. Par who put the whole matter from standpoint of the East London w ing woman.

Then came an appeal for m from the chair. The response prompt and generous, several che being handed up in addition t ordinary collection.

Miss Evelyn Sharp was the speaker, she also spoke as a wit of the events on the night of Pankhurst's arrest, and dwelt on significance of the large numbe working men whose presence on occasion proved that they are ma this question their own.

As she concluded with a tribu George Lansbury and his ga challenge to his namesake Geor the challenger himself appeare the platform, and was greeted vigorous applause. His appeal especially to the men, and he u upon them to call at the Hous Commons to see their respe members of Parliament, and ask t to put pressure upon Mr. Asp He satirised the Press for their h ual misrepresentation of everyt in connection with the movemen Freedom.

Miss Amy Hicks made a appeal for workers, and empha the need for immediate action at crisis.

The resolution was carried un mously and before the meeting b up the enthusiasm that aroused found an outlet in m promises of very practical help.

McKENNA'S TRIBUTE THE MILITANTS.

On Thursday, June 11th, the de on the Home Office took place. T was chiefly concerned with the S ragettes and the methods to be ployed to stop their activities.

Mr. McKenna said that: "The pre situation was a phenomenon absol ly without precedent, and then cussed four alternatives for dea with it.

1. Let them die (which was most popular).
2. Deport them.
3. Treat them as lunatics.
4. Give them the franchise.

LET THEM DIE.

"Those who say 'Let them di they choose to starve themsel usually base their views on the c viction that if they themselves w

IS SHE TO DIE ?

not get the vote even if the WSPU won all its demands.

The branch soon came into conflict with WSPU H Q . Organising continued, however: Dora Montefiore, who left the WSPU at the time, in protest at its lack of democracy, continued to work in the area. The major turn to the East End occurred when George Lansbury, the socialist MP for Bromley and Bow, resigned his seat to fight a by-election on votes for women and opposition to forced feeding of imprisoned, hunger-strik- ing suf-

The front page of the Woman's Dreadnought *20 June 1914. Sylvia is in prison, hunger and thirst-striking, at the time*

fragettes. The WSPU returned to the East End.

The East End was "colonised"; suffragette societies from Kensington to Bethnal Green, from Chelsea to Limehouse, and from Paddington to Poplar were given the job of building up support in specific areas of east London. Initially they met with much hostility, including violence. Even George Lansbury's local Labour Party branch in Bromley and Bow was at first unfriendly. But they persevered and won solid local support by involving themselves with the problems of the East End people. "Troubles with landlords, employers, Government departments, were brought to me for solution and exposure," reported Sylvia Pankhurst.

The Bromley and Bow by-election was, however, something of a fiasco. Lansbury supported Christabel's policy of voting against every measure in the House of Commons — that is, attempting to bring everything else to a standstill until votes for women were conceded. In addition, he was strongly critical of the Labour Party's support for Lloyd George's National Insurance Act. A volatile, sentimental and gesture-prone Christian socialist, Lansbury had initially been elected with Liberal support.

Though he had consulted Christabel and Mrs Pankhurst (the latter advising against resignation), he had not consulted the local trade unions who had been backing him, nor even his local Labour Party.

The local labour movement and the WSPU, which flooded the area with its organisers, did not make congenial allies. Many of the WSPU campaigners were politically miles from the labour movement and from George Lansbury's general politics. The WSPU organisers, according to Sylvia, had no sympathy with labour politics, nor any understanding of the movement. They were used to campaigning in elections but in a negative way, not actually supporting candidates.

The local Labour Party (Lansbury was to run an independent local labour organisation for the next few years) were suspicious and hostile to the WSPU, which, after all, had suborned its MP away from what was felt to be his first loyalties. Yet there was labour movement support for what George Lansbury stood for. Poplar Trades Council "heartily congratulated" George Lansbury for denouncing the Prime Minister Asquith as a torturer of women. Sylvia Pankhurst's East London franchise campaign would forge an alliance between dockers and suffragettes, but Emmeline and Christabel Pankhurst's followers could not do that.

The labour supporters of Lansbury and his WSPU "supporters" found themselves competing viciously for meeting pitches. The WSPU organiser devoted her meetings to inveighing against "the men". On the morning of the election, a fleet of Tory cars were getting out the vote; Lansbury had few cars; a fleet of WSPU cars lay idle on the Bow Road. The Labour Party Secretary, Banks, wouldn't give the electors' lists to the WSPU; the organiser refused to make her fleet of cars available to "the Men's Party". Not surprisingly, Lansbury lost the election and was out of the Commons for 10 years.

Yet the need for adult suffrage is starkly depicted in the figures for the Bromley and Bow by-election. Fifty thousand supporters of George Lansbury attended a rally at Victoria Park. But most of them, men and women, could not vote. Lansbury got 3,291 votes to his opponent's 4,042.

After the defeat the word went out from WSPU HQ to vacate the area. Sylvia persuaded her mother to allow her to remain in the area as an unpaid organiser – the unpaid status was her own choice – to organise a deputation of East End women to the Home Secretary. In fact this became eventually a national deputation consisting of Newham fish wives, Lancashire pit brow women, textile operatives and others, known as Mrs Drummond's deputation of working women.

The East End where Sylvia chose to remain was a docks community. Most male workers were dockers. Women workers were domestic servants or clothing workers. East End people became involved in the suffrage movement, engaging in street fights with the police to prevent Sylvia being arrested and to protect her meetings.

No other comparable mass active support was built up by other suffragettes. And though there were large scale pro-suffrage societies in the north of England, they were not linked to militancy.

Sylvia's extra-legal activities, the hunger striking and the aftermath – she was carried around to meetings on stretchers and chairs – captured the sympathy and evoked the active support of many in the local area. Mass meetings and demonstrations were held, usually with labour movement support, with George Lansbury on the platform.

Sylvia breaks with the WSPU

AFTER the experience of the Bromley and Bow by-election and further experience with supporters of Lansbury in Leicester, the WSPU turned to the demand that Labour supporters should vote Tory to hit hardest at the Liberal government. No labour movement people would stomach that.

The break between Sylvia and the WSPU came at the end of 1913. It was precipitated by Sylvia's involvement in work to support the Dublin labour movement during the 1913-14 lockout. The East London WSPU helped organise an attempt to evacuate hungry Dublin children to British working class homes. After Sylvia appeared at a giant support meeting for Dublin on the same platform as Jim Larkin, she was summoned to meet Christabel in Paris and, being on the run, went in disguise.

Christabel demanded a "clean cut" between the WSPU and the East London Federation. Sylvia had ideas of her own: the East London group was run on a democratic basis, contrary to HQ policy. Christabel said: "You have a democratic constitution and we don't agree with that." When Sylvia had appeared on platforms to support the workers of Dublin, newspapers had begun to speak of congruence between the streams of industrial and suffrage militancy: Christabel insisted that the WSPU should remain free of "all men's parties". The WSPU would not share a platform with men.

More than that: Christabel had no use for working-class women either. She was opposed to organising working-class women. A working women's movement was of no value, she told Sylvia. Working women were the weakest of their sex. How could it be otherwise? Their lives were too hard and their education too meagre to equip them for the contest. "Surely it is a mistake to use the weakest in the struggle," argued Christabel. "We want picked women [who are] the very strongest and most intelligent."

No doubt she was speaking to a central theme of her thinking. The Tory party and the upper classes in general were considered the strongest sisters, and the strongest brothers too. She despised the Lib-Lab politicians like Ramsay MacDonald and had contempt for Lansbury and Hardie.

Sylvia was weak after her recent hunger and thirst strike, and too dispirited to argue with Christabel. The latter suggested that they should meet occasionally as sisters. Sylvia wrote later: "To me the words seemed meaningless; we had no life apart from the movement".

Christabel's "glorification of autocracy" seemed to Sylvia "remote from the struggle we were waging, the grim fight even now proceeding in the cells". By this time the WSPU had long merited the following description: "...a non-party, classless, but centralised authoritarian body carrying out a militant yet initially a constitutional policy..."

In February 1914 Christabel announced to the press that the East London group was no longer part of the WSPU. The members of the Federation decided at a meeting to be known as the East London Federation of the Suffragettes (ELFS). When Mrs Pankhurst protested that they, the WSPU, were the Suffragettes, Sylvia replied that it had been decided democratically and was out of her hands. Red was added to the purple, white and green colours of the WSPU to make the banner of the East London Federation. The ELFS had men members, unlike the WSPU.

The East London Federation of the Suffragettes

I N HER work in the East End, Sylvia Pankhurst had evaded the controversy over adult suffrage versus votes for women on the existing franchise, essentially by avoiding the issue for as long as possible. But the very fact of organising women who could only benefit from adult suffrage implied a quite different trajectory to that of the WSPU for the East London group. Sylvia was in the grip of the same logic that had led Mrs Pankhurst away from the labour movement, but travelling in the opposite direction. Sylvia reports that once, when she cited the East End as an example of mass support for the suffragettes, the Bishop of London replied: "Oh, yes, but this is the dear, chivalrous East End; it will always fight for the bottom dog." It could scarcely be expected to fight for precisely the suffrage demand that would exclude the women of its own class, and in a lot of cases would continue the exclusion of their men as well.

In 1911 the population of Poplar was 75,614: there were only 9,519 registered voters. In Bromley and Bow there were only 10,669 registered voters out of a population of 86,994.

In the summer of 1914, the ELFS organised one of the most successful events associated with the Suffragette movement – a mass movement to send a deputation of delegates elected at mass meetings to see Prime Minister Asquith. After initial refusal to see them, followed by mass demonstrations of women and men, battles with the police and a threat by Sylvia to starve herself to death outside the House of Commons if the PM did not receive the deputation, Asquith finally did see them. On the eve of World War I, the PM made remarks to the delegation that many considered to mark a change in attitude to the demand of the Suffragettes (see below).

The activities of the ELFS around this deputation show us what the ELFS was and how it differed from the approach of the WSPU.

Mass meetings were held to elect the delegates – two women and one man from each meeting – and to decide by voting what specific suffrage demand to put to Asquith.

Writing in the *Women's Dreadnought*, Sylvia Pankhurst dismissed the disputes around adult versus limited suffrage as barren: the mass meetings should decide which demand to make, or whether to just make a general demand and leave the details to the government. All, she wrote, immediately came to the same thing: now was not the time for hair-splitting but for closing ranks.

"And we... shall be fighting, fighting, fighting to get the best terms for women that we can, for we know that every woman in the country has a right to the vote, and that the poorest need it most" (*Women's Dreadnought*, 6 June, 1914).

Of course, the meetings decided by very large majorities to demand adult suffrage, which was what Sylvia expected.

How did the ELFS present itself and its suffrage demands to the East Enders? The best representation of this is in a speech made by Julia Scurr, the wife of docker John Scurr and Labour Party activist, who would go to jail and hunger-strike alongside Sylvia in the battles for the vote. Official spokesperson for the deputation that met Asquith on June 20 1914 (*The Suffragette Movement*, p.479/80), Julia Scurr began with a tribute to Sylvia Pankhurst, regretting that she was not present (as she was in jail), speaking of "...the work she has done in arousing the women of the East End to the importance of the vote in their daily lives".

She told Asquith that it was common in the East End for a woman to earn seven or eight shillings for a full week's work. They were told, she said, that throughout the country the average wage for women was but seven shillings. It was "impossible... to live decently on such a miserable pittance".

Next, she asked him to consider the position of married women: "Any rise in the price of rents, foods and other household commodities affects us women vitally, and we need not point out that these are intimately bound up with the question of free trade versus protection, which bulks so largely in the political programme of today".

And Parliament constantly dealt with questions of care and protection of children "and more and more with every item of our daily lives". In deciding questions like the Insurance Acts and questions connected with sickness and maternity benefit, "we claim that our point of view should be represented".

She went on: "The position of working-class women is one that we all feel deeply. Our husbands die on the average at a much earlier age than do the men of other classes. Modern industrialism kills them off rapidly both by accident and by overwork.... we are left often with a family of young children to support... The Poor Law has treated us mercilessly. It is hated by every poor woman. In many cases outdoor relief is altogether denied to the widow, as it is to the deserted wife, and only the Workhouse is offered, which means separation from the children. Where out-relief is given it is surrounded by the most humiliating conditions, which cause us, as self-respecting women, very great indignity and distress."

Without women, Parliament was unfit to legislate on "questions of morality" and the white slave trade [prostitution], which were rooted in the social and political status of women. Women were taxed but had no voice in these questions.

"We women of east London are much concerned with regard to social conditions in our district. There is very great poverty around us and rents are high. There is much unemployment amongst men and a very large proportion of the wives are the principal breadwinner, though they are both the childbearers and keepers of the home." Women in the home were as much wage earners as those in the factory, and they gave a child-bearing service to the state. "They have the greatest of all reasons to desire [the state's] security and welfare. In our opinion our country, especially in districts like east London, is in many ways grossly unfit to receive the children that we bring into the world. We feel that we have a right to help in improving the conditions under which we and our children live." Some dismissed representative government, and thought the vote useless, but the Prime Minister could hardly be amongst their number.

"The demand which we have come to make to you today is one that we believe has not hitherto been made by any women's suffrage deputation... It is the form of the franchise which you have declared your intention of establishing for men in the near future. It is the one for which your party is said to stand – a vote for every woman over 21."

She claimed that they had mass support behind them. Organised labour throughout the country had for long been making this demand. Where popular unrest existed, she said, all great statesmen knew that the remedy was to remove the cause. If Asquith himself had fixed objections to votes for women she asked him to act in the tradition of Wellington who brought in Catholic Emancipation [1829] against his own personal convictions when the good of the country demanded it, as did Robert Peel when he repealed the corn laws [1846].

She ended with an appeal for the "political prisoners".

Women and men fight for the vote

THIS summary of Julia Scurr's speech allows us to get a clear view of how the vote question appeared to the members and supporters of the ELFS, and also a view of their general political outlook and concerns. It shows the gulf that separated them and their demand for the vote from the "ladies" of the WSPU. While the WSPU went off on a petty terrorist campaign, Sylvia Pankhurst built a mass movement of women and men that became a powerful force. While the ELFS concerned itself with the things Julia Scurr outlined, Christabel Pankhurst was making crazy propaganda that "75-80% of all men" had gonorrhea, deliberately infected women and opposed votes for women for fear of legislation (*The Great Scourge*, 1913).[3]

Yet Julia Scurr's message and the ELFS's approach was not unique to the ELFS. On the contrary, it was from a stock common to working class groups concerned for the suffrage, in Lancashire for example. Even the WSPU from the beginning had attempted to present its demands in terms of the needs of working women. Groups like the Women's Labour League and the Women's Co-operative Guild all approached the suffrage question in this way.

Where the ELFS differed was in that it roused large masses of women and men into active support of a group of WSPU women, most notably Sylvia Pankhurst, but others such as Nora Smyth as well, practising WSPU militancy and in conflict with the police. Great masses of men and women flocked to the meetings, organised to protect them from the police and to prevent them arresting Sylvia. And the democratic structure of the ELFS allowed the radical suffrage demands appropriate to the self-interest of the ELFS constituents to find full expression.

In addition, the alliance with the labour movement, despite the initial frictions, and the active support of men like George Lansbury and dockers' leader John Scurr, and of local women who had been formed politically during dockers' strikes and who now developed as effective mass agitators, led the ELFS to broaden the base of its concerns: the demand for the vote was closely and explicitly linked with the social purposes for which the members and supporters of the ELFS of both sexes wanted to use the vote.

For the ELFS, the vote was a means to ends which were generated from the social conditions of the East End. Increasingly, especially when war intensified the problems of the supporters and members of the ELFS, the Federation began to address itself directly and to evolve do-it-yourself approaches to some of the "ends", the social problems. In this

---

3. Quite what a strange cult the WSPU was is sometimes lost sight of. It was a personal dictatorship of Christabel Pankhurst's long before the petty terrorism might have required autocratic leadership. Its leading layer subscribed to an "Amazonian" ethos and was militantly hostile to "the men". Barbara Winslow speculates that a subtext in the split between Sylvia Pankhurst on one side and Emmeline and Christabel Pankhurst on the other was Sylvia's heterosexuality, which cut her off from the "Amazons". In 1913, Christabel published a small book, *The Great Scourge*. Speaking for the suffragettes, she argued that "75-80%" of all men suffered from gonorrhea and secretly infected women. Commitment to "sexual vice" was the root cause of male opposition to votes for women. The conclusion was summed up in a WSPU slogan, "Votes for women and chastity for men". Crazed stuff like this occupied the place in WSPU concerns, apart from the vote, that concern for the interests of working-class women occupied for Sylvia Pankhurst. In 1914 the WSPU became the most jingo of the jingos, rabid warmongers, working closely with the then equivalent of the Murdoch press. In 1918, the WSPU, as the Women's Party, stood in the general election on an extremely authoritarian platform. Christabel, who had the endorsement of Prime Minister Lloyd George, came within a few hundred votes of winning a seat. Immediately after that, Christabel Pankhurst became convinced that the "return" of Jesus Christ was imminent and wrote books to prove it. Emmeline Pankhurst stood as a Tory Parliamentary candidate in a by-election in, ironically enough, east London just before her death, in 1928.

way it evolved into an organic part of the working class East End community and labour movement in the early war period.

From its inception, the ELFS combined the labour movement attitudes and concerns that the founders of the WSPU – except Sylvia – had moved so far away from, with the attitudes, techniques, methods and the heroically militant spirit of the WSPU. One might say that it was a higher dialectical synthesis, combining the strength of both WSPU militancy and the broader-based suffrage concern of the labour movement, with Sylvia as a charismatic catalyst. The personal quality over and above those of the other WSPU militants which allowed Sylvia Pankhurst to play this role was the fact that neither in her feelings nor in her thoughts had she broken, as did her mother and Christabel, with the working class movement.

Sylvia Pankhurst's own account of what she thought she was doing is worth quoting: "I was anxious... to fortify the position of the working women when the vote should actually be given; the existence of a strong, self-reliant movement amongst working women would be the greatest aid in safeguarding their rights on the day of settlement. Moreover, I was looking to the future; I wanted to rouse these women of the submerged mass to be, not merely the argument of more fortunate people [surely a reference to the WSPU], but to be fighters on their own account, despising mere platitudes and catchcries, revolting against the hideous conditions about them, and demanding for themselves and their families a full share in the benefits of civilisation and progress" (Sylvia Pankhurst, *The Suffragette Movement* pp.416-417).

It is impossible not to be reminded here of the spirit in which socialists – Sylvia's friend, James Connolly, for example – involved themselves in national liberation movements. (And indeed when Connolly and his friends proclaimed the Irish Republic they also proclaimed universal suffrage – something whose radicalism is less apparent now than in 1916). In the fight for a "bourgeois revolution" for women, Sylvia stood for and with the submerged proletarian women – for their immediate interests and their ultimate emancipation.

In March 1914 Sylvia and her comrades started *The Women's Dreadnought*, which (with a change of name to *Workers' Dreadnought* in 1917) she was to publish until 1924. It was part of the attempt to develop the ELFS into a powerful mass organisation. It reported on the struggles for the suffrage and also on labour struggles under titles like "What a strike means to the woman at home". It ran reports on the experiences of women as trainee nurses, jam-makers, etc. Gradually, it broadened its scope until it became a general left socialist newspaper in World War I.

No public recriminations were entered into with the WSPU. Activities of the WSPU, including the small-scale terrorism (for example, the bombing of empty houses, such as one being built for Lloyd George), were reported sympathetically. On the first anniversary of Emily Davidson's death under the hooves of the King's horse at Epsom racetrack, Sylvia wrote: "Oh deed majestic! oh triumphant death" (*Women's Dreadnought,* 16 May 1914). The Federation even began to organise its own "People's Army", consisting of both men and women, in line with the fashion for private armies set initially by Edward Carson's Ulster Volunteers. The People's Army, like the Irish Citizens' Army set up by Jim Larkin in Dublin during the 1913-14 lockout, protected east London suffrage demonstrations. It was a sort of organised counter police force against the police. A sweated trades exhibition was held. And always demonstrations, meetings and conflicts with the police – which eventually began to recoil from repeated clashes with the numbers that the ELFS was able to bring on to the streets armed with sticks.

By August 1914, when war started, the ELFS was firmly anchored in the working class East London community and proclaimed itself part of the labour movement. *Women's Dreadnought* explained that, in the May Day procession 1914, "the ELFS procession will follow the labour procession to the park... We women of the East London Federation are workers and we mean to demonstrate on the day on which the workers all over the world hold a festival of Labour".

The legend is that the WSPU won the vote. That is not at all clear. When women eventually got the vote (women over 30), they got it as part of a package that expanded the franchise for men – many of the soldiers in the trenches had no vote. On the eve of war, when Prime Minister Asquith had met the delegation of working-class women from the

East End, Pankhurst was on hunger strike. He told them: "If change has to come, we must face it boldly and make it thoroughgoing and democratic." A few days earlier Lloyd George told Sylvia Pankhurst that he would introduce a Private Member's Bill in the next session and resign if it was not passed. Then war intervened.

Politically, in World War I Sylvia Pankhurst was broadly part of the pacifistic, non-doctrinal, emotional, socialist left whose spirit was best expressed by Keir Hardie. Hardie was Sylvia's political mentor (and, for a decade, lover). We shall see by what stages she developed beyond Keir Hardie.[4]

The impact of World War I

THE VAST majority of the British labour movement supported Britain at the outbreak of the war. The Labour Party did and so did the trade unions. Sections of the Independent Labour Party (now one of a number of socialist societies affiliated to the Labour Party) including both Ramsay MacDonald and Keir Hardie, denounced the war on pacifistic and liberal cosmopolitan grounds; and not always consistently at that. Their position essentially was one of harking back to the conditions of an earlier stage of pacifistic, free trade capitalism, whose passing was vividly demonstrated by the World War itself. The stand taken by *Women's Dreadnought* placed it broadly in the latter's company.

Women's Dreadnought carried a long article, written by Sylvia (from Dublin): "War — at home and abroad". The "Home" war was the shooting down of Irish nationalists at Howth outside Dublin, when they openly attempted to copy Ulster Unionist Edward Carson style gun-running, just before war broke out.

"Europe indeed is rattling back to the barbarism that should be passed and gone. It is many years since the machinery for settling international disputes was created, but arbitration has not even been attempted..." Democracy is discarded "and our people plunged into war with as little choice or foreknowledge as is allowed to those who live under the most absolute of old despotism". Her conclusion: "All the women of the world need votes. They need a powerful voice in moulding the policy of nations... The men-made governments of Europe rush heedless on to war" (*Women's Dreadnought*, 8 August 1914).

This was the same tone and message — except for the comment about votes for women — as Keir Hardie and Macdonald adopted. It was quite a long way from the reaction of the revolutionaries, and very far from Lenin's response. Specifically, it lacked any view of imperialism and of the relationship of the war to a *new stage* of capitalism; it lacked any appreciation of why the labour movements in most countries followed their native ruling classes to war, despite many pledges to do otherwise.

Like the WSPU, the ELFS abandoned militancy on the vote question at the outbreak of the war, probably because it could hope to have little impact against the background of the cataclysm that was engulfing Europe. Unlike the WSPU, the ELFS did not abandon agitation for the suffrage: on the contrary, the search for a workable form of representative democracy was to be a central part of the politics of the ELFS and its successor organisations up until Sylvia decided she had found it in workers' councils (soviets).

Under the impact of war, the Federation immediately broadened its activities and launched a campaign for a programme of immediate action to protect working class families from such consequences of the war as rising food prices. The Federation now stepped up its direct concern with achieving immediately some of the ends for which its supporters had wanted the vote.

The ELFS set to work organising a delegation to Lloyd George and Asquith to make the following demands:

1. Food supplies to be controlled by the government during the war so that all may feed or starve together: "To make sure that the food supply is properly controlled we demand that working women should be called into consultation in fixing the price to be charged for food, and the way in which the food shall be distributed."

---

4. Keir Hardie's obituary by Sylvia Pankhurst said "Keir Hardie has been the greatest human being of our time" (*Women's Dreadnought*, 2 October 1915).

2. Committees with government power to provide employment for men and women at trade union rates, with equal pay for men and women.

3. That there be a moratorium on debts of working people.

4. That working women should be placed on all committees for fixing food prices, and for providing employment and relief.

5. Immediate women's franchise: "That [women] may help in minimising, as far as possible, the horrors of war" (*Women's Dreadnought*, 15 August 1914).

During the war, millions of women workers moved into the factories to replace men gone to the trenches. Unskilled, unorganised, and without a tradition of organisation, they were particularly vulnerable to exploitation. *Women's Dreadnought* ran exposés of the conditions they suffered, and of the deteriorating social conditions. For example, in Sheffield, where large numbers of women moved into the factories, the infant mortality rate almost doubled immediately. In 1913, it was 11,912; in 1915, it was 22,281. The *Dreadnought* tried to raise a fightback against these conditions. It attacked other features of wartime, such as the "stupid" persecutions under the enemy aliens regulations.

Sylvia Pankhurst organised cost-price restaurants and other social amenities. The ELFS took part with labour organisations in rallies.

Women's Dreadnought used the conditions of war to plug away for votes for women: for example, a cartoon showed a woman in the trenches, shells exploding all around her and the caption "Does she deserve the vote?" (*Women's Dreadnought*, 14 November 1914).

The Workers' Suffrage Federation

ON 18 March 1916, the ELFS announced in the *Women's Dreadnought* that it had changed its name to the Workers' Suffrage Federation (WSF). The WSF's object was to secure human suffrage, a vote for every woman and man of full age [21]. It explained how the new organisation differed from the old suffrage and suffragette movements. This was Sylvia Pankhurst settling some of the account with the old, middle class suffrage movement:

"They refuse to set themselves free to say that universal suffrage must be introduced for all, and hold, instead, to the merely negative course of opposing universal suffrage for men until women are enfranchised.

"The unsatisfactory result of confining suffrage propaganda to the idea that two million women possessing the present property qualifications shall be given the vote, is clearly demonstrated by the fact that when the last Government Franchise Bill, which would have given practically manhood suffrage, was before the country, a large proportion of the members of women's suffrage societies were not prepared to agree to womanhood suffrage at the same time.

"The suffrage question can never be disposed of until the entire adult population is enfranchised" (*Women's Dreadnought*, 18 March 1916).

The WSF supported the struggles of the conscientious objectors, and the fight against conscription. They held anti-war meetings at the gates of the East London and other docks. In April 1916, 10,000 people took part in a demonstration against conscription. The WSF campaigned for peace. In 1917 they picketed the Labour Party Conference, (Labour MPs were in the government). The WSF made connections between the industrial strength and militancy of the working class movement, now giving rise to the shop stewards movement, and the fight against war. For example, on 15 September 1916 *Women's Dreadnought* said that the recent miners' strike showed how to fight conscription and that conscription could be opposed by the force of organised labour: "Organised labour has declared against conscription... but what will organised labour do if the government takes steps to introduce it?" (*Women's Dreadnought*, 15 September 1916).

Sylvia Pankhurst looked at the issues facing the labour and socialist movement with the eyes and spirit of a "militant".

The same militancy and contempt for legalistic inhibitions were dominant when the British government used fierce repression in the wake of the Dublin uprising of Easter 1916. *Women's Dreadnought* was foremost of the British socialist papers sympathetic to the insurgents in denouncing the government and exposing its repressions. It carried on-

"HANDS OFF THE RING"

Principal Scene in the GRAND CHRISTMAS PANTOMIME *~ European Theatre*
Continuous performance ~ Prices as usual

Anti-war cartoon by Herbert Cole, from the *Workers' Dreadnought*

the-spot reports of conditions in Dublin, written by an 18-year-old, Patricia Lynch.

By 1917 the WSF was campaigning for a new People's Charter, modelled on that of the 1830s and 40s, under the slogan "Peace. Socialism. Votes for all!". Advertisements had the following message: "Stop the hideous slaughter by ending the war! Down with profiteering! Secure food and necessaries for all! Not votes for some but adult suffrage! Down with the House of Lords!" (*Women's Dreadnought*, 26 May 1916).

By 1917 the WSF had spread outside London, where there were 10 branches listed, to Birmingham, Bradford, Durham, Doncaster and other places in the provinces (*Women's Dreadnought*, 24 February 1917).

The Workers' Suffrage Federation and the Russian Revolution

THE Russian February Revolution that overthrew the Tsar had an enormous impact on Britain, and on the WSF too. There was almost universal enthusiasm for it. The Government and its supporters welcomed the fall of the decrepit and inefficient monarch, in the hope that now the war would be vigorously prosecuted by the new government. Liberals and socialists welcomed the fall of an age-old tyranny. Socialists welcomed the prominence of socialists in the leadership of the revolution. In the labour movement there was great enthusiasm for workers' councils (soviets) which had erupted all across Russia and in fact held much of the power relinquished by the Tsarist state.

In June 1917, at a Convention in Leeds, 1,150 delegates from labour movement bodies adopted a resolution calling for the formation "in every town, urban and rural district of Councils of Workmen's and Soldiers' delegates for initiating and co-ordinating working class activity".

Soviets were seen as a supplementary form of democracy, not as something counterposed to parliamentary or bourgeois democracy; not as the specific form of working-class democracy, of working-class rule, nor yet as the best organisational form for an aggressive working class offensive to take state power. Soon, in Russia, the working class soviets would find themselves counterposed to bourgeois democracy in the form of the Constituent Assembly, and, led by the Bolsheviks, they would not hesitate to strike down the weak Russian bourgeois democratic institutions and establish the more democratic soviets. Sylvia Pankhurst would stick with the soviets.

The new form of democracy must have seemed especially attractive to the editor of *Women's Dreadnought*, who had formulated what was needed like this in January 1917: "The two great questions of the day are peace and an equal share of the power to decide the issue of war and peace for every one of us."[5]

The Annual General Meeting of the Workers' Suffrage Federation held in May 1917 transformed the organisation into the Workers' Socialist Federation, and decided to change the name of the paper to the *Workers' Dreadnought*. The following resolution was passed:

"That this Conference, realising that the existing system of society is irreconcilable with the freedom and the just demands of the workers, urges the WSF to work for the abolition of that system, and the establishment of the socialist Commonwealth in which the means of production and distribution shall be employed in the interests of the people."

More useful for assessing the state of the political development of the WSF, and of Sylvia Pankhurst, are the other declarations of the Conference, on war and peace. It declared its opposition to all wars and for the abolition of armies and navies. All the belligerents in the war fought for capitalist interests, and nothing else: "The war is in its every aspect antagonistic to the workers of the world, to popular and personal liberty and to the general welfare of humanity."

The WSF demanded peace negotiations, no annexations and no indemnities. But, "while private competitive trading continues, the danger of war will not be entirely wiped out. What was needed to guarantee peace was an International Council to settle disputes

---

5. *Women's Dreadnought*, 27 January 1917. The same issue said of US President Wilson, a few months before America entered the war: "President Wilson has spoken with the calm voice of reasoning humanity, untouched by war."

(to be elected on an adult suffrage basis from the various nations; decisions of the International Council to be ratified by the national Parliaments). As well as this there should be established international free trade, spheres of influence should be abolished, there should be internationalisation of trade routes and narrow seas, and freedom of the sea" (*Women's Dreadnought*, 26 May 1917).

This was a programme for, in effect, world government. As such, and seemingly looked to as the way out of the bloody morass in which the world had landed, it was a utopia: for how were these things, the reversal of the actual trends dominant in the world, to be achieved? In so far as the answer to that question might be that the working class would achieve this as part of its fight for socialism, the programme is remarkable for its lack of attention to the working class struggle, and its strategic and tactical problems. All that was said above about the response of the *Dreadnought*, Keir Hardie, etc., in 1914 would still be relevant to this programme.

The 1917 WSF Conference passed resolutions on the suffrage question stating "that no franchise measure will be acceptable to the working class unless it includes complete adult suffrage". It called for an end to plural voting in local elections, where business premises carried an extra vote, and of property qualifications. It pledged the WSF to campaign with others, especially socialist and labour bodies whose programme includes adult suffrage, on a democratic basis.

It also demanded democratic reforms to (a) establish the referendum as a normal part of political life, (b) establish the right of popular initiative in starting legislation, (c) a system of recall and re-election of ministers and judges by referendum vote (*Women's Dreadnought*, 26 May 1917).

These proposed democratic reforms would in some aspects merely have brought Britain to the level of such a bourgeois democracy as that of America. But the general "package" probably amounts to an initial WSF attempt to assimilate the experience of Soviets to its still prevalent concerns with Parliament.

Perhaps most striking in general are the number of points the 1917 resolutions have in common with the radical platform on which Richard Pankhurst had stood for election in the year 1883.[6]

The Workers' Suffrage Federation had now taken its place with the British Socialist Party, the Socialist Labour Party and others as one of the galaxy of militant socialist organisations in Britain. In April 1917, it had 300 members. When it changed its name to the "Communist Party, British Section of the Third International" in June 1920 it had 150 members.

When the February Revolution occurred Sylvia Pankhurst had responded with a sharp and perceptive question: whose Russian revolution? The October 1917 Revolution proclaimed unambiguously whose Revolution it was: that it was a workers' revolution and that the working class had taken power.

The Bolshevik government proclaimed itself ready to make peace immediately, published the secret treaties of the Allies and appealed to the workers in the belligerent countries to turn the war into civil war against their rulers. Lenin now had the ears of many millions throughout the world, war weary millions ready to draw revolutionary conclusions from their experience of the bloody impasse in which world capitalism had been bogged down for over three years.

The militants and the left rallied to the Bolshevik Revolution; those who wanted to emulate Lenin and Trotsky attempted to learn from them. The militant doctrines of the class struggle were proclaimed with a starkness and a vigour that had long been absent in the west European labour movement; to many militants who had been on political wavelengths similar to that of Sylvia Pankhurst, the vigour and the starkness seemed appropriate to the times.

---

6. Richard Pankhurst's 1883 election platform included: removal of non-representative elements from the British constitution; payment of MPs and Ministers; disestablishment and disendowment of the Church of England; free compulsory secular education; nationalisation of land; transfer from executive to the legislature of power of war and peace to make treaties; an international tribunal (at first voluntary); the United States of Europe leading to the World Commonwealth; drastic military and naval reductions; home rule for Ireland (*The Life of Emmeline Pankhurst*, Sylvia Pankhurst, pp.19-21).

Sylvia Pankhurst welcomed the October Revolution unambiguously. She proclaimed that the Revolution had been brought about in order that the workers of Russia might no longer be disinherited and oppressed as they had continued to be after the February Revolution.

"Our eager hopes are for the speedy success of the Bolsheviks of Russia: may they open the door which leads to freedom for the people of all lands..." ("The Lenin Revolution — What It Means for Democrats", *Workers' Dreadnought,* 17 November 1917).

The WSF and the small "DeLeonite" sectarian organisation, the Socialist Labour Party, were the only groups on the British militant left which gave the October Revolution a complete and unreserved blessing, and tried to assist the Bolsheviks by their own revolutionary activity in this country.

Sylvia declared: "I am proud to be a Bolshevik." The defence of the Revolution — "Hands off Russia" — in propaganda, and in attempts to organise working class action to stop intervention by capitalist armies to strangle the revolution, became the central activity for Sylvia for the next two years. In 1920 her work in the East End helped persuade dockworkers to refuse to load ammunition for Poland's war with Russia onto the ship Jolly George.

Bolshevik

WITH a certain arbitrariness, perhaps one can take as marking Sylvia Pankhurst's definitive transition to Lenin-Soviet-Communism the events at the beginning of 1918 when the Russian soviets suppressed the Constituent Assembly.

The Constituent Assembly, elected before the October Revolution, had a majority hostile to the Revolution and to the policies of the majority that had been elected out of the vast network of workers', soldiers' and peasants' councils that covered Russia. The majority party in it, the Social Revolutionaries, had just split into Left and Right, with deputies on Right and Left in inverse proportion to the support for Left and Right policies on the land question. The left would enter into a coalition with the Bolsheviks. When the Constituent Assembly met, the question arose: which was the sovereign power, Soviets or Constituent Assembly? The Soviets, under the leadership of the Bolshevik Party, answered that they were, and proceeded to dismiss the Constituent Assembly.

For Sylvia Pankhurst, who had fought so hard for Parliamentary democracy, it may have been the point where she made her mind up definitively about the Russian Revolution. She gave the Bolshevik-led Soviets complete support in their action.

She wrote: "The old bourgeois parliamentarianism has seen its day that is unable to cope with the tasks before socialists". The Revolution created the Soviets "as the only organisation of all the exploited working classes in a position to direct the struggle of those classes for their complete political and economic emancipation.

"But some people complain that the Soviets only represent the working classes... and if they are to rule then the opinion of other classes will be ignored. Yes, that is so; and that is what the Bolsheviks desire.

"To those who object we need only ask but one question: are you socialist?

"If you are not a socialist, of course, you object to a system which gives all power to the workers; we understand the ground of your objection, and realise that until you are converted to socialism your objection cannot be overcome.

"But if you are a socialist you must recognise that under socialism everyone will be a worker, and there will be no classes save the working classes to consider or represent. Under socialism no-one will live on profits and dividends drawn from the labour of others; there will be no leisured classes.

"As a representative body, an organisation such as the All Russian Workers', Soldiers', Sailors' and Peasants' Council is more clearly in touch with, and more directly represents, its constituents than the Constituent Assembly or any existing Parliament." ("What About Russia Now?", *Workers Dreadnought,* 26 January 1918).

Looking back

ET US look back along the road Sylvia Pankhurst had travelled. The WSPU and its characteristic tactics of militancy, and then small scale terrorism against property, developed from a sense of outrage at the reactionary inertia which kept women disenfranchised, despite the fact that there was a variable but more or less perennial House of Commons majority platonically committed to votes for women.

Its focus on the form of women's suffrage deemed most acceptable to most members of the social and political establishment, with the intention (on the part of the ILPers who started the WSPU) of first establishing the principle of votes for women, inexorably led it away from the labour movement. The nascent Labour Party got caught in the crossfire between the WSPU and the Liberal government, to which the Labour Party chose to tie itself. The social and political background of most of the women attracted by the WSPU's specific combination of limited immediate suffrage demands and militancy, bourgeois and aristocratic women, and women who did not have a socialist or labour movement background, led to the transformation of the WSPU into an organisation alienated from the labour movement, and ultimately hostile to its concerns and aspirations.

Sylvia Pankhurst, by starting to organise a mass agitational propaganda campaign at the point where the WSPU moved to petty terrorism, and by focusing on the East End of London, began a process which reversed for her section of WSPU activists the trajectory of the WSPU. The turn to proletarian women led her to centre her concerns on the fact that votes for these women were inseparable from their social concerns. That led to increasing involvement and concern with the daily problems and struggles, as such, of the East London proletariat, and, inevitably in the circumstances, not just those of women. Adult suffrage implied organising men too, in an area where most men did not have a vote. The turn to the general problems brought socialism to the fore, and that led to a complete broadening of the Federation's concerns: for women alone could not transform society. The movement was first to proletarian women and then to the proletariat.

Rooted in the east London community and labour movement, and subscribing to the ideas of the Keir Hardie segment of the labour movement, Sylvia's evolution during the war was part of, and characteristic of, the development of a trend of socialists who learned to look to industrial direct action militancy, when that showed its strength and power in resistance to wartime conditions (with the Labour Party, the "political wing of the movement", in the government). The terrible slaughter for four years hardened a bitter resolve to finish off the capitalist system as quickly as possible. They turned with hope and enthusiasm to the Russian Revolution and set out to re-educate themselves politically on the basis of Russian experience and the politics of those who led the revolution.

To judge by the positions taken by her paper and by organisations in which she was the most influential figure, Sylvia Pankhurst was, in her basic political outlook, a consistent radical democrat until 1917/18. The ideas and proposals, and even the implied conception of the world, in the initial "programme" of the Workers' Socialist Federation owed more to the rationalist world outlook of the liberal Enlightenment than to Marxism. In 1917 Lenin and his supporters were with bitter invective denouncing similar notions as utopian. And, indeed, they were utopian in the prevailing world conditions: the point at issue for socialists was how to get out of and beyond those conditions.

In addition to her basic underlying ideas, there was Sylvia's wholehearted commitment to the working class and reliance on its victory as the only way to ensure human progress; and her belief that society must be reorganised on socialist lines so as to satisfy the fundamental needs of the majority. Yet, though the WSF was a militant socialist organisation, its politics at its formation had no more than elements of Marxism. Its eclecticism and dependence on the ideas of left-wing liberalism was, of course, not unique on the British far left then.

Sylvia's political concern remained centrally, though not exclusively, focused on problems of democracy. Her first words at the outbreak of war had commented on the practical emptiness of the democracy of the parliamentary system. At the beginning of 1917, the central question, linked with the problem of peace was presented by her as one of getting an effective mass democracy. As the attempt to assimilate the experience of Soviets to the British Parliamentary system in the programme of the WSF testifies, her concern with effective democracy was still focussed on Parliamentary forms as late as mid-1917.

A few months later at the beginning of 1918, Parliament was removed from the equation under pressure of the unfolding in Russia of the sort of mass working class struggles which Sylvia hoped for in Britain as the culmination of struggles already in being, and which had already, during the war, partly displaced her focus from votes to direct action.

In 1918, when she sided with the Soviets against the Russian Parliament, she in fact *chose*, under the pressure of events and her deep-rooted impulse to side with the workers and their struggles, *a new form of democracy* – soviet as distinct from parliamentary democracy. It was the form of democracy which, through recallability of delegates, most eliminated the separation of electors and legislature. At the same time, it was a network of mass organisations for struggle. It was the most developed political form of the sort of mass working class struggles Sylvia had been committed to even before the war. And, of course, the Soviets of 1917/18 enfranchised women completely and drew them into political action.

Sylvia Pankhurst's conviction that the Soviet was the best form of representative democracy and answered the problems which she had spent much of her life grappling with was a major element in her evolution to communism, and to the specific, anti-Parliamentarism on principle, communism which she embraced.

Epilogue

IN MID-1918 Sylvia Pankhurst started the Russian People's Information Service, with Bolshevik money, and launched into a great campaign in defence of the October Revolution.

She belonged to the ultra-left wing of the Communist International. Once she had embraced the Soviets as the best system of popular democracy, she turned her back completely on Parliament, opposing in principle any working class involvement in bourgeois parliaments or in electoral activity. She refused an invitation to contest a Sheffield seat for the Labour Party in the 1918 election.

Thus, when the Communist International had to concern itself with going beyond propaganda for the soviet system, and find ways to develop working class political activity within the bourgeois political system as a means of building up and educating support for an eventual transition to a system of soviet democracy, Sylvia Pankhurst found herself much out of sympathy with tactical manoeuvrings, and, essentially, with involvement in the bourgeois political system.

Her method had been – up and straight at 'em! Now, paradoxically, that meant confinement to mere propaganda for soviets. Sylvia was part of the Council Communist current associated with the names of Anton Pannekoek and Herman Görter. Lenin wrote a pamphlet against them, amongst others, in 1920, *Left Wing Communism: A Disorder of Infancy*. Her comrades and Sylvia were in many ways close to syndicalism.

Retrospectively, they sided with anarchists who had been opposed to the whole course of development of the working class movement in the 40 years before 1914. They opposed not only participation in bourgeois parliaments – that is, effectively, in politics – but also trade unions. They were against fighting for reforms.

Sylvia Pankhurst broke with the Communist International in 1921 and was a founder of a "Fourth International" led by Herman Görter, which seems to have gone out of existence in a few years. (Van Dere Lubbe, who stood in the dock with Dimitrov at the Reichstag fire trial in 1933 and was found guilty and beheaded, was a council communist.)

In a dispute about control of *Workers' Dreadnought*, she was expelled from the Communist Party of Great Britain, in September 1921. She continued to publish *Workers' Dreadnought* until 1924; but now what had been a splendidly alive paper was a very dull, rather "literary", review. In 1921 she published the platform of the "Workers' Opposition" in Russia, which said much of importance about the way things were going, but had no solution (its leaders, Shlyapnikov and Alexandra Kollontai, author of the platform, went over to Stalin in the mid-20s). Sylvia Pankhurst moved out of east London after 12 years in 1924. She had her first child in 1927 at the age of 45. She then wrote a book about mothers and children, advocating reforms. She was no longer a council communist...

Thereafter she wrote a number of valuable books on the history of the suffrage struggle.

In the 1930s, she returned to a sort of politics as an anti-fascist campaigner in the Popular Front period, and especially as a champion of Ethiopia, invaded by Mussolini's Italian armies in 1935. She started a paper, *New Times and Ethiopia News* in 1936, that survived for 20 years. She allied loosely with the "anti-fascist" Communist Party, but also with dissidents to the left of the party, such as the black ex-CP militant George Padmore.

She denounced the Moscow Trials; and she sided against the anarchists and the POUM of Barcelona in May 1937 during their battle with the Stalinists, saying that these victims of Stalinism should have waited until General Franco was defeated...

For her last quarter century she was a devotee of the Emperor Haile Selassie, who from 1935 to 1942 was an exile in Britain.

Selassie gave his personal name Ras Tafari to Rastafarianism, whose devotees made a god of this Christian king of an ancient, feudal African state. Sylvia Pankhurst, one could say, was amongst the first rastas! She was a tireless propagandist for Ethiopia, championing, amongst other things, its right to control Eritrea.

There may have been elements of rejection of capitalism in her devotion to feudal Ethiopia. Here Sylvia's political fate was a variant of the fate of so many of her contemporaries and ex-comrades, like Harry Pollitt, who became General Secretary of the Stalinised CPGB, who looked to the USSR and to Stalin's and other bureaucratic dictatorships as the hope of the socialist future, embracing a reactionary, historically regressive anti-capitalism. If there is anything good in Sylvia's variant of it, it is that she can't have told herself that Ras Tafari represented either socialism or the future of humanity.

She died in Ethiopia in 1960, aged 78.

Reading

Ray Challinor, *The Origins of British Bolshevism*
G D H Cole, *British Working Class Politics, 1832-1914*
Mary Davis, *Sylvia Pankhurst: A Life in Radical Politics*
Richard J Evans, *The Feminists: Women's Emancipation Movements in Europe, America and Australasia, 1840-1920*
George Lichtheim, *Europe in the 20th Century*
Rosa Luxemburg, *The Belgian General Strike*
Ralph Milliband, *Parliamentary Socialism*
David Mitchell, *The Fighting Pankhursts*
Dora Montefiore, *From a Victorian to a Modern*
A L Morton and George Tate, *The British Labour Movement, 1770-1920*
R S Neale, *Class and Ideology in the 19th Century*
E Sylvia Pankhurst, *The Life of Emmeline Pankhurst*
E Syliva Pankhurst, *The Home Front*
E Syliva Pankhurst, *The Suffragette Movement*
Harry Pollitt, *Serving My Time*
Antonia Raeburn, *The Militant Suffragettes*
Patricia Romero, *E Sylvia Pankhurst*
Barbara Winslow, *Sylvia Pankhurst: Sexual Politics and Political Activism*

Lenin and the myth of revolutionary defeatism
By Hal Draper

"When Vladimir Ilyitch once observed me glancing through a collection of his articles writ-ten in the year 1903, which had just been published, a sly smile crossed his face, and he remarked with a laugh: 'It is very interesting to read what stupid fellows we were!'"

Karl Radek[1]

Introduction to the myth

SINCE the First World War, Marxists, would-be Marxists, and even many non-Marxist socialists have gained a good part of their political education through a close study of Lenin's anti-war writings of 1914-1918. In fact, even much of anti-Marxist and anti-Leninist literature is often based on an unexamined acceptance of Lenin's account of ideas, even when these writers change all the value signs from plus to minus.... Myths about Lenin's views on war policy during the First World War have a very tenacious hold on life...

Since our subject concerns a *peculiarity* of the Lenin group, we need to be aware of the other anti-war socialists for purposes of comparison, and to this end we will largely use two who denounced "social-patriotism" (pro-war socialism) as sternly as did Lenin. These were Leon Trotsky, then an independent in the Russian Social-Democratic factional situation, and Rosa Luxemburg, best known as a leader of the left wing in the German party...

As Lenin himself saw the problems of theory and political policy, his historical role in the socialist movement was to revive and reanimate the revolutionary substance of Marxism that had been overlaid by the creeping social-reformism of the Second International. In respect to anti-war policy, however, he – along with Luxemburg and the whole left – had to do more than revive. They had to *readapt* Marxism and its policies to the realities of a new epoch. From the First World War on, the Marxist view of war had a new starting point. Even if we eliminate revolutionary defeatism from this package, Lenin made the major contribution to this end, with Luxemburg (as author of the *Junius Pamphlet*) running second.

The old Second International had never worked out a clear line on the fight against war. By and large, its resolutions had repeated that war flowed from the capitalist system and would disappear along with that system, and had vaguely recognised the right of nations to defend themselves from attack by another power acting from presumably reprehensible motives. When the day came that saw all participants in the world slaughter "defending" themselves against some attack or other, this principle was no help by itself. It was not until the 1907 Stuttgart congress of the International that a new note was injected: the threat of socialist revolution, not through the empty brandishing of a general strike threat on the outbreak of war, but the threat of revolution developing as the outcome of the disaster. This was expressed in the amendment to the main resolution submitted by Lenin, Luxemburg and Martov. It simply said that if war should break out despite all, the socialists should intervene "with all their powers to utilise the economic and political crisis created by the war to rouse the masses and thereby to hasten the downfall of capitalist class rule". This passage was included also in the resolution adopted by the next International congress, the last regular congress, held at Copenhagen in 1910...

For most of the delegates it was a matter of some more verbiage about revolution to scare the bourgeoisie with a threat they scouted. For the left, it was a challenge – once war had bro-ken out – to work out the practical and tactical meaning of the statement.

In August 1914... Lenin worked out the view that "revolutionary defeatism" was a necessary part of the socialist anti-war riposte...

Abridged from Hal Draper, *War and Revolution, Lenin and the Myth of Revolutionary Defeatism* Edited by E Haberkern, Humanities Press, New Jersey, 1996.

Content of the myth

BEFORE recounting what Lenin did and thought, let us present the myth itself, which has blanketed socialist history on this point since it was invented in 1924...To begin with, the myth claims that "revolutionary defeatism" became a permanent and fixed part of the Lenin canon, and that to question it was to question a "fundamental principle" of Leninism. We will see that it was not only not permanent or fundamental, but it was not even a "principle".

The rest of the myth includes the following:

● During the war Lenin alone adopted a completely consistent and uncompromising policy of opposition to the war, all others among the anti-war socialists being guilty of some "centrist" deviation or similar unclarity.

● This defeatist principle comprises the very heart of Lenin's anti-war position; or, as it has sometimes been put, this defeatism of Lenin's "summed up" his anti-war politics.

● This "revolutionary defeatism" is the necessary alternative to defencism — these two being the only consistent choices. To reject defeatism means to make some degree of concession to social-patriotism...

So goes the myth. When we look at some of Lenin's writings of 1914-1915, we will find a variety of shifting and inconsistent formulations on defeatism, but the part that has entered into the canonical concept of defeatism includes the following: *in a reactionary war you must desire the defeat of "your own" government*, wish defeat, favour nothing less than defeat.

It was not enough, then, merely to condemn the war, or condemn the voting of (say) war credits; it was not enough to organise or favour the organising of mass struggles against the war; it was not enough to denounce "defence of the fatherland" and its social-patriotic proponents; it was not enough, certainly, to denounce the consequences of military *victory* by "one's own" government, since there were "centrist" positions that were "against both victory and defeat". In fact, an anti-war position that fell short of avowed defeatism was either "left-centrist" or tinged with pacifism, or, at the very best, it was an "unconscious" defeatism which could not be carried out consistently and fearlessly in action until the "slogan of defeat" itself was embraced.

These were Lenin's claims during the 1914-1916 period, and he counterposed them in polemic not only against the pro-war social-patriots but also against the views of other anti-war socialists such as Luxemburg and Trotsky. These two not only agreed with Lenin on war policy in general but also on the main organisational conclusion, i.e., the call for a new revolutionary International. The main difference was on Lenin's "slogan of defeat", which Trotsky specifically attacked; and Luxemburg, who possibly never even heard of it during the war, wrote along a line that precluded any sympathy for it...

Lenin's combination

IN sum, we are faced with the following counterposition. On the one hand, we have the leading anti-war internationalists like Luxemburg and Trotsky who were against both imperialist camps in the war; against voting for war credits; in favour of irreconcilable class struggle during the war; in favour of transforming the fight against the war into a fight for socialist power; in favour of breaking with the International of the social-patriots of both camps. Against the military victory of their own government's imperialism, they counterposed the victory of their own working class struggle for socialism. Against the military victory of their own government, they did not counterpose a desire for its military defeat. They counterposed their own socialist solution to *any military outcome, victory or defeat, on the plane of the inter-imperialist conflict.*

These antiwar revolutionary socialists were not "defeatists"...

In the case of the position peculiar to [him], Lenin... sought to combine some variety of "defeat of your own government" with the anti-war policy of opposition to both war camps.

Lenin attempted to *combine* defeatism and an anti-war line.

Note that this is worded in a manner precisely opposite to that of the Lenin myth, which paints defeatism as the inescapable and necessary expression of antiwar policy and which therefore recognises no problem at all about making such a combination...

Lenin in 1914: the four formulas

BEFORE 1914, without any exception known to me, [defeatism] meant *defeat by the enemy government* – what we have called pro-war defeatism – because it also meant victory for the enemy government. It was not a policy capable of international application, but could be held by one side of a given war between a despotic, backward state and a capitalist state considered "progressive".

As we raise the curtain on Lenin in August 1914, preparing the first document to state the anti-war position of the Bolshevik Party, it was *this* tradition and *this* meaning that was in his consciousness. Shocked and appalled not only by the onset of world slaughter but also by the collapse of the Socialist International, he saw a line of blood not of his making: the line of blood between those socialist leaders who were whipping their parties and workers into line in favour of the imperialist chauvinism of their own ruling class, under the slogans of "civil peace" and "defence of the fatherland", and, on the other hand, those relatively few socialists who maintained the class struggle against the war and sought to carry out the International's injunctions of 1907-1910 to utilise the war crisis for the overthrow of the capitalist system that was setting workers against workers to cut each other's throats.

He reacted in a fashion that was characteristic of Lenin the man, and not merely Lenin the Marxist.

For example: over a decade before, he had had to raise a great hue and cry in order to bring together the atomised Russian Social-Democratic groups and circles into a modern centralised party with a central organ. At the time, he thought, this was the great next step that had to be taken; it was "what is to be done". Since it was the key, it had to be pounded home into the consciousness of every comrade; everything had to be subordinated to emphasising it. How do you emphasise it? By repeating it a thousand times in every conceivable way? Yes. By explaining it patiently over and over? Yes. By piling up argument after argument, seizing on every fact and every problem and converting them into lessons on centralisation? Yes. But that was not all. The problem was greater centralisation, as compared with the existing looseness, when no party existed at all. Then put "Centralisation!" on a banner, on a pedestal; emphasise it by raising it to a principle. But the opponents of this elementary step of centralisation covered their political objections – objections against having any organised party at all – by demagogically yelling "Bureaucratism! Lenin wants more bureaucracy while we are for democracy!"

Lenin reacted typically. Yes, he retorted, "Bureaucracy *versus* democracy" – that is the revolutionary organisational principle.[2] The whole passage made fairly clear how he used the initially shocking statement to underline, with heavy strokes, the task of the day, by exaggerating in every way that side of the problem pointing in the direction where it was necessary to move now. Tomorrow the balance could be recaptured, but first you put the weight on where it was needed. That was Lenin's way of doing it.

He did it again in 1921, at the Third Congress of the Comintern, when Lenin (together with Trotsky and the Bolshevik leadership) was fighting the ultra-leftist trends that he had attacked in his book *Left-Wing Communism*. At a meeting of key delegations, Lenin told them – in words virtually made to be wrenched out of context: "Our sole strategy now is to become... more sensible, more 'opportunistic', and that is what we must tell the masses."[3] The point was, of course, that the ultra-leftists were accusing him of becoming "opportunistic". Therefore, "Become opportunistic!" was sloganised onto a banner, and waved in a spirit of bravado. Lenin had done this all his political life.

It was undoubtedly with relish that an article by Lenin in 1915 used a quotation "by a French philosopher" which obviously had impressed him. The quotation went this way: "Dead ideas are those that appear in elegant garments, with no asperity or daring... Strong ideas are those that shock and scandalise, evoke indignation, anger, and animosity in some, and enthusiasm in others."[4] The other side of this virtue has been shown by the large number of passages in Lenin in which he resorted to exaggerated one-sided generalisations in order to give emphasis, temporarily seeing only the one-sidedness. Whatever benefits there were in this method were garnered by his contemporaries; the same cannot be said for the generations that tried to learn from his writings without understanding that, in reading Lenin, one must know not only what he was saying but also what he was polemically concerned about at the moment. This is a case where "authority by quotation" can be quite misleading. Tendentious historians have naturally found that this offers opportunities for tendentious misinterpretation, but it is a pitfall for honest students too.

In 1914 the people whom Lenin considered traitors to international socialism were yelling "Civil peace!" Well then, said Lenin, *No! Civil war!*

In 1914 these traitors were yelling "Defence of the fatherland!" No, said Lenin, *defeat* of your own fatherland!..

Formulation No. 1: the "Lesser Evil" formula

IN early September 1914 Lenin presented his draft thesis on the war to his Bolshevik Party comrades in Bern. In this document – in a subordinate place, to be sure, but still included – was this statement:

"From the viewpoint of the working class and the toiling masses of all the peoples of Russia, the defeat of the Tsarist monarchy and its army, which oppress Poland, the Ukraine, and many other peoples of Russia, and foment hatred among the peoples so as to increase Great-Russian oppression of the other nationalities, and consolidate the reactionary and barbarous government of the Tsar's monarchy, would be the lesser evil by far."[5]

What role did this statement play in the thesis? It was *not* in the point (No. 7) that presented the general line and slogans on the war. It was in the section (No. 6) which related the war to the *national question* in the Tsarist prison of the peoples; which argued that Russian socialists must "wage a ruthless and all-out struggle against Great-Russian and Tsarist-monarchist chauvinism". In this connection, Lenin argued, defeat was the "lesser evil" *for the oppressed nationalities.*

Lenin had remembered the idea and stuck it in at this point. This was the starting point of a development which we will now have to follow step by step, as it evolves and changes and shifts. It can be done only step by step because, as we have indicated, we are not dealing with a clear political idea that can be easily discussed pro and con, through "examples" and "illustrative quotations", but with a theoretical snarl that has to be disentangled.

We get a hint of what was working in Lenin's thinking, as he remembered the concept of defeat, by his rough notes for an unfinished article which he jotted down at about the same time.[6]

"...if Russian Tsarism is particularly infamous and barbarous (and more reactionary than all the rest), then German imperialism too is monarchist: its aims are feudal and dynastic, and its gross bourgeoisie are less free than the French. The Russian Social-Democrats were right in saying that *to them* the defeat of Tsarism was the lesser evil, for *their* immediate enemy was, first and foremost, *Great-Russian* chauvinism, but that in each country the socialists (who are not opportunists) ought to see their main enemy in their 'own' ('home-made') chauvinism."[7]

This gives us a train of thought. Note the criteria with which he compares Russian Tsarism and German kaiserism. Tsarism is the most reactionary regime. But... he recalls that the enemy government, Germany, is also dominated by pre-capitalist reaction (it is monarchist, feudal, dynastic, etc.). In this comparison, it is not imperialist-*capitalist* Germany that is examined...

The emphasis limiting the concept to the *Russian* socialists was brought out very sharply in Lenin's next mention of defeat as a programmatic idea. This was in his letter to Shlyapnikov of October 17:

"...in order that the struggle should proceed along precise and clear lines we need a watchword which generalises it. That watchword is: for us *Russians,* from the point of view of the interests of the working masses and the working class of *Russia,* there cannot be the smallest doubt, absolutely any doubt, that the *lesser* evil would be now, at once the *defeat* of Tsarism in this war. For Tsarism is a hundred times worse than Kaiserism. Not sabotage of the war, but the struggle against chauvinism... It would be a mistake both to call for *individual* acts of shooting officers, etc., and to tolerate arguments like the one that 'we don't want to help Kaiserism'."[8]

It was now a watchword, a slogan. And when Lenin wrote that there could not be "the smallest doubt, absolutely any doubt" about it, it was his way of reacting vigorously to the fact that it had already been attacked in the Bolshevik ranks.

The letter made very clear that by "defeat" Lenin meant defeat *by the enemy government,* by the German armies. It was this that was the "lesser evil". (Later reinterpretation sometimes claimed that Lenin meant defeat *by the workers' revolution*; but in the first place, this was no "evil" at all, and in the second place the whole business about defeat would be totally incomprehensible if that were all he intended to say.)

It is not breaking in an open door to insist on this point, since odd interpretations of Lenin's "revolutionary defeatism" have been legion. *At this stage, defeatism had no other meaning than military defeat by the enemy camp...*

This was what gave the "lesser evil" formulation the sense it had: defeat by Germany would be an evil, yes, but the greater evil would be the victory of the Tsar's army; and we choose between these two evils.

This made sense of the *reason* given by Lenin for the slogan: "For Tsarism is a hundred times worse than Kaiserism." This defeat slogan depended for its rationalisation not on balanced opposition to both camps but on a "lesser evil" *distinction* between the two camps. Tsarism was the worst: this plainly could not apply in Germany, where Kaiserism was a hundred times better than Tsarism. It could apply only for "us *Russians*".

Moreover, Lenin never did apply this "lesser evil" formulation of the defeat slogan to any other country. When he tried to internationalise the concept, it became something else.

The slogan of defeat began, therefore, as a *special Russian position* on the war. Like the motivation for it, it had its roots in the "special Russian position" that had developed in the Second International. Without this background, the very idea of a "special Russian position" on the war in 1914 would be strange. Here was a general world war, where in every other respect Lenin was driven to emphasise the inextricable entangling of all the threads of world imperialism, and yet he proposed that the socialists of one of the belligerents should adopt a position which he did not propose for the others.

For these socialists, the next question raised by the proposal leaps to the eye. If the defeat slogan meant defeat *by Germany* (whose victory is the lesser evil), then didn't this mean preferring the victory of Germany? But – that was exactly what the German social-patriots preferred. Yet the bulk of Lenin's writing at this time was devoted to marshalling the arguments *against* the social-patriots (the Germans above all). Clearly the slogan of defeat could not have the simple and clear meaning that it had in 1904-1905. How could this contradiction be resolved?

Out of the attempt to resolve this contradiction came the wavy course of Lenin's defeatism in 1914-1916.

Rejection of defeatism in the Bolshevik ranks

IT turned out that the defeat slogan was the one aspect of Lenin's war position that immediately met with the widest opposition in the ranks of the Bolshevik Party itself. In his letter to Shlyapnikov, Lenin had asked for "*More details* about the views and reactions of the workers". Others reported also.

Shlyapnikov's memoirs recount that when Lenin's first official statement on the war was brought to Petersburg, it was generally acceptable to the "party workers", "but the question of 'defeatism' did cause perplexity"...

Bukharin and Piatakov criticised the defeat slogan in the emigration...

Shlyapnikov's memoirs give other indications of at least uneasiness about the defeat slogan...

Shlyapnikov never reports that *he* ever raised the defeat slogan, in the course of great and varied activity as a party activist, in touch with Lenin as we have seen. He quotes the longish texts of anti-war declarations he wrote and circulated and not one of them shows a wisp of defeatism...

In fact – outside of Lenin's immediate co-workers on the Central Organ in Bern, particularly Zinoviev in his own peculiar way – we cannot cite any known leading Bolshevik who defended the defeatist slogan, or any section of the party that came to its defence against its critics; though one imagines there must have been such people, to one degree or another, since at different times different formulations of the idea were approved or compromised on.

The Geneva section of the Bolshevik emigration sent their objection in to Lenin...

The passage had meant to the Geneva Bolsheviks exactly what it had meant in the past of the movement: a wish for the victory of the enemy government. They could not answer the question: if we Russian Bolsheviks see reason to wish this, why attack the *German* Social-Democrats for wishing the very same thing? So they proposed that a different statement should be made about defeat, a statement about the *objective consequences* of defeat. What they had in mind was merely the idea that "defeat facilitates revolution". And they wanted to strip the passage down to this.

Whittling down the "Lesser Evil" formula

BUT when the Bolshevik Central Committee adopted its thesis on the war for publication as the position of the party on November 1, the change proposed by the Geneva Bolsheviks was not made. The "lesser evil" formulation went into the document – but in modified form.

Now it was not merely tied up with the nationalities problem; it was directed more generally. And it was preceded by a sentence (whose idea had already been somewhat indicated in Lenin's rough notes[9]) which doubly underlined that this was a notion for *Russian* socialists only, and which warned that it could not be applied for the international socialist movement as a whole. The passage in the party statement began as follows:

"In the present situation, it is impossible to determine, from the standpoint of the international proletariat, the defeat of which of the two groups of belligerent nations would be the lesser evil for socialism...

"But to us Russian Social-Democrats there cannot be the slightest doubt that, from the standpoint of the working class and the toiling masses of all the nations of Russia, the defeat of the Tsarist monarchy, the most reactionary and barbarous of governments, which is oppressing the largest number of nations and the greatest mass of the population of Europe and Asia, would be the lesser evil."[10]

This "special Russian position" now became the public position of the party. It repeated Lenin's tell-tale emphasis that Russia was "the *most* reactionary and barbarous government" in order to justify this special Russian policy as such, echoing the thought that "Tsarism is a hundred times worse than Kaiserism".

The next step that had to be taken was a step that followed *politically* from this statement of the "lesser evil". Surely the "lesser evil" opinion could not remain simply an interesting thought in a thesis. Though the thesis did not say so as yet in so many words, what followed was that socialists had to *wish* for this "lesser evil", actively *desire* it. Otherwise, why was it brought up in that way?

In fact, Lenin put this down in black and white in his next mention of the defeat concept, published on December 12:

"We say that the Great-Russians cannot 'defend the fatherland' otherwise than by desiring the defeat of Tsarism in any way, this as the lesser evil to nine-tenths of the inhabitants of Great Russia."

So socialists now "wished defeat"; and this conclusion could hardly have been avoided. But the "lesser evil" notion had depended for its political motivation on nothing else than the idea that Tsarism was "worst", "most reactionary", "most barbarous" and so on. This motivation was surely inseparable from the formula. But when Lenin *now* stated the reason (to continue the quotation where we broke it off) it was watered down to a statement *that could apply to any of the imperialist powers and not only to Russian Tsarism*:

"For Tsarism not only oppresses those nine-tenths economically and politically, but also demoralises, degrades, dishonours, and prostitutes them by teaching them to oppress other nations and to cover up this shame with hypocritical and quasi-patriotic phrases."[11]

But this was agitation; it was no longer a motivation for the *special* position. The motivation for the special Russian position had disappeared, and, as we will see, it will soon be specifically repudiated. Only the formula was left, and this too will soon be changed.

Formulation No.2: "Defeat Facilitates"

THE big contradiction remained: if the Russian socialists could wish the military defeat of Tsarism (*everybody understood: by German arms*), then what was so terrible about the German socialists wishing for the same outcome? Very likely Lenin confronted this objection within Bolshevik ranks where criticisms of the defeat slogan were being raised. But we do not find him taking note of it until February 1915 – and then in a polemic against the Menshevik Axelrod. Lenin had accused Axelrod of being an apologist for the German social-patriots; and, as his critics had warned, he found this apologist *utilising his own methodology*.

Axelrod's assertion [wrote Lenin] that "the defeat of Russia, while unable to hamper the organic development of the country, would help liquidate the old regime", is true if taken by itself, but when it is used to justify the German chauvinists, it is nothing but an attempt to *curry favour* with the Südekums.[12] Recognition of the usefulness of Russia's defeat, without openly accusing the German and Austrian Social-Democrats of having betrayed socialism means *in reality* helping them justify themselves, wriggle out of a difficult situation, and deceive the workers. Axelrod's article is a double obeisance — one to the German social-chauvinists, the other to the French.[13]

No doubt Axelrod was using the argument to justify the Germans, but *what was wrong with the argument* that could be so used? Lenin had replied in effect: "When the Germans said what we say, it's because *they* merely wanted to find a pretext for their betrayal of socialism." True, of course. But is it a *cogent* pretext? Is the pretext justified *politically*? Had not Lenin lent colour and strength to this pretext with his insistence, *as a basic political concept governing war policy*, that "Tsarism is a hundred times worse than Kaiserism" or at any rate "most reactionary", and with his formula of the "lesser evil"? Lenin had no reply to this argument. He was being confronted with the other side of his formula as it looked from the German angle, and against Axelrod he did not repeat the formula. Instead, he ran for defence to precisely the line which the Geneva Bolsheviks had recommended in its place, which he had refused to accept: he proceeded to write as if all he had said was that Russian defeat had its "usefulness". ("Objectively")...

And so we find Lenin going over to what we may call Formula No. 2 — the idea that "defeat facilitates revolution" (objectively). As will typically happen again on this question, it is a shifting of ground in the face of the insoluble contradiction...

Formulation No. 3: "Wish Defeat In Every Country"

LENIN'S Formula No. 2 was in fact internationally applicable and not special to Russia. At this same time (February 1915) Lenin explicitly launched his "defeatism" as an international policy.

"Present-day democracy [i.e., socialism] will remain true to itself only if it joins neither one nor the other imperialist bourgeoisie, only if it says that the two sides are equally bad,[14] and if it wishes the defeat of the imperialist bourgeoisie in every country. Any other decision will, in reality, be national-liberal and have nothing in common with genuine internationalism."[15]

This was the end of the road for the *politics* which had given birth to Lenin's defeatism. Lenin was specifically repudiating, in so many words, the whole motivation which had brought it on in the first place: both sides were "equally bad," or more exactly, "both are worst". Only a few months before, the basic thought had been that "Tsarism is a hundred times worse than Kaiserism"; "most reactionary"; "more reactionary than any", etc. Not only had the original motivation been abandoned, but now the formula itself had been changed. The "slogan of defeat" remained as the smile without the Cheshire cat. What remained was a running polemic but not a political line.

The new formula was now: "wish the defeat of the imperialist bourgeoisie in every country." Superficially it sounded as if he had said it before, and he had indeed used the phrase "wish defeat". But that was only as part of the "special Russian policy", as a conclusion from the lesser-evil formula; it was only Russian socialists who were supposed to "wish defeat" because of the uniquely reactionary character of their own government.

The phrase was the same, but the political content was now entirely different. "Wish defeat" was a *consistent* conclusion from the lesser-evil formula. But what did it mean once it was internationalised? Something different, at any rate. It was, in fact, a new formulation, Formula No. 3.

Let us now see how the insoluble problem of what it meant gave rise to the fourth and last switch in the formulation of defeatism.

"Wish defeat" was, as a matter of historical fact, the necessary kernel of any defeatism properly so called... One may say anything one wants about "defeat", but not every statement about defeat is a "defeatism". Defeatism means *favouring* defeat, *desiring* defeat, *calling for* defeat, *working for* defeat, or something akin, or else one is simply inventing misleading and useless terminology.

In the experience of the Second International and in the tradition established by socialists in the Russo-Japanese War, by Lenin as well as others, "defeat" meant defeat by the enemy government, the government whose victory we support. And when this concept was revived in Lenin's thinking in 1914, it still meant defeat by the enemy government. This was what we called (redundantly, it is true) pro-war defeatism.

Entirely unaware of what he was getting into, Lenin in 1914 was trying to work out a way of preserving the sharp anti-war flavour of the term defeatism on the basis of a political position that left no room for this meaning. A new one had to be invented.

The Baugy Group's attack

AT precisely this point, the pertinent political problem was raised by a section of the Bolshevik emigration led by Bukharin. On February 27 to March 4 1915, the Bolsheviks convened a Conference of the Foreign Sections of the Party in Bern. The Bolshevik group from Baugy (Switzerland) presented a document with a number of criticisms of the party's war thesis. Point 11 of the Baugy resolution dealt with the slogan of defeat. Although it stated opposition to any form of the slogan, it balked particularly at the formulation "wish defeat", more than at the "lesser evil" formula.

"11. The group denounces positively any advancing of the so-called slogan 'the defeat of Russia', particularly in the manner in which it has been advanced in No. 38 of the Central Organ [*Sotsial-Demokrat*].[16]

"In the manifesto of the Central Committee as well as in the reply to Vandervelde, the defeat of Russia is described as being the 'lesser evil', after an objective evaluation of the other issues of the war. The editorial of No. 38, on the other hand, says that every revolutionary is obliged to *desire* 'the defeat of Russia'.

"Such a consideration of the question, in the judgement of the group, is not only devoid of practical sense but also introduces into the question an undesirable confusion. If a revolutionary is obliged merely to 'desire' the defeat, then there is no use in writing leading articles about it in the Central Organ of the political party; but if he is obliged to do more than merely 'to desire', then this would be not simply an objective evaluation but the preaching of an active participation [i.e., taking of sides – H.D.] in the war, which participation would hardly be approved by the editorial board of the Central Organ.

"Still more unsatisfactory, according to the opinion of the group, is the consideration of the same question in the third and concluding paragraph of the article, when the desirability of the defeat is explained by the revolutionary uprisings which may follow. The absolute impossibility of practical agitation in this sense compels the rejection à *limite* of such agitation for the defeat. We record that in the article referred to, the boundary line between the objective, fully admissible, and correct evaluation of the situation and the *agitation for the defeat* has not been traced at all; the group believes that it is an urgent necessity to have all confusion and obscurity in this question removed in a most decisive manner."[17]

The challenge was plain: if you really "desire" it, then you work for it. (Especially if it is so important to "desire" it that you write resolutions, articles, editorials and polemics about it.)

But what does "*work* for defeat" mean?

Remember that, in spite of the tentative "internationalisation" of the defeat slogan in one article so far, "wish defeat" still carried the meaning of "wish military defeat by the enemy government". More than once Lenin will have to stress that he did not mean "blowing up bridges", helping the enemy, etc. The reason he had to insist that he did *not* mean this was simply that the slogan he was using *did* mean this to the movement.

His comrades knew what it meant to "work for revolutionary action"; but "work for defeat" in this war in which we did not support either camp – what was that? To be sure, agreed Bukharin and the Baugy people, revolutionary action might *objectively* be related to defeat, but what we *worked* for was not "defeat" but the socialist aim.

There is no recorded answer by Lenin to this political refutation of the defeat slogan. Certainly none was recorded in connection with this Bern party conference; and none can be found in Lenin's collected works, down to manuscripts and rough notes published as supplementary material at a later time. He simply never faced up to it.

Formulation No. 4: "Don't halt before the risk"

EVEN more important is a fact that can be ascertained more easily: in the face of the Baugy group's criticism, *Lenin dropped the formulation they had attacked.* The resolution adopted by the conference said absolutely nothing about "wish defeat" or "desire defeat". Instead, for the second time, confronting a difficulty with the formulation of the defeat slogan, Lenin abandoned the formulation that was criticised and invented a new one.

The final resolution was adopted unanimously... Besides eventually agreeing on the resolutions, the disputants agreed to consider the differences as a mere matter of emphasis, and parted amicably. But Bukharin and Baugy had won their point.[18]

The Bern resolution, written by Lenin, said on this point, under the heading "The Defeat of the Tsarist Monarchy":

"In each country, the struggle against a government that is waging an imperialist war should not falter at the possibility of that country's defeat as a result of revolutionary propaganda. The defeat of the government's army weakens the government, promotes the liberation of the nationalities it oppresses, and facilitates civil war against the ruling classes.

"This holds particularly true in respect of Russia. A victory for Russia will bring in its train a strengthening of reaction, both throughout the world and within the country, and will be accompanied by the complete enslavement of the peoples living in areas already seized. In view of this we consider the defeat of Russia the lesser evil in all conditions."[19]

This seems to have been a compromise. A kind of "lesser evil" formula was still in it. To be sure, its "special" motivation was still dead and would never be disinterred; but a version of Formula No. 1 was indubitably there.

No. 2 was there also: "defeat facilitates."

But instead of No. 3, precisely the one that had been vigorously attacked, there was a totally new formulation of the "internationalised" defeat slogan: viz, the class struggle must not falter (or halt, to use another translation of this passage) before the possibility of defeat brought on by "revolutionary propaganda". Or, as it will read when we meet it again: do not halt (falter, etc.) before the *risk* of defeat. This was Formula No. 4.

It is one of the curious features of the history of the defeat slogan that this last formulation has been so widely accepted as simply the equivalent, or restatement, or variant of a "wish for defeat", or even of the "special Russian policy" of the lesser evil. Formula No. 4 is not only completely different from a "wish for defeat", but in implication it is precisely the reverse.

"Do not halt before the risk" implies that we do *not* wish defeat. What we wish is a continuation of the class struggle to socialist victory; and we pursue this wish *in spite of* the fact that it may have an objective effect on the military plane.

This is especially clear when the word "risk" or an equivalent is actually used, as Lenin did more than once. In these cases it *specifically* repudiated Formula No. 3. In other cases the same thought might be implied. Yet it is possible to find – in scholarly histories or *soi-disant* Leninist expositions – that both meanings are quoted indiscriminately as equally "illustrative" of Lenin's defeatism, plus (more often than not) the special *Russian* formula of the lesser evil thrown in for good measure.

In Formula No. 4, as in No. 2, there is the positive element which we noted before. It would play a part in the analysis of socialist war policy quite apart from the confusions of "revolutionary defeatism". But for our present purposes we want only to emphasise the formulation's limitations.

"We do not halt (or hamper) the socialist struggle before the risk (or possibility) of defeat..." Very well; but the same socialists might make similar statements of policy. We will not halt the struggle before the risk or possibility of – say, personal injury or loss; or before the risk or possibility that an intensified class struggle will stimulate fascist elements to organise; or before the risk or possibility that our struggle will lead to persecution by the government; or before a number of other contingencies – contingencies which we certainly seek to take into account, but which *we* do not "wish", which we do not turn into a slogan or an "ism" or a new political "principle".

But Lenin had pushed himself into an impasse, from which he refused to extricate himself by dropping the whole business. He was seeking the sharpest ways to separate the sheep from the goats, and "defeatism" became a *point d'honneur* of the Bolshevik war line. Later it became a shibboleth.

Summary: the four formulas

BY this time, March 1915, the four different formulas of "defeatism" had been created out of Lenin's attempts to meet the insoluble contradiction without solving it. Let us summarise them.

No. 1. The special Russian position: defeat of *Russia by Germany* is the "lesser evil".

No. 2. The objective statement that "defeat *facilitates* revolution".

No. 3. The slogan: *wish* defeat in every country.

No. 4. Do not halt (falter, etc.) before the *risk* of defeat.

These are four *different* political ideas. Only three of them are meaningful for the international movement. Only two of them involve any wish for defeat (No. 1 and No. 3). Only one of them can actually be put forward in the form of a "slogan" (No. 3).

Even if we assumed that all of them had some self-consistent meaning of their own, we could ask: which one expressed Lenin's position? The answer is this: from this point on, Lenin juggled all four interpretations depending on his polemical aim and convenience – until by the end of 1916 he dropped all references to defeatism at last...

The rest of the record: before 1917

WE now come to the only article published by Lenin written solely to expound his defeat slogan; all his references to defeatism had previously been in passing paragraphs... Lenin... wrote his article "The Defeat of One's Own Government in the Imperialist War" as a blast against Trotsky.

This article was easily the biggest muddle of any we have so far encountered. Because it is a whole article discussing "defeatism", and therefore appears to be *the* authoritative statement on the subject for handy reference, it has undoubtedly played a major role in disorienting investigators of the present subject.

To understand this article and how it was written, it is necessary to present its immediate background, which fortunately is known. The background was the clash between Lenin and Trotsky on issues *not* involving defeatism.

Trotsky was at this time the leading leftist spirit of the Russian anti-war paper *Nashe Slovo*, published in Paris as a daily of the revolutionary emigration. On the paper collaborated also a number of dissident Bolsheviks, a number of internationalist (i.e., anti-war) Mensheviks – including Martov, up to almost the Zimmerwald Conference – and a number of unaffiliated Social-Democrats (the latter category including Trotsky himself). Its technical spark plug was Antonov-Ovseyenko; a partial list of its contributors would include a roster of later leaders of the Russian Revolution. It was the leading anti-war organ of the Russian movement.

At the beginning of 1915 there were tentative efforts made between the *Nashe Slovo* group and Lenin's Bolsheviks to collaborate in anti-war propaganda...

Nashe Slovo sent invitations to both the Bolsheviks and the Menshevik "Organisation Committee" to get together to prepare a joint statement against the war... Lenin agreed, and drew up a draft statement. The joint action never took place, with some accompanying hard feeling, but we can note here that it was *not* because of the question of defeatism. It couldn't have been, for the good and sufficient reason that Lenin's draft did not include a wisp of the defeatist idea, not in any of its protean forms...[20]

Yet *Nashe Slovo* had been taking pot-shots at the Bolsheviks' defeat slogan ever since it had been launched. According to the account by Alfred Rosmer, who was himself a *Nashe Slovo* contributor and a collaborator of Trotsky's, "The polemic [on defeatism] developed between Lenin and *Nashe Slovo*, most particularly Trotsky."...[21]

He mentioned these political differences and commented on them. In this context, the following was his comment on the defeat slogan, as a subordinate matter:

"...under no conditions can I agree with your opinion, which is emphasised by a resolution, that Russia's defeat would be a 'lesser evil'. This opinion represents a fundamental concession to the political methodology of social-patriotism, a concession for which there is no reason or justification, and which substitutes an orientation (extremely arbitrary under present conditions) along the lines of a 'lesser evil' for the revolutionary struggle against war and the conditions which generate this war."[22]

In my opinion, Trotsky here hit the nail on the head. He pointed to the fundamental identity in methodology between the "lesser evil" formulation of defeatism and that of the social-patriots. *Nashe Slovo* had pointed out that this defeatist concept was simply *defencism turned inside-out*. Trotsky pointed precisely to the *social-patriotic potential* which resided in the defeat slogan...

Lenin versus Trotsky on defeatism

L ENIN'S anti-Trotsky roast was published on July 26. Following are important points about the article "The Defeat of One's Own Government in the Imperialist War"... At Zimmerwald in September 1915, the Bolsheviks' position was put forward in the documents of the "Zimmerwald Left", which brought several non-Russian left-wingers to support of these views on the war, as distinct from those of other anti-war and "centrist" elements at the conference. While Lenin supported the majority resolution after his own was rejected, the resolution and manifesto of the Zimmerwald Left were intended to put on record what the Bolsheviks considered the *complete* anti-war position.[23]

These documents as introduced by the Zimmerwald Left, and as introduced to the Left by the Bolshevik delegation, did not mention defeatism or the defeat slogan.[24]

It appears that the Bolshevik delegation to Zimmerwald rejected Lenin's draft in favour of one by Radek (who was representing the Social-Democracy of Poland and Lithuania), but their preference had nothing to do with defeatism: Lenin's draft had no mention of it. Neither did his speeches at the conference, according to the minutes; nor did other notes of his, collected in a supplementary volume of Lenin's *Collected Works*.[25] There is an unclear exception which may be mentioned only for the sake of completeness: in a (probably unfinished) manuscript article on "The Draft Resolution Proposed by the Left Wing at Zimmerwald", there is a subordinate clause lost in a long sentence, about "not shying away in that [revolutionary] agitation from considerations of the defeat of their 'own' country".[26] Was this, the weakest form of Formula No. 4, directed against the Radek resolution? It said nothing about "defeatism" being lacking from that resolution...

The social-patriotic version of defeatism

W E have pointed to the relationship between the defeat slogan and the "methodology of social-patriotism". We have seen how easily one could turn into the other. Now, finally, we can show how it did turn into a clearly social-patriotic idea — in the hands of Zinoviev.

This will be shown by an idea that Zinoviev repeated a number of times, in three different articles; it was no passing slip of the pen. In its own way it was perhaps the most surprising aspect of what happened to the defeat slogan. Although these articles came from Zinoviev and not Lenin, we must add that they went through Lenin's editorial hands.

In these multiple cases, Zinoviev slipped a single word into the formulation on defeat — a single word with a political meaning as devastating as the insertion of a "not" into a clause.

It was a question of his repeated limitation of his argumentation to *despotic* governments.

For example, in his historical article on "'Defeatism' Then and Now", Zinoviev wrote the following when he got down to formulating the principle:

"All other things being equal,[27] the defeat of a despotic government in foreign war always helps the people to overthrow the government. It is absolutely impossible to seriously deny this principle... The whole modern history of Russia admirably illustrates this truth that the defeats abroad of reactionary governments redound to the benefit of the democratic movement inside the country."[28]

That said it twice in a short passage: the "truth" was limited to "despotic" governments, "reactionary" governments. Was it possible for a sophisticated writer to set this down without understanding that the principle did *not* apply to a democratic capitalism?

Similarly, in another article, where "Russia" (in quote marks) was used to mean theTsar's regime while Russia (unquoted) meant the country of the Russian people:

"Yes, we are for the defeat of 'Russia', for this would further the victory of Russia, its breakaway from slavery, its liberation from the chains of Tsarism. Where are the cases in the recent history of Europe where the victory abroad of a reactionary government led to democratic freedom within the country?"[29]

The counter-position was just as clear here: "reactionary" versus "democratic". In immediate illustration, Zinoviev gave the quotation from Wilhelm Liebknecht that will be found below.

In his long article on "The Russian Social-Democracy and Russian Social-Chauvinism", where he gave his most elaborate polemic in favour of defeatism, the same thought abounded.[30] The first occasion came when he attacked Plekhanov:

"Plekhanov maintains that only the liberals were given to desiring a defeat of their despotic government, in the hope that this would broaden the possibility of political freedom, while they themselves had neither the strength nor the inclination to fight for it."

And Zinoviev replied with the same language:

"Of course, Plekhanov is completely wrong. That the defeat of a despotic government in war can further a democratic transformation in the country, this idea is not in the least peculiar to the liberals."

In proof of this, he brought a couple of "defeatists" onto the witness stand, citing their words triumphantly. One was Wilhelm Liebknecht, who (according to Plekhanov) had written these words:

"Has anyone ever heard of a despotic government that became liberal after it won a victory? With defeated governments this has happened on occasion for a short period."

He adduced August Bebel as a "defeatist", quoting these words:

"It is my opinion that for a nation which lives in an unfree condition, a military defeat is more a help than a hindrance for its internal development."

Bebel was referring to Prussia as distinct from bourgeois democracies like France or England.

This takes us quite a distance beyond the mere "methodology" of social-patriotism. If the formulas of defeatism were to be limited to "despotic" governments, to "reactionary" regimes needing a democratic transformation, to nations "in an unfree condition", then certain consequences followed: defeatism could not be internationalised; it could not be the policy of socialists in all the belligerent countries. And if, simultaneously, one insisted that defeatism was the only consistent anti-war policy and that the only consistent alternative was defencism (social-patriotism), then it was scarcely a short step to draw social-patriotic conclusions for the socialists of *non-despotic* governments. The governing slogans became "Democracy versus despotism" and "Progress versus reaction". And these were already familiar to Zinoviev when he wrote these articles.

Furthermore, we should note that Zinoviev (as well as his authorities W. Liebknecht and Bebel) applied the "despotic" limitation not even to the formulation "wish defeat" but to the idea "defeat facilitates revolution". The muddle was thereby raised to the second power. What special reason was there to believe that "defeat facilitated revolution" only in despotic countries? Wouldn't it have a similar impact in bourgeois-democratic countries ("all other things being equal")?

Historically speaking, there was no mystery as to why Zinoviev fell into this strange formulation, even if it remained surprising that he was not caught at it. His thinking was a reflection of the situation in the Russo-Japanese War; he was reproducing it, transplanting it to the World War. In 1904-1905, for Lenin (as for most of the Second International) it *had* been a question of "despotism" versus "progress", and defeatism *had* been the other side of a wish for Japan's victory. *But Lenin's defeatist position of 1904-1905, transplanted to the World War, was – social-patriotism.*

What was the significance of Zinoviev's strange mistake? He found himself, perhaps quite unawares, playing with a "defeatism" that would apply to only one side of an imperialist war. It was not thought out; it teetered on the edge of political *débâcle*. It was in reality not a "position" at all, except insofar as one can be said to be in a certain "position" when on the edge of a cliff and swinging arms wildly to recover balance.

To be sure, neither Lenin nor Zinoviev were subjectively "teetering on the brink". Their anti-war position was in fact anchored in a quite different analysis, which kept them on the ground with only occasional gyrations around the defeat slogan. It was not fatal for them; but it bore the seed of considerable confusion.

"Neither victory nor defeat"

THE defeat slogan led Lenin (with Zinoviev trailing along) into a swamp. Others did better in analysing the relationship between defeat and revolution from the standpoint of Marxism. This was especially true, during the war, of the two outstanding leaders of anti-war socialist opinion outside the Bolshevik ranks: Rosa Luxemburg and Trotsky.

Luxemburg and Trotsky differed from Lenin at this time on certain points; perhaps the most important concerned raising the slogan of peace as an integral part of a revolutionary platform.[31] But we will not examine these questions. What united the anti-war wing was essentially two points: rejection of "civil peace", the aim of turning the imperialist war into a struggle for a revolutionary outcome; and the perspective of building a new International.

Still, an investigation of the defeat slogan must look at the alternatives to it proposed by the revolutionary wing, not only the attack on it by the pro-war proponents of victory for one or the other side of the imperialist powers. One of the alternative slogans that Lenin criticised most often was the idea sloganised as "Neither victory nor defeat!"

We saw in previously that Lenin made that concept a whipping boy especially in his anti-Trotsky polemic. But in fact Trotsky did not raise that slogan. The Menshevik leadership, including Martov, did indeed raise this idea as their slogan, especially in the form "Neither victor nor vanquished!"[32]

It was against the Mensheviks that Lenin emphasised what was wrong with "Neither victory nor defeat". This conception of the tasks before revolutionaries presupposed a return to the *status quo ante bellum* as the aim of socialists, as against the struggle for a revolutionary outcome of the war. Everything was supposed to return to Square One, to the pre-war status quo that had produced the holocaust, after untold sufferings that were now to be ignored, and regardless of the revolutionary crisis that the war itself had produced.

The same political development had occurred to the Mensheviks in the Russo-Japanese War, when they likewise accepted the dilemma of victory-or-defeat *within the framework of the existing governments*. But Trotsky had not taken this line then, as he did not in the world war.

Far from using "Neither victory nor defeat" to summarise his war policy, Trotsky levered powerful attacks on it, from his own point of view. He was able to do this without in any way falling into the "defeatist" quagmire of confusion. To the in-betweeners' cry of "Neither victory nor defeat" he did not reply "We must wish defeat" (like Lenin). He did not reply "We must wish for victory" (like the social-patriots). He argued that *the question itself was a trap*. "Victory or defeat" meant: victory for one government over the defeated enemy government, and these were simply not the alternatives accepted by revolutionary socialists. For they counterposed a different alternative, a third way: the utilisation of the war crisis to overthrow both ruling classes.

Thus his approach undercut the defeatist line as well as that of the Mensheviks. This difference in "methodology" went to the root of the war question.

This analysis was put forward in a work by Trotsky written during the 1915-1916 period, one which specifically took up the question of victory-or-defeat. It was published as a series of articles in *Nashe Slovo*, directed against the Mensheviks. Under the title *What Is a Peace Programme?* it was later republished in pamphlet form after the Russian Revolution.

In this work Trotsky showed in some detail how the *total* consequences of the victory of either side (which meant also the defeat of either side) would be reactionary from the viewpoint of the socialists' aims. He devoted special attention to the slogan "Peace without annexations" in order to show that this aim could be realised neither through the victory (or defeat) of one side nor the victory (or defeat) of the other side of the war camps.

He presented "three typical possibilities" for the outcome of the war:

1. A decisive victory by one of the camps.

2. A general exhaustion of the opponents without the decisive dominance of one over the other.

3. The intervention of the revolutionary proletariat, which forcibly interrupts the development of military events.[33]

On the first: "Only charlatans or hopeless fools can believe that the freedom of the small nations can be secured by the victory of one side or the other", he summarised. "A like result," he argued, would follow if the war ended in something like a draw, as envisioned by the Menshevik slogan "Neither victors nor vanquished".

"The absence of a pronounced preponderance by one of the combatants over the other will only display, all the more clearly, both the dominance of the strong over the weak within either one of the camps, and the preponderance of both over the "neutral" victims of imperialism. The ending of the war without victors or vanquished is no guarantee for anybody."[34]

He made it explicit that he looked to "the third power, the revolutionary power":

"The second possible ending of the war, which mainly those depend on who seek to promote the narrow programme of 'peace without annexations and nothing more', presupposes that the war, exhausting as it does all the resources of the warring nations, will end in general lassitude, without victors or vanquished, without the intervention of the third power, the revolutionary power. To this very condition, in which militarism is too weak to effect conquests and the proletariat is too weak to make a revolution, the passive internationalists of the Kautsky type adapt their abbreviated programme of 'peace without annexations', which they not infrequently present as a return to the *status quo ante bellum*."[35]

But this was only "apparent realism", for under the conditions of imperialism, "an indecisive outcome" of the war does not "exclude annexations but on the contrary presupposes them". It was only the third way, the revolution, that could really paralyse the war and "finally stop it from the bottom up".

"A powerful movement of the proletariat is thus a necessary prerequisite for the actual realisation of a peace without annexations." The Menshevik programme assumed such a movement but it was inadequate "in that it accepts the restoration of the order which prevailed prior to the war and out of which the war broke out". The only positive content of the slogan "Peace without annexations" turned out to be "the European *status quo ante bellum*."[36]

From this standpoint Trotsky had no difficulty rejecting both Lenin's "defeat as the lesser evil" and the Mensheviks' slogans that meant return to the pre-war status quo. Trotsky, to be sure, wished "neither victory nor defeat" for either of the war camps, but this could not be his slogan. *He rejected the disjunction that it posed.*

In another valuable article, published in *Nashe Slovo* in late summer 1915, Trotsky made an important survey of "Defeat and Revolution", that is, the historical relationship between these phenomena.[37] It was not formulated as a critique of Lenin's defeat slogan, but it demands reading as part of the bigger question which, we have said, lies behind the present issue. In August 1916, an article by Trotsky on the factional situation in the Russian movement devoted a couple of paragraphs to the two errors in the Bolsheviks' war line. One was Lenin's hostility to the peace slogan, and the other was defeatism (in the form of Formula No. 3, which Lenin had emphasised in his anti-Trotsky polemic):

"Finally, the paradoxical and internally contradictory formula 'the defeat of Russia is the lesser evil' creates difficulties for our German co-thinkers and does not enrich but rather hampers our agitation. It has provided the social-patriotic demagogues with a most important weapon in their struggle against our common banner. Such an exaggeration of revolutionary slogans is all the more dangerous since *Sotsial-Demokrat* [the Bolshevik organ] is quick to turn these formulas into the absolute test of internationalism."[38]

Luxemburg on victory and defeat

ROSA Luxemburg took a position on the victory-or-defeat dilemma that was identical with Trotsky's — entirely independently. When she discussed this question in her anti-war argument (the *Junius pamphlet* of 1915), she was probably not even aware of Lenin's defeatist line, but even so she demolished it in advance. We need do little in this section but quote her at some length, from her last chapter, Chapter 8.

"Victory or defeat" is the watchword that the Social-Democratic leaders have adopted: "yet, what can victory bring to the proletariat?" Either of the two alternatives will mean for the people impoverishment, economic ruin, an intensification of militarism. Here is the general line of her analysis:

"...even before any military decision of victory or defeat can be established... the result of the war will be: the economic ruin of all participating nations... This, in the last analysis, neither victory or defeat can alter; on the contrary it makes a purely military decision altogether doubtful and increases the likelihood that the war will finally end through a general and extreme exhaustion."[39]

We may note parenthetically that during the war Trotsky also expressed the opinion that this was the most likely military outcome. The consequences for the working class would not depend on the political character of the belligerents as "democracies" or "absolutisms". Preparations for a new imperialist world war would begin on the morrow of the peace. The consequences of either victory or defeat would be reactionary, she concluded after an examination.

"Under the circumstances the question of victory or defeat becomes, for the European working class, in its political exactly as in its economic aspects, a choice between two beatings. It is, therefore, nothing short of a dangerous madness for the French socialists to believe that they can deal a death blow to militarism and imperialism, and clear the road for peaceful democracy by overthrowing Germany. Imperialism and its servant militarism will reappear after every victory and after every defeat in this war. There can be but one exception: if the international proletariat, through its intervention, should overthrow all previous calculations. The workers must not 'become the uncritical echo of the victory-or-defeat slogan' in any of the warring countries, for the content of this slogan is really identical for each of the imperialists with another question: 'gain or loss of world political power, of annexations, of colonies, of military supremacy.'"

Conclusion:

"For the European proletariat as a class, victory or defeat of either of the two war groups would be equally disastrous. For war as such, whatever its military outcome may be, is the greatest conceivable defeat of the cause of the European proletariat. The overthrow of war and the speedy forcing of peace by the international revolutionary action of the proletariat alone can bring to it the only possible victory. And this victory alone can truly rescue Belgium, can bring democracy to Europe.

"For the class-conscious proletariat to identify its cause with either military camp is an untenable position. Did this mean advocating a return to the pre-war status quo, in 'the fond hope that everything may remain as it was before the war?' No, that would be impossible; we cannot go back to the old Europe.

"In this sense alone is it possible for the proletariat to oppose with its policy both camps in the imperialist world war."[40]

Thus her "methodology" excluded the slogan of defeat; it was, in contemporary terms and almost in her own terms, the methodology of the Third Camp. It was equally hostile both to social-patriotism and to the latter's bisymmetric opposite, the swamp of defeatism...

The abandonment of defeatism in 1917

WHATEVER defeatism meant to Lenin in 1914-1916, it was in 1917 that the pay-off came on the whole question: *with the March Revolution in Russia and the overthrow of Tsarism, Lenin dropped defeatism and the defeat slogan completely.*

"We were not defeatists"

BUT in fact all the Bolshevik slogans on war line did not remain the same. Lenin (if not all the Bolsheviks) remained consistently opposed to the war, even now when it was being conducted by a democratic republic under capitalist domination, the party had to re-emphasise its opposition to defencism twice as energetically. But on certain points where, during 1914-1916, the Bolsheviks had differed from other left-wing Marxist internationalists, Lenin revised his distinctive positions, in content or in scope: the peace slogan; the application of the slogan "turn imperialist war into civil war"; and the defeat slogan. These shifts took place in stages, not suddenly; and mostly implicitly, not by overt statement.

Lenin's explicit statement about his abandonment of defeatism in this period came... after the November Revolution: in March 1918. Let us record it now. The subject came up, perhaps accidentally, at the special Congress of Soviets called to ratify the Brest-Litovsk treaty of peace with Germany. The Socialist-Revolutionaries (S-Rs) were against peace — for continuation of the war in spite of the complete exhaustion of the country. In reply to a speech by the Left S-R Kamkov about disrupting the army, Lenin remarked that Kamkov was confused:

"He [Kamkov] has heard that we were defeatists, but he has recalled this when we have ceased to be defeatists."

And he immediately re-emphasised this in still another way:

"...alright; we demoralised the army and we must recall that now. But how did we demoralise the army? We were defeatists at the time of the Tsar, but at the time of Tsereteli and Chernov [i.e., under the Kerensky regime] we were not defeatists."[41]

Here Lenin used "under Tsereteli and Chernov" (S-R ministers in the cabinet) to denote the period from March to November 1917 because of the context of Kamkov's speech, not for any reason that need concern us.

Lenin never explicitly discussed this change, any more (for example) than he ever discussed the coeval revision of his views on Trotsky's theory of permanent revolution. But even without the categorical statement of March 1918, his abandonment of the defeat slogan would have been clear, simply because it was no longer put forward. There were no exceptions that really change the picture...

Summary

To sum up, it is not enough merely to point out that Lenin dropped defeatism after the March Revolution. Why he did so and the programme he replaced it with make clear what was wrong with the mistake of 1914-1916.

1. Lenin dropped defeatism in the face of the realisation, made vivid to him for the first time, that the defeat-slogan broke all links between the sentiments and interests of the masses and the programme of consistent revolutionaries. In this sense, it was *sectarian;* and in my opinion the defeat-slogan deserves to be recorded as a classic example of a sectarian shell built around an opportunistic (in this case social-patriotic) theoretical core. It is an example of the oft-repeated Marxist truism that there is a dialectic relationship between the sectarian-opportunist opposites.

2. Lenin discovered in practice that the defeat-slogan was incompatible with a living Marxist approach to the problem of the *defence of the nation*, conceived not in the social-patriotic sense as the "defence of the fatherland" but in the light of a Marxist *class* understanding of the *nation*.

3. Lenin's change of line after the *democratic* revolution (not socialist revolution) of March 1917 reflected an important fact. The defeat slogan had a meaning only in terms of a war by the Tsarist pre-bourgeois autocratic despotism against a progressive capitalist revolutionary force. This was the situation that Lenin *thought* obtained in 1904-1905, and though he was wrong even then, at least the defeat slogan had a clear meaning for him. It was the same *arrière pensée* that had led Zinoviev to write the qualification "despotic" into his defeatist formulations.

The March democratic revolution erased the basic motive leading to the defeat slogan in the first place — the "special Russian" consideration of Tsarism as the unique menace, the worst evil. Naturally, this did not bear on the conscious motivation but only on the real theoretical underpinnings, which have their effect despite consciousness.

4. Lenin's course in 1917 proved that defeatism was and is not any necessary element in a consistent revolutionary anti-war position...

After Lenin: the revival and reinterpretation

The revival of defeatism did not take place while Lenin was alive, that is, during the first five years of the Comintern... A check of the resolutions and theses, major documents, and publications of the Comintern permits the confident statement: if anyone referred to defeatism at all, it certainly played no role in the programme, policy and principles of the Communist International under Lenin.

The first four congresses of the Comintern (from 1919 to 1922) adopted a large number of long, detailed, analytical theses on all the major questions of revolutionary policy and many minor ones. And these documents were not infrequently marked by discursive historical sections.

Especially at the Second Congress in 1920, the aim of these defining documents was not to make it easy for individuals or groups to adhere to the new revolutionary International, but on the contrary: the Bolsheviks thought one of the main dangers was the tendency of centrists and other dubious elements to flock to the new banner, now that the Second International was thoroughly discredited; too many were only too anxious to cover their pasts with present acceptance of the most revolutionary-sounding slogans. To bar these elements the Second Congress adopted the famous "21 Points" as conditions for admission.

Yet there was not a hint of any kind of defeat slogan in any of the documents of the first four congresses of the Comintern.

By 1924 the International and many of its parties were considering the question of new overall programmes. Even at this date (which is after the period we are now discussing, as we will see) the draft programme for the Communist International presented by Bukharin ignored defeatism. Even at the Fifth Congress in 1924 the reports on the Programme Question delivered by Bukharin and August Thalheimer ignored defeatism under the head of the war question. At the same time the Young Communist International, the German party, and other parties were also developing new draft programmes – without defeatism.

From the November Revolution up to Lenin's death, a flood of books and pamphlets were issued by the Communist movement, presenting discussions of the war positions of the First World War period as well as current policies, usually prominently displaying Lenin's ideas. I have checked a large number of these, including a number by Zinoviev. In not one case have I found a recollection of defeatism.

There was the monthly organ of the International, called *The Communist International*. From 1919 to 1923 inclusive, there was no lack of articles reviewing the war question, the World War period, Lenin's distinctive ideas, and so on. Not once was the defeat slogan raised, either as a reminiscence of the war or as a current view.

It would be nice to cite one or two exceptions, since the complete disappearance of the defeat slogan seems almost preternatural. If it was a question of finding the defeat slogan *raised,* there were no exceptions. But the rule was "proved", nevertheless, by a couple of mentions of *defeat* that deserve quoting.

1. Karl Radek

IN the April-May 1921 issue of *The Communist International*, an article by Radek painted the consequences of defeat, and they were not very happy. He wrote about the post-war world:

"Not a proletarian revolution but Wilsonianism was the slogan of the working masses in the victorious countries. In the defeated countries on the contrary the thirst for peace and quiet predominated over all other proletarian feelings; a morsel of bacon was of more value than dreams for the liberation of mankind..."

And so on along the same lines. This distorted picture, reflecting Radek's journalistic subjectivity at its worst, was no contribution to history; but more important for present purposes: the man who wrote this could not have had the slightest recollection that the Bolsheviks had called for defeat in the war.

2. August Thalheimer

IN issue No. 25 of 1923, *The Communist International* reprinted a polemical exchange of articles that had appeared in the German organ *Die Internationale* between Thalheimer and a critic named Sommer, on policy regarding the French invasion of the Ruhr. (This was the tense situation which evoked the notorious "Schlageter" speech by Radek heavily tinged with a sort of "national-Bolshevism".) In this dispute with Sommer, Thalheimer came little short of taking a defencist position, that is, for defence of Germany against French rapacity. In this context, *one of Thalheimer's articles mentioned the defeatism of 1914-1916 – in order to reject it for now!*

This was a fascinating case, for once again it illustrated the social-patriotic potential in the notion of defeatism. What was operative here was the dichotomy: if not defencism, then (horrors) defeatism; and if you can't swallow *that,* then it has to be – defencism. We will see this methodology again.

How Zinoviev revived defeatism in 1924

WELL then, when do we find defeatism raised again? The facts so far have been bound to awaken a certain suspicion in the minds of all who know the history of this period. And there is strong documentary evidence to substantiate this suspicion.

Defeatism was revived as a "principle of Leninism" in the beginning of the Stalinist counterrevolution, specifically by Stalin's partner in the "troika" (triumvirate) that succeeded to Lenin's leadership, namely Zinoviev.

The sign under which this "troika" of Stalin, Zinoviev and Kamenev took over was the fabricated struggle against Trotsky and "Trotskyism". The background history of the "invention of Trotskyism" can be read in many works, and will not be given space here.[42] Defeatism was only one of the levers set in place for this struggle. The ideological cover under which this anti-Trotsky coalition operated, created by Zinoviev, was the slogan of "Bolshevisation" of the cadres of the Comintern. *Defeatism was revived as one of the elements in this anti-Trotskyist "Bolshevisation".*

By the time of Lenin's death in January 1924, after his lingering incapacitation, Stalin was already in control of the main levers of the party apparatus; Zinoviev, his accomplice, was the "boss" of the Comintern and public ideological mentor of the anti-Trotsky cabal. They were ready to go into high gear before Lenin's body was cold. They had, in fact, had a rehearsal in the factional "literary discussion" (so-called) over Trotsky's *Lessons of October*.

The first time that we find defeatism recalled as a "principle of Leninism" in the pages of the Comintern organ was in the very first issue published after the death of Lenin.

This number of *The Communist International* was, naturally, mostly made up of articles on Lenin, his ideas, his role and so on. One of the most prominent of these articles was signed by Martynov, on "The Great Proletarian Leader". Martynov had been a leading Menshevik up to yesterday, and presently he was a hatchet man for the troika; he had joined the Bolshevik bandwagon with the New Economic Policy wave. Now he loaded his gun with the defeat slogan and fired its shot openly and by name – straight at Trotsky.

We here give its essential passage at a little length, because of the crucial historical role it played. Not only Lenin opposed the war, wrote Martynov; so too did other "internationalist minorities" of socialist parties. But –

"...the slogans launched by Lenin at that time were so daring, I should say so defiant, that they contained a challenge not only to the social-patriots but also to all the internationalists... He said: 'In order to put an end to the imperialist war, it should be transformed into civil war. Those who will start the civil war may be menaced by defeat in the imperialist war, but we have no fear about that. Particularly to us Russian Social-Democrats, defeat in the war is the lesser evil.' This 'defeatism' aroused the protests not only of social-patriots but even of all the internationalists, including the most Left ones, as for instance Comrade Trotsky. He [Lenin] was told: 'You want Russia to be defeated, consequently you want Germany to win, and in this case it is social-patriotism inside out! You reason the same way as the social-patriots, but for another country, not your own.' This accusation, as everyone can now see, was quite beside the mark."

The small amount of theoretical rationalisation that Martynov tried to insert was no brighter than his old efforts as a Menshevik theoretician. Thus:

"Lenin knew and did not disguise the fact that if we start the revolution during the war, it will lead directly to our military defeat. But he knew more than that; he knew that the revolution started by us will spread also to Germany and that our defeat like the German victory will be but short-lived. He therefore said: 'Dare!' and he was fully vindicated by history... Lenin could see farther than his nose, and he therefore launched such slogans as appeared rather unreasonable to the other socialists."[43]

Let us note by the way that (1) the defeat formula resurrected here was Formula No. 1, the "special Russian" version which Lenin dropped most decisively; but in my opinion there was no significance in this bit of incompetence beyond its reflection on Zinoviev's or Martynov's ability to remember political ideas. (2) In giving Lenin's alleged reply to Trotsky's argument, Martynov here invented a motivation for defeatism based on the expectation of international revolution; and while this was not encountered in Lenin's argumentation on the subject, it did smack of *Trotsky's* theory of permanent revolution. It would be superfluous to underline the convolutions of the Stalinist mind in intrigue.

Thus, all of a sudden, after six years of silence, the defeat slogan got more space in this article than any other element in Lenin's war position.

A few issues later, likewise in the Comintern organ, Zinoviev himself picked up the campaign which he had put Martynov up to launch. His article was specifically on "War and Leninism". Here too the sharp point of the reference was turned against Trotsky, this time without openly naming him; but the dig was lost on no-one, especially since Martynov had already done the naming:

"Leninism was much taken to task for its 'defeatism'. Even some of the internationalists, on reaching this point, would turn their backs on Bolshevism and their faces to social-chauvinism. Nevertheless, Leninism, remaining true unto itself, said... "

Then Zinoviev quoted the sentence on defeatism from the pamphlet *Socialism and War*, which just happened to be the one which he had signed together with Lenin. The meaning was: "This was how I, Zinoviev, stood at Lenin's side while Trotsky was attacking him..."[44]

This was the beginning.

It was not until the Sixth Congress of the Comintern (1928) that defeatism was canonised as an article of programme for the Communist movement. (By the Fifth Congress, in 1924, the sly references were only getting under way.) At the Sixth Congress, the resolution on "The Struggle Against Imperialist War and the Tasks of the Communists" put defeatism almost at the head of "the political programme of the Communists in an imperialist war". It defined "Defeatism, i.e., to work for the defeat of the home imperialist government in the war".

We need not follow the further progress of defeatism in the Communist movement as an article of faith. The more interesting question is the reaction to the revival of defeatism by the man who was the target of the exercise, Trotsky himself.

Trotsky: dodging the bullet

OBVIOUSLY the whole point of Zinoviev's resuscitation of this old difference between Lenin and Trotsky was as a part of what Zinoviev later confessed to be "the invention of Trotskyism". This bogey was to be brandished in the power struggle launched by the Stalin-Zinoviev group to oust Trotsky from the party leadership, even though Lenin's death left him the single most popular leader of the revolution.

Every difference that Trotsky had ever had with Lenin was revived, and if defeatism has the distinction of being the very first one to be given the treatment after Lenin's death, it was not the most important. The theory of the permanent revolution, the peasant question, the dispute over the role of trade unions, Trotsky's "organisational" criticisms of the Bolsheviks before 1917, the conflict over Brest-Litovsk, and so on – all of these were systematically recalled and put to work for factional purposes. Trotsky was not an "old Bolshevik" but a comparative newcomer to the Bolshevik ranks, in spite of his already pre-eminent position; and the leaders of the bureaucratic counter-revolution struck the pose of "old Bolsheviks" who were defending historical Leninism against an old foe. Thus they threw up a smoke screen of old and outlived differences in order to press forward their new course of national-socialism and bureaucratisation.

As these old issues and disputes were artificially revived one after the other, Trotsky's reaction was, in general, to minimise the significance of the differences. On some he openly admitted that he had been wrong and Lenin right, as on his pre-1917 "organisational" differences. On others, as on the theory of permanent revolution, he fought back vigorously, while maintaining that the difference had never been as fundamental and irreconcilable as the Stalinists made out.

But on defeatism, he "passed", as they say in poker...

There was no reply from Trotsky on the substantive point. Still, if only for himself and aside from polemical purposes, Trotsky had to face the question in his own mind. His own course in the matter had been a model of clarity. He had always been against the defeat slogan. When he joined the Bolshevik Party in 1917, the slogan was dead; and for the next six years it remained effectively buried. *He* certainly had no reason to change his opinion.

But now, along with the rest of the anti-Trotsky fabrications, the disloyal revival of the defeatist issue was tactically embarrassing, even though all political logic and truth was on his side. Plainly he decided that he could not meet this assault head-on. As mentioned, he sought to minimise his historical differences with Lenin, hopefully within the limits of honesty and political clarity. On the subject of defeatism, it would seem, he managed to convince himself, under the difficult circumstances, that there was no real difference at all...

Trotsky in the Trotskyist movement

DID, then, Trotsky come to agree with Lenin's defeat slogan? Or did he refrain from indicating any criticism of it purely for "diplomatic" and tactical reasons, that is, insincerely and in defiance of elementary political honesty? All one has to judge by is the record of what Trotsky did in the 1930s, as the theoretical leader of the Trotskyist movement, in formulating "defeatism" or the defeat slogan for programmatic purposes.

From this examination, we must come to the following conclusion: Trotsky persuaded himself to accept the *term* "defeatism," or "revolutionary defeatism"; but he never did accept it in any sense ever given to it by Lenin – or by anyone else. What happened was that he sought to reinterpret it in a peculiar fashion that not only deprived it of Lenin's content but sometimes of any content whatever. If the history of defeatism has been one of confusion and muddle up to now, with this period of Trotskyist reinterpretation the muddle reaches awe-inspiring proportions.

Under the pressure of the Stalinist campaign against his Bolshevik credentials, Trotsky tried to be "orthodox" (that is, to bend before the pressure) but he also wished to write nothing that he did not believe, or could not persuade himself to accept. Therefore none of his formulations of "defeatism" came within a mile of "wishing defeat". Of Lenin's four formulas, he sometimes paraphrased the one that was furthest away from "wishing defeat", namely, No. 4: "Do not halt before the risk of defeat". But in addition, and mainly, he developed for his purposes an ingenious formula of his own devising that had the advantage of *sounding* like the "lesser evil" formulation.

This ingenious contrivance may be found in his document for the fundamental programme of his Fourth International, the theses called "War and the Fourth International" (1934), under the heading "'Defeatism' and Imperialist War". This is what he worked out:

"Lenin's formula *'defeat is the lesser evil'* means not that defeat of one's own country is the lesser evil as compared with the defeat of the enemy country but..."

Pausing for a moment at this point, what we have is already rather odd. We are told here what the formula does not mean; and this meaning which is not Lenin's is also not anybody else's. Whatever it may mean, which is moot, the counter-position was not "Defeat of one's own country" against "defeat of the enemy country", but rather this: "defeat of one's own country" is the lesser evil as compared with the "victory of one's own country". The latter was so indubitably Lenin's explicit idea that we need not prove it all over again at this point.[45]

The odd thing that Trotsky did here was to invent a brand new set of words in order to deny that Lenin ever said it! – in which he was undeniably right since he had just invented it himself. Why? Perhaps because the necessary conclusion from Lenin's actual formula was "wish defeat", and this was the last thing that Trotsky wanted to suggest.

Now, to continue Trotsky's new set of words: Lenin's formula means –

"that a military defeat resulting from the growth of the revolutionary movement is infinitely more beneficial to the proletariat and to the whole people than military victory assured by 'civil peace'."[46]

Of course, we have seen that there is nothing in Lenin's writings (or in anyone else's) that corresponds to such a bowdlerised version of defeatism. This is a fabricated meaning which is arbitrarily assigned to Lenin; Trotsky wanted to convince himself that it had some relation to Lenin's slogan because he managed to use the words "defeat" and "lesser evil" in close association. Let us see how Trotsky has juggled the words to get his effect.

"Military defeat *resulting from growth of the revolutionary movement* is better than military victory *assured by civil peace.*"

The italicised qualifiers are what do the trick. To see how little it actually says, let us put other terms into the same algebraic formula and note the effect:

"Hunger *due to continuing a hard strike* is better than getting a raise *which is conditioned on the capitulation and destruction of the union.*"

This is obviously the analogous slogan of "hungerism", which proves that "hunger is the lesser evil". And there is no doubt that hunger *is* a lesser evil, as compared with a great number of other evils. If this is all that is proved about "defeat", then an open door is being kicked to splinters. But above all, the exercise in words does not convince us to "wish" hunger any more than to "wish" defeat. The case is, as it were, that we "continue the strike even at the cost of hunger".

(Or try this: "Defeat of a socialist party [in an election] *resulting from a revolutionary programme* is better than its victory *assured by compromising deals and class collaboration.*" Then call this the principle of "electoral defeatism", and you have Trotsky's formula.)

Secondly: however indubitable Trotsky's well-qualified version may be in itself (in the case of defeat as in the case of anything else), such a formula is *no positive guide whatever* on the war question, and this is fundamentally because it poses the question in terms of a defeat or victory *of the government*. For this reason it is not itself a "formula of proletarian policy" but, at best, a warning against a bad one. Trotsky fell into the methodological error of putting the question in terms of a choice between *military outcomes* on the governmental plane. This was the error that he saw so clearly in Lenin, before he started to invent "orthodox" formulations.

Thirdly: Trotsky limited his formula to "military defeat *resulting from the growth of the revolutionary movement*". Lenin never did so. Lenin thought in precisely the reverse terms: growth of the revolutionary movement *resulting from military defeat* at the hands of the enemy government. The hollowness of Trotsky's attempt at a paraphrase (or parody) should be apparent.

This same limitation of Trotsky's does not make sense when we apply it to the formula "defeat facilitates revolution". *What* defeat "facilitates"? Only that defeat "which results from the growth of the revolutionary movement"? Of course not.

Fourthly and finally: Trotsky presented his set of words as a formula for defeatists. Yet it clearly applied also to situations in which Trotsky (among others) was a defencist! Consider, for example, Trotsky's position on the Spanish Civil War, in which he advocated a form of revolutionary *defencism* in the Loyalist camp fighting Franco. Yet, as a defencist with revolutionary aims, he would say that "military defeat which results from the growth of the revolutionary movement" was, at any rate, the "lesser evil" as compared with "military victory which is assured by" the left's abandonment of its revolutionary role and its support to popular-frontism and the bourgeois-Stalinist government...

What this illustrates is that the truth which is contained in Trotsky's formula is of so general a nature, indeed so fundamental, that it applies not only when we oppose a war but even when we are supporting a progressive war. It is not a formula for "defeatism" at all; it is not even a formula for an anti-war policy *without* defeatism; it is a general formula for proletarian class independence.

It simply has nothing to do with defeatism...

Exegesis in the Trotskyist movement

TROTSKY'S course of dealing with the defeatist orthodoxy, by interpreting it away, was reflected in all the products of the Trotskyist movement. Alfred Rosmer can be considered an exception, as a friend of Trotsky's outside the organised movement. He is worth mentioning also for the light he threw on the significance of the question.

Rosmer has already come up as a collaborator of Trotsky on *Nashe Slovo*, and his point of view no doubt stemmed from that period, "unreconstructed". In his great historical work on France, *Le Mouvement Ouvrier Pendant la Guerre*, there is a short passage which stands out in the post-war literature of the *soi-disant* Marxist movement, as one of the few (if there are any others) indicating the hollowness of Lenin's wartime defeat slogan. Rosmer argued that there was no validity to Lenin's claim that defeatism was *necessary* to a fearless and consistent anti-war fight. Besides —

"I see clearly the dangers it involves. The word 'defeatism' is very widely used during war. The press utilises it unceasingly to scare and frighten. It is useless to reinforce this if it is not absolutely necessary. I will recall here a retort by Noah Ablett that I mentioned in 1915. When the Welsh miners went out on strike, all of chauvinist England rose up against them, crying: 'You are helping the enemy! You are pro-German!' And Noah Ablett, in the name of the miners, calmly answered: 'We are not pro-German; we are working class.' I believe that is the best basis, a sure and sufficient basis to carry on the working class struggle against war and justify it in the eyes of all workers. 'Defeatism', even though preceded by the qualification 'revolutionary', puts the accent on defeat while we ought to put it on revolution."[47]

Rosmer also cited a recent (1935) case in which the German CP leader Pieck invoked Lenin's defeat slogan "to justify the absurd tactic adopted by his party in the question of the Saar plebiscite" — that is, to cover a defencist position...

Perhaps this is the point to mention the absolute opposite extreme in Trotskyist politics, in a segue from wits to witlings. A sect that split off from the Trotskyist movement, generally called the "Oehlerites", put out a pamphlet on war policy which set down the defeatist concept in its crudest form: defeatism meant "to work for the military defeat of their 'own' army by the 'enemy' army".[48] This flat-footed version cannot be found in regular Trotskyist literature.

About 1935-1936 a pamphlet by James Burnham, published by the then Trotskyist group which called itself the Workers' Party, gave a version of defeatism that had been hovering on the fringes as the "authoritative" meaning:

"The Marxists fight, but within each country they fight not for the victory but for the defeat of their own government — not for its defeat by the opposing capitalist powers but for its defeat by its own working class."[49]

We have seen that this effort at a reinterpretation had already surfaced now and then. It was an "acceptable" formula since it made defeatism mean nothing special — nothing except "the revolution". Now, as before, no-one wondered why the revolution should be relabeled "defeat". The term was retained only as a ritualistic bow to Lenin and to the myth that no war position was completely "revolutionary" without something called defeatism.

On the other hand, another prominent Trotskyist writer, CLR James, could not ignore Lenin's world war slogan entirely since he was producing a history of the Comintern: *World Revolution, 1917-1936* (published in 1937). He wrote of 1914 that Trotsky and Luxemburg

"had early called for the new international, but Trotsky refused to accept Lenin's uncompromising demand that each socialist should fight for the defeat of his own country."[50]

Aside from the common gaffe ("country" for "government"), we should note that this ritualist, only a couple of pages before, had devoted a long passage to summarising Lenin's position on the war — and had not even mentioned defeatism at *that* point.[51] He had remembered the defeat slogan only when it was a matter of showing Lenin to be more "revolutionary" than other anti-war socialists, in line with the myth. Indeed, this was the pattern that defeatism played with Lenin himself, who "forgot" it on more than one occasion.

At the end of 1937 the newly formed Socialist Workers' Party (henceforth the official Trotskyist group in the United States) adopted a basic programme in which the defeat slogan was formulated as a variant of Formula No. 4:

"The SWP will advocate the continuance of the class struggle during the war regardless of the consequences for the outcome of the American military struggle..."[52]

Neither the word "defeatism" nor "defeat" was used. From this time on, the Trotskyist movement in general (with the possible exception of those with unusual memories) came to regard this formula as if it were the classical and canonical meaning of defeatism, and as particularly "authentic" in some sense. The "dirty words", at any rate, had been shoved under the table.

The confusion over defeatism came up for another workout in 1939, when the outbreak of the Second World War — and Russia's role in it — precipitated a fierce political conflict in the SWP; a split in the Trotskyist movement followed, and the formation of the Workers' Party (later called the Independent Socialist League). In this conflict, Trotsky's line of "defence of the Soviet Union" in the war, that is, support of Moscow's invasion of Poland and Finland, was captained in the United States by JP Cannon.

You are against the defence of the Soviet Union? said the majority-Trotskyists. *Then that means you are defeatists in Russia. That means you wish the defeat of Russia by reactionary Finland and Poland. It means you wish the victory of imperialism against the "workers' state"!*

The minority, opposed to "defence of the Soviet Union" and its invasions, was faced with the task of defining defeatism. The situation was ironic. The followers of Cannon knew well enough that *they* had never considered defeatism to mean favouring the victory of the enemy side; yet they began to insist that defeatism meant just that. (Demagogy, to be sure; yet it happened to be basically true, as we have seen, in terms of how defeatism had been developed by Lenin.) On the other hand — such things were possible only in the muddle of ideas known as defeatism — these same Cannon followers considered themselves to be defeatists with respect to *American* imperialism, and nevertheless indignantly denied that this made them favour the victory of an opposing imperialist camp. Unwittingly the Cannonite-Trotskyists had developed a double-barreled concept of defeatism: it meant one thing for one war camp and a different thing for the opposing war camp...

In response, the minority — upholding a "Third Camp" anti-war position— sought to make clear its belief that "defeatism" did *not* mean favouring the military victory of the other side. It even coined a new set of terms to make the distinction. In a document entitled "War and Bureaucratic Conservatism", the new terminology (which has since been heard of, here and there) went like this: the kind of defeatism where you do wish the other side's victory was tagged "military defeatism"; the kind of defeatism where you don't was simply left to stand as "revolutionary defeatism". What was here called "military defeatism" (favouring the military victory of the other side) was obviously related to what we called "pro-war defeatism" in Chapter 1.

As for the meaning of "revolutionary defeatism" in this terminology, the document "War and Bureaucratic Conservatism" explained:

"Does revolutionary defeatism mean the defeat of "our" army by the "enemy" army — the American army by the Japanese, the British army by the German, the Italian army by the French? Not at all. It means the defeat of one's "own" government by one's own proletariat."[53]

From this point of view, "defeatism" more and more was stripped down to mean nothing more than non-defencism. In conjunction with the development of the Third Camp position in the Cold War ("Neither Washington nor Moscow") all use of the term virtually died out. Even in the "official Trotskyist" circles of the SWP, *without* any re-examination, references to the word also virtually disappeared.

The revival by Shachtman

IN the early 1950s the picture changed through a development in the Independent Socialist League.[54] The best-known leader of this group from the beginning had been Max Shachtman. By 1950 Shachtman began a slow process of political collapse which was going to bring him, in 1956, to the overt abandonment of his long-standing revolutionary Marxist views. In brief, Shachtman went through the classic breakdown pattern from left-wing socialist to right-wing social-democrat. From his standpoint, the war question was prominently involved in this trans-mogrification (he wound up, for example, as a supporter of the Vietnam War)...

Shachtman set out to work up a "revolutionary" justification for abandoning revolution; and to this end struck out on a course where we have seen a predecessor. The interest of this tale is that Shachtman's road to social-patriotism was going to be — the concept of "revolutionary defeatism".

In a two-part essay on "Socialist Policy and the War" in the 1951 *New International*, Shachtman revived the old exegeses on "what Lenin meant" by defeatism in 1914-1916 — precisely in connection with the question: Will this "defeatism" apply in the next, Third World War? Woven into the structure of his essay was a basic ambiguity: *he presented Lenin's concept of defeatism as the correct and necessary policy for 1910-1916, but he rejected it as inapplicable to the looming Third World War* (the one to make the world safe from Stalinism)...

What was the meaning of the split-up position that Shachtman proposed, and which put forward a brand-new variant on the whole defeatist muddle?

Obviously its political meaning was to provide a justification for supporting war by the capitalist democracies against Russia. Since Shachtman was, at this point, not yet ready to come out openly with this proposition, he drew a slightly different conclusion: namely, in the looming Third World War by our American democrats against Stalinist Russia, *we cannot be "defeatists" at home*, even though "defeatism" was the correct policy in 1914-1916 and even though Russians must be for the defeat of *their* government in the same war...[55]

What the difference was, in these two different versions of allegedly opposing the war, was impossible to explain; and indeed when another ISL leader directed this inquiry to Shachtman, formally in the pages of the *New International*, Shachtman retreated with the claim that he had been misunderstood.[56] All that is unimportant now: water under the bridge — arguments invented when the arguer did not want to look his own views in the face.[57]

What remains worthy of continued emphasis is the meaning of what may be called "one-way defeatism". The proposal for a sort of "one-sided" defeatism, the kind of proposal exemplified by the "Palestine Trotskyists" and by the Shachtman episode, raises this question: can a distinction be invented between a "defeatist" *anti-war* policy and a "non-defeatist" *anti-war* policy?

No such distinction can be fabricated; no such distinction has ever been devised that made sense...

The concept of "revolutionary defeatism" is an untenable position, and like many another untenable position it gives rise to opposite errors as a way out. On the one hand, it may encourage a tendency, in reaction, to cling to Lenin's defeat formulas in all their crudity, in the hope that at least these will "guard against social-patriotism" like a blessed medallion (though they will not). And on the other hand, as an equal and opposite reaction, it may encourage a tendency to press from a "one-sided" defeatism to a politically disastrous end.

Bury the dead. The tradition of Lenin's defeatism was born in a political mistake in 1904-1905; it was revived in confusion in 1914, to be shelved without stock-taking in 1917; it was revived again in malice and reaction in 1924; it was turned into a hollow phrase by "explaining away" in the 1930s; it was ignored in the 1940s; and muddled into a pro-war stew in the 1950s; and any war policy based on it can only be disorienting or worse. In a world like ours, which at any time can blow itself to smithereens, revolutionaries of any persuasion or politics have only to start with the traditional policy of Marxism on the war danger: the policy of the Third Camp, which was the real content also of Lenin's war policy when he ignored the hollow formulas of defeat.

Appendix 1: Some Authorities on "Defeatism"

Isaac Deutscher: The Prophet Armed

DEUTSCHER'S first consideration of the defeat slogan is in connection with Zimmerwald. Deutscher writes that Lenin "urged the conference to adopt a defeatist attitude towards all warring governments".[58] Besides being false, and neglecting to explain what a "defeatist attitude" was, it limits its attention to the internationalised version, ignoring the "lesser evil" and special Russian position.

Ten pages later we learn that there was a disagreement over defeatism between Lenin and Deutscher's subject, Trotsky. Deutscher does not give Trotsky's line of argumentation against revolutionary defeatism, which permits him to argue that this disagreement was merely "one of propagandist emphasis, not of policy". Defeatism is treated as the "defeat facilitates" idea, i.e. "risk" of defeat.

"Trotsky, and with him many of Lenin's own followers, refused to tie the fortunes of revolution so exclusively to defeat."[59]

Deutscher winds up with a justification of defeatism: it made a revolutionary "immune from warlike patriotism", an "insurmountable barrier...".[60] (Trotsky, not quoted by Deutscher, argued that this was not so, and he was right.) Deutscher has nothing more on revolutionary defeatism.

Possony: A Century of Conflict

WHEN I first started investigating this question, one academic authority had recently published a book titled *A Century of Conflict: Communist Techniques of World Revolution* with an unusual feature: a whole section on "The Theory of Revolutionary Defeatism." According to the erudite scholar Professor Stefan T. Possony: "In July 1915, 11 months after the outbreak of World War One, Lenin outlined the doctrine of revolutionary defeatism for the first time,"" whereas Zinoviev had written about it in February. Therefore the *savant* found it "interesting to note that Sinovyev [sic] rather than Lenin seems to have been the originator of revolutionary defeatism."

Since this statement of Possony's is quite false (as we have seen), one may wonder how an eminent expert could go so wrong. It is clear that this devotee of scholarship did not bother to check Lenin's collected writings before announcing his discovery, but limited his research to the articles by Lenin and Zinoviev which in 1916 were collected in the book *Gegen den Strom*. This indubitably saved him a lot of trouble. The rest of his pages on the subject are not less (or more) illuminating, up to and including his sole word of political analysis: "Treason!"

Tony Cliff: Lenin Vol. 2, All Power to the Soviets

CLIFF'S treatment throughout is simply a repetition of the orthodox myths, uncritically. In Chapter 1, "The War", he asserts: "Throughout the war, Lenin stuck to the policy line which he had developed at this time." Specifically, "this time" is the first Bern conference of the Bolsheviks after outbreak of war. As he expounds Lenin's war line through uncritical citations of the usual documents, he writes:

"And Lenin was not equivocal. To aim at overthrowing one's own ruling class through civil war, one must welcome the defeat of one's own country."

But the citation he immediately gives says nothing about welcoming. It is the one about "defeat facilitates". He then asserts, having ignored Lenin's first formulations: the line of "revolutionary defeatism" is a universal one, applicable to all imperialist countries.

And lastly, he brings up the denunciatory rhetoric, and summarises: "Any retreat from 'revolutionary defeatism' might lead one to hesitate in carrying through the class struggle, in case this would weaken national defence."[61]

This statement about why the defeatist slogan is necessary (the necessity of firm purity) makes explicit what was only implicit in Lenin: the typically sectarian approach. This line must be correct because it is soul-saving...

At the end of this chapter, he criticiszes Trotsky for disagreeing with Lenin on revolutionary defeatism, giving two passages from Trotsky's view. He says nothing about why Trotsky was wrong, only again making the sectarians' soul-saving argument: this position "was better calculated to create a clear division between revolutionaries and social patriots." And then he asserts:

"What he [Lenin] said could not be misinterpreted. Where he stood nobody could mistake. There was no room for equivocation."[62]

In Chapter 2, he recounts some of the known information about disagreement with the defeat slogan inside Bolshevik ranks. There is no evaluation of the criticisms. The implicit politics is that any criticism of the defeat slogan meant only that the critic was wavering or uncertain in his anti-war politics.[63] Among the prominent examples of this internal disagreement was that of the Baugy group led by Bukharin, whose criticism obviously rocked Lenin and affected his approach; but precisely this case is prominent in Cliff by its nonexistence; Cliff pointedly ignores it.

David Shub: *Lenin...* [Unabridged Ed.]

A good example of the Stripped-Down Mode of reference to defeatism: a minimum. In his Chapter 7, "From War to Revolution".

In the course of two substantial passages from Lenin's anti-war documents, the defeatist concept appears as part of the quotes, with no comment on it by the author, no analysis, no link-up with the rest of contemporary history, etc. The two defeatist formulas that are embedded in the quotes are, as it happens, No. 1 and No. 2.

Leonard Schapiro: *The CPSU...*

NATURALLY Schapiro makes a tangle of it; for one thing, he wants to make the majority of the Mensheviks (not merely Martov) "internationalist". This Menshevik majority of "internationalists", he says, included the view of "limited approval of the war". It would seem you are a "defencist" only if you approve of the war *sans limites*. A writer who can pull off this sleight of hand, what can't he do with a slippery term like defeatism! But in fact he does nothing with it, except a gaffe:

"Lenin's simple formula that Russian defeat was the lesser evil was both more direct and, as time went on, more popular..."[64]

More popular than what? Apparently, than the Mensheviks' position, though there "all shades of opinion prevailed"... It would be hard to be wrong from more directions.

—About defeatism in the Russo-Japanese war? As far as I can make out from Schapiro's book, this war didn't exist, so there could be no question of mentioning war policy.

Dan: *The Origins of Bolshevism*

REGARDING war policy: nothing, or next to nothing, in the whole book. This book is not concerned with such matters, only with polemicising for the Menshevik factional view of the Russian Revolution as a bourgeois revolution only. It would be misleading to mention that revolutionary defeatism is not mentioned, for it is the whole war question that Dan finds irrelevant.

Notes

1. This passage is from an article by Karl Radek published in the magaazine *Current History* for March 1924, translated from *Pravda*, there noted as "written shortly before Lenin's death".

2. Lenin: *One Step Forward, Two Steps Back* (1904), in *LCW* 7:396. For the meaning Lenin attached to "bureaucracy" in this context, see not only the immediate context but also the preceding discussion from p.392 on.

3. Lenin, "Speeches at a Meeting of Members of [various] Delegations", July 11, 1921; in *LCW* 42:326.

4. Lenin, "The Voice of an Honest French Socialist", *LCW* 21:353.

5. Lenin, "The Tasks of Revolutionary Social-Democracy in the European War", in *LCW* 21:18; written not later than 6 September.

6. The current *LCW* gives the time of writing as "late August-September". The original Russian is a good deal rougher than this smoothed-out translation shows.

7. Lenin, "The European War and International Socialism:, in *LCW* 21:22f.

8. Lenin to Shlyapnikov, 17 October 1914, in *LCW* 35:162f.

9. That is, the piece referenced in note 5, above.

10. Lenin, "The War and Russian Social-Democracy", in *LCW* 21:32f.

11. Lenin, "On the National Pride of the Great Russians", in *LCW* 21:104.

12. Südekum's name was often used by Lenin to represent the especially vulgar pro-war wing of the German Social-Democrats.

13. Lenin, "The Russian Brand of Südekum", in *LCW* 21:123f.

14. This is the translation in the current *LCW*. As explained in the Foreword, the more exact version is the one in the old collected works: socialism will be true only "if it says that 'both are worst'." This deliberately repudiated the original formulation, about Tsarism being "a hundred times worse than kaiserism".

15. Lenin, "Under a False Flag", not published until 1917; in *LCW* 21:144.

16. No article by Lenin was published in No. 38. The reference seems to be to an unsigned leading article on the war, said to have been written by Zinoviev. Note that the Baugy people did not limit themselves to Zinoviev as the target; they went on to question also the party statements Lenin had written.

17. Gankin & Fisher, *The Bolsheviks and the World War*, pp.190-191.

18. Ibid, p. 182; for some other details on Bern, see Cohen: *Bukharin and the Bolshevik Revolution*, pp. 22-24, but unfortunately Cohen's account ignores the dispute on defeatism, and elsewhere he shows no grasp of it.

19. Lenin, "The Conference of the RSDLP Groups Abroad", published by the end of March 1915; in *LCW* 21:163.

20. For Lenin's draft, see *LCW* 21:165-68, or Gankin & Fisher, pp. 164-67; the latter's account of the affair begins on p. 162.

21. Rosmer: *Le Mouvement Ouvrier Pendant La Guerre*, p. 478.

22. Trotsky, "Open Letter to the Editorial Board of *Kommunist*", 4 June 1915, in Gankin & Fisher, p. 170; there is another translation in Riddell, ed.: *Lenin's Struggle* [&tc], p. 235.

23. The myth that defeatism was a basic element in Lenin's anti-war policy was well exemplified when even Isaac Deutscher stumbled over it. In his great biography of Trotsky (*The Prophet Armed, Trotsky: 1879-1921*, p. 226) telling of the Zimmerwald Conference, Deutscher related that "A minority, grouped around Lenin... urged the conference to adopt a defeatist attitude towards all warring governments..." Not so.

24. The documents giving the position of the Bolsheviks and the Zimmerwald Left are found in the appendix of the old collected works of Lenin 18:477-81, or in Gankin & Fisher, pp. 349-53.

25. For Radek, see Gankin & Fisher, 348; for the supplementary material on Zimmerwald, see *LCW* 41:349-57.

26. Lenin, "The Draft Resolution Proposed by the Left Wing at Zimmerwald", in *LCW* 21:347.

27. Aside from the present point under examination, note this qualification: it covered a lot of territory. In effect, it hedged on the categorical principle that "defeat facilitates revolution", recognising that the idea had to be historically conditioned. Zinoviev showed sensitivity to this point more than once, whereas Lenin did not waver on the unqualified assertion.

28. Zinoviev, "'Defeatism' Then and Now", in *Gegen den Strom*, p. 438.

29. Zinoviev, "The War and the Fate of Our Liberation", first published 12 February 1915; then in *Gegen den Strom*, p. 56.

30. Zinoviev, "The Russian Social-Democracy and Russian Social-Chauvinism", in *Gegen den Strom*, p.243f.

31. Lenin used to charge that Trotsky (like "pacifists") failed to link the peace slogan up with class struggle and revolution, a charge I think was unjustified; and in practice Lenin adopted the attitudes he criticised when he returned to Russia in 1917 and confronted what he called "the social-patriotism of the masses". The same can be said, I believe, about the critique Lenin seemed to make against Luxemburg with respect to her analysis of "defence of the nation" in her Junius pamphlet; Luxemburg's theoretical approach to this difficult issue was brilliant, and Lenin's (in his review of the Junius pamphlet) was abstract. All this bears on the larger myth — that only Lenin followed a complete and thoroughgoing antiwar policy during the war. People who accept this myth (including academic historians who have swallowed the Lenin myths whole) tend to be unaware of how extensively Lenin changed his tactics and emphases when he returned from emigration and confronted a different practical situation — one that Trotsky and Luxemburg had been familiar with from the beginning. But these are side-issues in the present context.

32. Martov & Dan: *Geschichte der Russische Sozialdemokratie*, p. 276 (this section written by Dan); and Getzler: *Martov*, Chap. 7, esp. pp. 139-42.

33. Trotsky: *What is a Peace Programme?* p. 10.

34. *ibid* p. 6.

35. *ibid* p. 11.

36. *ibid* p. 12.

37. Trotsky, "Defeat and Revolution", trans. in Riddell, ed.: *Lenin's Struggle* [&tc], pp. 170-72.

38. Trotsky, "Groupings in Russian Social-Democracy", *ibid*, p. 405.

39. Luxemburg: *Rosa Luxemburg Speaks*, p. 320.

40. *ibid* pp. 321-24.
41. Lenin, at 4th Congress of Soviets, "Reply to the Debate on the Report on Ratification of the Peace Treaty", 15 March 1918; in *LCW* 27:193.
42. See, for example, Deutscher's second volume of his Trotsky biography, *The Prophet Unarmed*, especially Chapter 2; also many sections of Trotsky's *The Stalin School of Falsification*, esp. pp. 89-99.
43. Martynov, "The Great Proletarian Leader", in *The Communist International* (English ed.), No. 1 New Series (not dated: ca. Feb. 1924), p. 41.
44. Zinoviev, "War and Leninism", in *The Communist International* (English ed.), No. 5 New Series (not dated, ca. June 1924), pp. 6-7.
45. There is the minor point that Lenin never spoke of "defeat of one's own *country*", except in one slip. One was supposed to say: defeat of one's *government* or one's *bourgeoisie*. The reader should remember, also, that Lenin never proposed the "lesser evil" formula for international use. But in the attempt to be "orthodox", Trotsky combined the well-known "lesser evil" phrase with the equally well-known fact that Lenin internationalised the slogan – without being aware that these two features never came together in Lenin. (We have pointed out that Zinoviev made similar gaffes.)
46. Trotsky: *War and the 4th International* [1934 pamphlet], Sec. 58, p. 26.
47. Rosmer, *Le Mouvement Ouvrier Pendant la Guerre* (1936), p. 478.
48. Revolutionary Workers' League: *The Workers' Answer to Boss War*, a pamphlet.
49. "John West" [i.e., James Burnham]: *War and the Workers* (N.Y., Workers Party, 193?), p. 13.
50. James: *World Revolution*, p. 74.
51. *ibid*, pp. 71-73.
52. Socialist Workers' Party: *Declaration of Principles and Constitution*. (1938), p. 24.
53. "War and Bureaucratic Conservatism", issued by the SWP minority in the dispute, was a mimeographed document, [reprinted later as an appendix to James P Cannon's *Struggle for a Proletarian Party*].
54. Starting as the Third Camp minority in the Trotskyist Socialist Workers' Party, founded as the Workers' Party in 1940 in the subsequent split, the group adopted the name Independent Socialist League in 1949. Its weekly organ was *Labor Action*, its magazine was *The New International*.
55. Shachtman, "Socialist Policy and the War", in *The New International*, May-June 1951 (p. 164+) and July-August 1951 (p. 195+); these two parts constituted the complete essay.
56. A criticism of Shachtman's essay by Gordon Haskell, followed by Shachtman's reply, appeared under the same title, "Socialist Policy and the War", in *The New International*, September-October 1951 (p. 294+).
57. However, the original version of this essay, in 1953-54, did devote six or seven pages to detailing the course of Shachtman's argumentation, with emphasis on his special methodology. As the "Foreword" mentioned, the space dedicated to this episode has been sharply reduced, but the material is still there for anyone concerned with the history of the ISL.

Notes to Appendix 1

58. Deutscher: *The Prophet Armed*, p. 226.
59. *ibid*, p. 236.
60. *ibid*.
61. Cliff: *Lenin*, p. 4.
62. *ibid*, p. 21.
63. *ibid*, pp. 22-25.
64. Schapiro, *The CPSU*, p. 152

Subscribe to workers' liberty

● UK subs: £25 (8 issues)
£14 (students, unwaged)
Cheques to "AWL"
Send to Workers' Liberty, PO Box 823, London
SE15 4NA

● US subs: $63
Cheques to "Barry Finger"
From Barry Finger, 18 Cragswood Road,
New Paltz, NY 12561

● Australian subs: $63
Cheques to "Workers' Liberty"
From Workers' Liberty, PO Box 313,
Leichhardt, NSW 2040

● European subs: £34
Payment in British currency, payable to "AWL"
From the London address

W ATCHING the accelerating political and moral degeneration of the Stalinised "Communist International" in the mid-1930s, Leon Trotsky entitled one of his commentaries "Is There No End To The Fall?" Had he been forced to observe the contemporary "revolutionary left" during the Balkans war of April-May 1999 he might have addressed the same incredulous and bitter question to a large proportion of those who name themselves "Trotskyists". By way of campaigning "against the war", NATO's war, and "against imperialism", that is against the NATO powers only, many "Trotskyists" actively sided with the primitive Serb imperialism of Slobodan Milosevic and tried to whip up an "anti-war movement" in support of those engaged in war to kill or drive out 90% of the Albanian population of Serbia's colony, Kosova.

Some did this because they had not quite got rid of the idea that the "socialist" Milosevic regime, the most Stalinist of all the successor regimes in the former Stalinist states, was somehow "still" progressive. These ranged from the surviving Stalinist churches and chapels to the *New Left Review*. Others — the SWP — simply thought that a big anti-war movement on any basis would rouse young people to action and thus help build up the forces of the left. Yet others were one-sided pacifists, or old style Neanderthal anti-Germans. They spent the war re-enacting a foolish parody of the sort of Stalinist antics that over decades destroyed independent working class politics.

The state of the British left at the start of the 21st century is most horribly depicted in its antics and in the arguments it used to build a pro-Milosevic "stop the war" movement in April-June 1999. That is the main subject of the following article: the techniques of political deception and self-deception that during the Balkans war turned so much of the "left" into its opposite.

The Degradations of "Apparatus Marxism"

By Jack Cleary

"Now it is clear that the decline of a language must ultimately have political and economic causes: it is not due simply to the bad influence of this or that individual writer. But an effect can become a cause, reinforcing the original cause and producing the same effect in an intensified form, and so on indefinitely. A man may take to drink because he feels himself to be a failure, and then fail all the more completely because he drinks. It is rather the same thing that is happening to the English language. It becomes ugly and inaccurate because our thoughts are foolish, but the slovenliness of our language makes it easier for us to have foolish thoughts. The point is that the process is reversible."

George Orwell, _Politics and the English Language_

"Borodin... is characterised in the novel as a 'man of action', as a living incarnation of Bolshevism on the soil of China. Nothing is further from the truth! [Borodin was no old Bolshevik]... Borodin, appeared as the consummate representative of that state and party bureaucracy which recognised the revolution only after its victory... People of this type assimilate without difficulty the gestures and intonations of professional revolutionists. Many of them by their protective colouring not only deceive others but also themselves. The audacious inflexibility of the Bolshevik is most usually metamorphosed with them into the cynicism of the functionary ready for anything. Ah! To have a mandate from the Central Committee! This sacrosanct safeguard Borodin always had in his pocket..."

Trotsky, discussing André Malraux's novel about the 1925-7 Chinese Revolution, _The Conquerors_.

Introduction

THE Comintern functionary whom Trotsky discusses, using Malraux's fictionalised Borodin as an example, was a "revolutionary" James Bond figure – a "superman" raised above the organic processes of the labour movement and the working class, and above mundane restraints and moralities. In the service of "the cause" he could say and do anything – so long as his superiors approved. As Stalinism progressed in the Comintern, there was literally nothing such people, and the working-class organisations they controlled and poisoned, would not for an advantage say and do. There was nothing that had been unthinkable to old socialists and communists that they did not in fact do.

They could ally with fascists to break socialist strikes, suppress the proletarian revolution in Spain, become rabid chauvinists for their own countries (so long as that might serve the USSR), turn into anti-semites... Nothing was forbidden to them. Nothing was sacred, and nothing taboo. Any means to an end.

Old agitational and propagandist techniques of manipulation were brought to new levels of perfection by the Stalinist rulers and their agents and allies across the world. Politics, history and, they thought, "History", were freed from the primitive slavery to facts. Politics that were virtually fact-free and virtually truth-free became possible on a mass scale. Great political campaigns could now be lied into existence. To be sure, this was not something unknown before Stalinism; but the Stalinists, beginning with their lies about what the Soviet Union was, made it an all-embracing permanent way of political life.

Truth did not exist, only "class truth", which meant "party truth", which meant Russian bureaucratic truth... Consistency was a vice of lesser, unemancipated mortals. You could say and do anything. Logic? Anything was logical so long as you got the "context" right and understood the "historical process". It was all a matter of "perspectives". Dialectics, comrade!

At different times Trotsky described this condition as "syphilis" and "leprosy". In the summaries of the proper revolutionary communist approach which he wrote in the 1930s, the demand to "be true, in little things as in big ones" is always central. The fact that such a "demand" had to be made and that it was made only by a tiny pariah minority, as incapable of imposing the necessary norms of behaviour as they were incapable of doing what they knew had to be done to defend the working class, was one measure of how far the "Marxist" movement had fallen, how deeply it had regressed, and how much had to be done to restore its health.

The "revolutionary superman" today is typically a "Trotskyist" builder of "the revolutionary party". One of the things trade union supporters of *Workers' Liberty* in Britain have to contend with – in the civil service union for example where the "revolutionary" left has had a presence for many years – is that many good trade unionists, honest, rational people, have come to hate the "revolutionary left" as liars, manipulators, people who place themselves outside the norms of reasonable political, moral and intellectual interaction. To a serious degree they do not have a common language with people who do not share their methods and habits of thought, or their special view of themselves and their "party".

II

TROTSKY himself commented more than once that the small groups of Trotskyists had sometimes absorbed too much "Comintern venom" into themselves. After Trotsky's death, not at once, but over many years, and not uniformly, organisation to organisation, but more in some "orthodox" Trotskyist organisations than others, a kitsch-Trotskyist political culture developed that replicated much that Trotsky had called leprosy and syphilis in the Comintern.

Its core was the development of the idea of a "revolutionary party" into a fetish, into something prised loose from both the social and historical context and the political content which gives it its Marxist meaning. For Marxists, the party and the class, though there is an unbreakable link between them, are not the same thing. "The Communists... have no interests separate and apart from those of the proletariat as a whole," as the *Communist Manifesto* puts it. The programme Leon Trotsky wrote for his movement in 1938 insisted that it was a cardinal rule for Marxists to "be guided", not by the interests of "the party", but "by the logic of the class struggle". And there is at any given moment an objective truth that cannot be dismissed if it is inconvenient to "the party".

In post-Trotsky "kitsch Trotskyism", the tendency over decades is for "the party" and what is considered to be good for "the party" to become the all-defining supreme good – to become what the USSR was to the Comintern and its Borodins. There are more limits than the Comintern functionaries had, but not too many limits. There are very few things people calling themselves Trotskyists have not done for organisational advantage. Much of the time, for many of the "orthodox" Trotskyist groups, everything – perceptions of reality, "perspectives", truth, consistency, principle – is up for "construing" and reinterpretation in the light of perceived party interest. Their "Marxism" is "Apparatus Marxism": it exists to rationalise what the party apparatus thinks it best to do.

Central to this pattern, of course, was the radical falsity of many of the axial ideas of the "orthodox" Trotskyist groups – on the USSR, for example, or on the "world revolution", of which the USSR's existence was both manifestation and pledge for its presently on-going "immanent" character; and on the linked idea that capitalism was perennially in a state of imminent 1930s level collapse. The survival and mutation of such ideas – the USSR is "in transition to socialism", capitalism faces immediate catastrophe – were themselves often shaped by organisational considerations.

Their "Marxist" ideas had become dogmas glaringly at odds with reality; to hold those ideas you needed a special way of construing the world; and thinking about it became a work of special pleading for the fixed dogmas, of rationalising to arrive at conclusions already set and inviolable. If "Marxism" is reduced to such a role, then there is no logical or psychological barrier against "Marxism" being used to rationalise whatever seems to "make sense" for the party on a day to day basis.

The German pre-World War One Social-Democrat, Eduard Bernstein, who proposed to shed the socialist goal of the Marxist labour movement and substitute for it a series of reforms of capitalism, notoriously summed up his viewpoint thus: "The movement is everything, the goal nothing." The kitsch-Trotskyists in their fetishistic commitment to creating an instrument, the "Revolutionary Party", that could make the socialist revolution, stumbled into a grim parody of Bernstein's notorious dictum: the party, short of the socialist revolution itself, is everything; all other things, including the actually existing working class, count for little and often for nothing. An obituary of Tony Cliff, one of the most seemingly successful proponents of the "Party First" approach in *WL*64-5 discussed this phenomenon.

[Cliff's] "was a refined, sophisticated variant of the approach developed by such orthodox Trotskyist tendencies as those of Healy and Lambert.

"These two, on the face of it, seem to be very different from Cliff. Not so. Gerry Healy came to dominate British Trotskyism from the late 40s, and Pierre Lambert much of French Trotskyism from about the same period, because in the 1940s and 50s the world posed big political and theoretical problems to the old-style Trotskyists, and most of the political leaders of the movement collapsed in demoralisation, confusion or perplexity. The Healys and Lamberts came to the fore because they cared about the ideas, and assessed them, only as crude working tools that did or did not help build the organisation. They could propose what to do on the basis of short term calculation without any political or intellectual qualms.

"The Trotskyists in Trotsky's time had drawn confidence, despite the gap between their tiny numbers and their very large perspectives, from the idea that 'the programme creates the party'. What might be called the 'organisation-first' schools of neo-Trotskyism turned this upside down. For them the old formula came very much to mean: arrange a programme and lesser postures, that will assist the organisation to grow. After he asserted his political independence in the early 60s, Healy's politics were blatantly cut, and frequently 're-cut', to fit his organisational needs and calculations. So were and are those of the Lambert groupings...

"Not 'the programme creates the party' but 'the needs of the party create and recreate the programme'. Not the unity of theory and practice in the proper sense that theory, which is continually enriched by experience, guides practice, but in the sense — Tony Cliff's sense — that 'theory' is at the service of practice, catering to the organisation's needs. "The very literary and 'theoretical' Cliff, on one side, and Healy and Lambert on the other, had a common conception of the relationship of theory, principle and politics to the revolutionary organisation..."

III

THIS approach led to the creation of a special sort of Marxism — "Apparatus Marxism" — the neo-Trotskyist version of which is really, all qualifications granted, a dialect of the old Stalinist Comintern "Marxism". It is the predominant revolutionary "Marxism".

Today Marxism has retreated deeper into academia — though there is a lot less even of that than there used to be — or, in a ridiculous parody of what Marxism was to the Stalinist organisations, into the cloistered seclusion of one or other "revolutionary party", where it exists to grind out rationalisation and apologia to justify the decisions of the "party" apparatus: "Marxism" with its eyes put out, chained to the millwheel — "Apparatus Marxism".

Apparatus Marxism is a peculiarly rancid species of pseudo-academic "Marxism" from which everything "objective", disinterested, spontaneous and creative is banished. Creativity is incompatible with the prime function of "Apparatus Marxism": rationalising. Creativity and, so to speak, spontaneity is the prerogative of the all-shaping, suck-it-and-see empirical citizens who staff the "Party" apparatus. Everything is thereby turned on its head. The history of the "Orthodox Trotskyist", or Cannonite, organisations is a story shaped by this conception of the relationship of Marxism to "the revolutionary party" — as a handmaiden of the apparatus. So, too, is the story of the the British SWP. "Party building" calculations determine the "line" and "Marxism" consists in "bending the stick" to justify it.

Lenin rightly argued that revolutionary theory without revolutionary practice is sterile and that revolutionary practice without revolutionary theory is blind. "Apparatus Marxism" is both blind and sterile because it is not and cannot be a guide to practice. It exists to rationalise a practice that is in fact guided by something else — usually, the perceived advantage of the organisation. For Marxists, the unity of theory and practice means that practice is guided by theory, a theory constantly replenished by experience. In "Apparatus Marxism", the proper relationship of theory to practice and of practice to theory is inverted.

Our predominant Marxist culture is largely made up of the various "Apparatus Marxisms", protected, as behind high tariff walls, by the "party" regimes they serve. Demurrers or questionings of cloistered certainties are inimical to that culture. This segmented "Marxism" stands in the way of Marxist self-renewal. The kitsch-Trotskyist conception of the "revolutionary party"

— which in fact is a conception closer to that of the Stalinists than to either Lenin's or Trotsky's conception — makes revolutionary Marxism impossible. It makes the cornerstone of *revolutionary* Marxism — as distinct from Academic Marxism and its gelded first cousin, "Apparatus Marxism" — the unity of theory and practice, Marxism as *a guide to action*, an impossibility.

Apparatus Marxism is self-righteous: it serves "the Party", which for now "is" "the Revolution", or, so to speak, its "Vicar on Earth"; it has few scruples, and recognises only those aspects of reality that serve its needs. Its progenitor is neither Marx nor Engels nor Lenin, but, ultimately, Stalin.

One reason why it thrives, even among anti-Stalinists, in our conditions, which are unfavourable to serious Marxism, is precisely its simple, uncomplicated, easily graspable logic and rationale. It is the way to "build the party", "catch the mood". You don't need background, study, work; and there aren't any very difficult or unanswerable questions — just three or four basic ideas and a willingness to listen to the Central Committee, or whomever it is that can "come up with a line" that lets "the party" have something plausible to say. This approach is much simpler and far easier than "full Monty" Marxism, for which reality cannot always be construed to fit what is best for "party-building". The contemporary kitsch-Trotskyist superhero embodies "Apparatus Marxism". From his collection of "Trotskyist" formulas, "lines" and rationalisation, he selects what will best advance the organisation — the "Revolutionary Party" which represents socialism — *whatever it says or does*. The kitsch-Trotskyist superhero has no time for Engels' comment in a letter to the German socialist Conrad Schmidt:

"The materialist conception of history has a lot of dangerous friends nowadays who use it as an excuse for not studying history. Just as Marx commenting on the French 'Marxists' of the late [18]70s used to say: 'All I know is that I am not a Marxist'...

"In general, the word 'materialist' serves many of the younger writers in Germany as a mere phrase with which anything and everything is labelled without further study, that is, they stick on this label and then consider the question disposed of. But our conception of history is above all a guide to study, not a lever for construction after the Hegelian manner. All history must be studied afresh, the conditions of existence of the different formations must be examined in detail before the attempt it made to deduce from them the political, civil-law, aesthetic, philosophic, religious, etc. views corresponding to them...

"You who have really done something, must have noticed yourself how few of the young literary men who attach themselves to the Party take the trouble to study economics, the history of trade, of industry, of agriculture, of the social formations... The self-conceit of the journalist must therefore accomplish everything and the result looks like it..." — the self-conceit of the "party-building" "Apparatus Marxist".

Apparatus Marxism in the Balkans War

I

WHAT THE "self-conceit" of the Apparatus Marxists "accomplished" during the Balkan war was to put their "Marxism" to the task of apologising for and making propaganda on behalf of Serbian imperialism attempting genocide in its colony Kosova.

In April 1999, as soon as NATO started to bomb Yugoslavia, a broad "Stop the War" alliance was formed. It ranged from Tony Benn MP to Bruce Kent of CND, to unreconstructed Stalinists of the *Morning Star* sort, and, at the organisational core of it, the SWP. The organisers of "Stop the War" rigorously excluded from their movement all demands for Serb withdrawal from Kosova. It was a rigorously pro-Serb campaign. Even supporters of the SWP and this campaign who "only" wanted to add a call for Serb withdrawal from Kosova, were hounded by the block of SWPers, Stalinists and confusionists*.

An understanding of what happened on the British left during the Balkans war, of how Apparatus Marxism operates, is best sought by looking at the problem that faced those whose instinct was properly to oppose "NATO", who saw great advantage for the left if a strong anti-war movement could be developed, and who, refusing to let the realities of what was happening in the Balkans inhibit them, then worked at the creation of an "anti-war" movement, attempting to lie a "stop the war movement" into existence.

You are assigned by The Party to "make the case against the war", NATO's war – to write a pamphlet designed to drum up an anti-war movement that will help to "build the revolutionary party". Ideally for this purpose you will want to make the case for some such slogan as "Down with NATO, victory to Milosevic" – something analogous to the slogans in Britain of the great anti-Vietnam war movement: "US troops out – victory to the National Liberation Front". How do you set about it?

You will survey the history, and the political and diplomatic and military realities. In the Marxist tradition you will start with the idea that "war is the continuation of politics by other means"; you will try to ground your "case against the war" in an examination of the politics whose pursuit has now taken the form of war. You will look at the developments that led to this particular war, uncover the hidden objectives, if they are hidden, being pursued by means of war; if there is a discrepancy, you will distinguish the real reasons from the given "good reasons". You will expose war propaganda, counterpose the truth to official lies, rip off the masks of righteousness and hypocrisy in which the rulers disguise their war aims and expose the less pretty face of reality. You will look objectively at both sides and at all sides.

Is there some hidden political design behind what NATO seems to be doing? For example, is NATO's concern with Kosova really a design to conquer Serbia? Is it tied into a broader network of conflicts and ambitions in which the Kosovars can only be saved if some other people is sacrificed to the same fate. What if you cannot find a hidden design?

You can of course argue that socialists and consistent democrats should not trust or support NATO, or give it credit in advance for being able to stop Milosevic's attempted genocide in Kosova, or trust it not to sell out the Albanian Kosovars in a rotten deal with Milosevic. But that is not enough. To do the assigned job, you need to be able to denounce and condemn without qualification what NATO is doing.

With the Marxist procedures outlined above, it would in the 1999 Balkans war have been far easier – although I am not advocating it – to make a case for backing NATO than for opposing it; and for a socialist or consistent democrat it was impossible to make any case in favour of Milosevic.

For truth-driven Marxist politics, making other than a pacifist case against this war presented impossible difficulties.

NATO's war aim was to stabilise the Balkans by forcing Milosevic to give Serbia's colony Kosova autonomy – not independence – and stop ethnic cleansing and the killing of Albanians. That was the substantial issue in the war. Milosevic could at any point have stopped NATO's bombs by ceasing his genocidal drive and withdrawing from Serbia's colony, Kosova, as he eventually did.

---

* This did not end with the war. At the SWP summer school Marxism 99 one new short-stay member of the SWP was driven out of the meeting with Alex Callinicos's cry "running dog of imperialism!" ringing in his ears! Honest!

"Stop the war, stop the bombing"? Whether or not ways less costly than bombing for Albanian and Serb alike might have been found, once the full-scale Serbian drive against Kosovar Albanians started, "stop the war, stop the bombing" meant and could not but mean: give Milosevic the victory in Kosova.

To be one-sidedly against NATO is in the existing relationships implicitly to be for Milosevic — to make the case for giving Milosevic a free hand to kill and drive out 90% of the population of Kosova. Even if you did not dare cry "Victory to Milosevic!" that is what such a campaign would stand for. There is the dilemma for those who want to build a "stop the war movement" in April 1999. Only a native or adoptive Serb chauvinist could argue the one-sided "case against NATO's war" or build a "mass anti-war movement" that could not but be a support campaign, a political foreign legion for Milosevic.

Your best "case against the war" is the perennial pacifist case against all wars. But Marxists are not against all wars. We are for wars of liberation — for wars such as the Kosovar Albanian war of liberation in Serbia's colony Kosova! So, go back to the Party and report that the assignment is an impossible one and offer the conclusion that the idea of building a pro-Milosevic "anti-war" movement is as daft as, say, campaigning in Britain in the early 1990s for a general strike to bring down the Tory government? You can't do that? It is not that kind of party.

Then you must use the tried and tested old high-Stalinist techniques yourself. Facts are not sacred; opinion — other than that of the "party leadership" — is not free. Where an old stick-to-the-facts Marxist or consistent democrat would find it impossible to complete a Party Assignment to make the required sort of "case against the war", the difficulty can be overcome. The complexities of the situation can help.

In Kosova the first NATO bombs triggered an enormous escalation of the ethnic cleansing that had been going on for many months — perhaps a quarter of a million Albanian Kosovars had been driven from their homes in 1998 — a killing and driving out of the Albanian Kosovars by the Serbian state and Serb paramilitaries that, within days, had more than half Kosova's population either uprooted and on the move or dead.

It is not NATO, whatever fault can be justly laid on it that is organising or "provoking" the horrors in Kosova. But confusion is fertile ground for "peace" propaganda. And the bombing of Serbia and Montenegro is repulsive and horrible in itself, whatever the issues. You can write your pamphlet! You can build an anti-war movement.

II

IN APRIL 1999, the Socialist Workers' Party published a commentary on the three-way Serb-Kosovar-NATO war, *Stop the War*, reputedly the work of the academic Alex Callinicos, as a basis of the mass anti-war movement they were trying to build.

In summary its argument is as follows:

1. War is bad; it kills people, makes refugees. NATO's claims that the war would quickly bring peace were false.

2. Milosevic is bad, but not *so* bad — not Hitler, not a fascist, not even as bad as Croatia's president Tudjman. The US used to regard him as a good man to do deals with.

3. Therefore, any connection of NATO's war to Milosevic's "horrible policies" is "spurious". Actually the driving motive of the war is that "Clinton wants to prove that the US through NATO is the world's policeman".

4. "However horrible the events in Kosovo", what Serbia was doing there was not as bad as the Nazi Holocaust. Moreover, the attitude of the British government and press to Kosovar refugees is hypocritical.

5. The break-up of Yugoslavia in the 1990s was due to economic crisis and the fact that "the rulers of each part of Yugoslavia turned to ethnic rabble-rousing in an effort to divert... class feeling into scapegoating".

6. "Milosevic can be toppled" — but by the opposition inside Serbia. And "the NATO bombing... has drowned out" that opposition.

7. The big powers have a bad record in the Balkans.

8. The answer to national conflict there is "to go beyond nationalism" by way of workers' unity.

9. The Labour Party has a bad record on Britain's wars.

10. Anti-war movements are desirable, and socialists "connect the struggles against war with struggles against poverty, bad housing, racism and all oppression".

Stop the War appeals to peace and to the desire for peace in general but in fact means only stop NATO attacks on Serbia and – the implication is unavoidable – give Milosevic a free hand in Kosova. That is all it can mean in context. That is all its authors and publishers intend it to mean.

Organised in eight chapters and an introduction, *STW* at no point presents an objective, overall, factual account of the Serb-Kosova conflict or of the development of NATO involvement. Facts and elements of the overall picture are doled out only as, when and as much as is necessary to allow *STW* to argue its case: thereby it does not "argue" its case in terms of reality, measuring itself against the facts and the full picture.

All through, it distorts the realities so as to favour Serbia/Yugoslavia and discredit its Kosovar victims.

This account of the war fades out both Serbia's long oppression of Kosova and its then current attempted genocide of the Kosovars. Shreds of fact in that connection are filtered into the pamphlet, but only negatively: Milosevic is not as bad as Hitler, the West's condemnations of him are hypocritical, his actions in Kosova are not as bad as the Nazi Holocaust, national conflicts in ex-Yugoslavia are the result of evil machinations on all sides – but, yes, it has to be admitted, as a fact now reduced to its proper insignificance, that Milosevic had "horrible policies" in Kosova. In place of the real history of national conflicts in the Balkans, and of Serbian imperialism, centre-place in the story is given to the idea that the US wants to be boss of the world and has seized on Kosova artificially as "another chance to show [the EU] it alone is capable of calling the shots".

The arguments here not only radically misrepresent the reality of Kosova, but pulp basic socialist concepts about imperialism, the national question, democracy, and workers' unity. Not only out of concern for the Kosovars, but also to set a sound basis for socialism in the 21st century, the arguments and methods deserve close critical discussion. There are more weighty renditions of what is discussed here than the pamphlet *Stop the War*. *Stop the War* is what it came down to in living politics and in ideas offered to what they hoped would be a large scale movement of youth against the Balkans war.

III

WHAT follows is an analysis and discussion of the SWP pamphlet *Stop the War* in the form of a fictional dialogue between "**Caliban**", an SWPer arguing the case made in *Stop the War*, "**Brownstone**", an independent working-class socialist, and "**Varga**", an analyst of political culture and propaganda methods. Our fundamental concern here is with the methods and techniques used in the shame-facedly pro-Milosevic "stop the war" movement.

Caliban: We are anti-imperialists, not moralists. We don't wring our hands, we build a movement that will eliminate once and for all such suffering as occurred on both sides in Serbia and Kosova! The first step in socialist education is hatred of NATO and opposition to our own rulers.

We made the case against the war as best we could. You stood there, wringing your hands – and objectively making the case for NATO's war. You accepted their basic lie – that it was for the Kosovars.

Brownstone: No, I accepted the basic fact that, since there was no NATO intention to conquer Serbia, and no people who would suffer the fate in Serbia that Serbia intended for the Kosovar Albanians, or anything remotely like it, the rights of the Kosovar Albanians were the immediate issue in the war, whatever NATO's motives.

NATO was not trying to conquer Serbia. It was trying to impose "Rambouillet" – NATO's terms for a Balkan settlement. Those terms fell far short of a consistently democratic policy because they upheld Serbian sovereignty over Kosova and denied self-determination to the Kosovars. But compared to the Serbian drive to wipe out the Kosovars as a nation, they represented survival, civilisation and limited national democracy for the Kosovar Albanians.

NATO acted with scant concern for the Kosovar Albanians. Its targets in Serbia progressively broadened beyond military installations. Political cowardice led Clinton and Blair to put avoiding casualties on their own side above everything else, and that led to many Serb deaths.

But once the bombing and full-scale *cleansing* started, for Milosevic to win the conflict could not but mean irreversible doom for the Kosovar Albanians as a people and death for large numbers of them. NATO's victory over Milosevic has made possible the return of the surviving Albanians to Kosova.

It is right to point out what NATO is and what the USA is, and to preach no confidence, endorsement or trust for NATO, the USA, Britain or the European Union. Yet, since you shared all the political assumptions of Rambouillet – for you, the Kosovars' right to self-determination was a question very much secondary to the big-power politics at stake – you criticised NATO only for its mode of action, for bombing, not for its basic politics. You detached that from any true picture of what Serbia was doing, and attached it – by way of essentially pacifist but one-sided anti-war agitation – to pro-Serbian apologetics.

Serbia was a colonial power in Kosova; an expansionary imperialism, albeit more akin to the imperialism of Tsarist Russia than to the big powers. The prime duty of socialists was solidarity with the colonial revolt of the Kosovar Albanians, and against the Serbian drive for genocide.

Socialists do not necessarily adopt the viewpoint of the Kosovars! But we are obliged not to dismiss them, or side against them with their would-be exterminators. Even if we grant that NATO is imperialist in Kosova, and that Serbia, by some quirk of pedantic definition, is not – from what point of view is imperialism in general, without more specifics, a worse evil than attempted genocide by this murderous "non-imperialism"?

Caliban: You are missing the big picture. I quote: "The war in the Balkans involves two evil forces. One, Slobodan Milosevic, has horrible policies but can only implement them in a fairly limited area. The other, US imperialism, is just as capable of evil but can do so on a world scale. Hundreds of thousands of dead in Central America, Africa, the Middle East and Indonesia are testimony to its crimes, just as the *thousands dead* in Kosovo are testimony to Milosevic's crimes."

Brownstone: When *Stop the War* was written, Pristina had already been emptied of 200,000 people at gun point...

Caliban: Ah, yes! "Every day since [24 March] the horror has worsened... Kosovo's capital, Pristina, has emptied as people flee in fear of Milosevic's paramilitaries and NATO bombs."

Brownstone: No, it was not NATO bombs, but Serbian state terror that forced people out of Pristina. Over half the Kosovar Albanians had already been uprooted and an unknown number killed. Your authors know what happened in the first half of the 1990s in Croatia and Bosnia. And they know that Britain colluded with Milosevic and the UN and bears criminal blame for what happened in Bosnia.

To talk of "thousands dead" in Kosova was grossly to minimise and to falsify the picture at the point in the war when *Stop the War* was written – not to speak of the prospects for Kosovar Albanians if the "anti-war" movement won its "demands" to leave Slobo alone. It was to try to persuade everybody the pamphlet reached to ignore the attempted genocide. You use the lie direct and couple that with comparing incomparable things – the crimes of the US over time and across the world with the bestial intensity of the immediate, short-term, racist Serb drive to kill and disperse Kosovar Albanians now.

Varga: Double standards are indispensable to Caliban. Without them, he thinks he will be conceding a little bit of the moral high ground to NATO or US imperialism.

Brownstone: You display great indignation against the "hundreds of thousands" of dead attributed to the USA, and so little indignation against the slaughter organised by Milosevic as to cover for its perpetration. Therefore in an auxiliary way, you collude in it. You help set up a propaganda smoke screen for Milosevic – specifically aimed at the working class and the left and, in the first place, the members and supporters of the SWP.

You exonerate Milosevic in Kosova by finding him not guilty of being Hitler, and not guilty of being the world's leading capitalist power. You deploy proper anti-capitalist humane outrage – in the propaganda service of people attempting genocide! You compare incomparables, dissolving the concrete now into world history and generalities. The horror wreaked by capitalism in the world is invoked to minimise and excuse the very specific horror of would-be genocide in Kosova.

Many evils are conflated with the intention of making distinctions impossible and so as to maximise the evil and guilt attributable to one and minimise that of the other. Invocation of the general evil is used to diffuse the impact of the concrete evil in Kosova. This is the intellectually and morally corrosive classic Stalinist method. For example, the old conflation of economic grinding down of people by capitalism with direct slaughter. It belongs intellectually to the same order of things as the argument that, all things on both sides taken account of, the USSR with its low rents, etc was more democratic than any capitalist country. The late Nahuel Moreno, one of the leading kitsch-Trotskyists, once wrote a book to prove it.

Why did NATO go to war? It had the general aims of policing and stabilising the region for maximum penetration by "the imperialism of free trade". Beyond that, European or American imperialist aims played no part in this war.

Caliban: That's what Ken Livingstone said in order to justify the NATO bombing! "'Western or Yankee imperialist' aims are not involved in the war, Labour MP Ken Livingstone claimed as he backed the bombing".

Varga: You deal with Livingstone's point, not by direct argument, but by using "guilt by association" with his pro-NATO conclusion. It is an old Stalinist technique. They would deflect true criticisms of the USSR by associating them with people who used them in the service of the Nazis, or Cold War arms build-ups or US imperialism.

Caliban: "Clinton wants to prove that the US through NATO is the world's policeman." That is what's central to the war. "The US has certainly been the driving force in pushing for war, just as in numerous other military adventures over the last two decades, from the invasion of Grenada and Panama in the 1980s to the recent bombing of Sudan and Iraq." The same people decided to bomb Yugoslavia. "The US does not have two rival sets of armed forces and intelligence agencies... the Clinton administration behind the bombing is the same Clinton administration that dances to the tune of agribusiness giant Monsanto or the Chiquita fruit company as it attempts to dictate trade policy to the Third World... [Its] policies on debts mean" — we quote Barton Briggs of Morgan Stanley, the bankers — "200 million sullen Latin Americans sweating away in the hot sun for the next decade so that Citicorp can raise its dividend twice a year".

Brownstone: Yes. That is capitalism! Having defined the US as imperialist around the issue of "Iraqi oil" (it was Kuwaiti oil, in fact), you admit no such issue exists in Kosova. ("There is no oil there like in Iraq"). You link Kosova to the aggressive economic policies of US corporations and banks in the Third World.

In most of the Third World today, imperialist domination is via "free trade". The policies imposed from gigantic economic strength on the poor countries of the world are indeed an obscenity. We can agree to denounce this "imperialism of free trade and usury". But how can that denunciation justify siding with Serb colonialism and would-be genocide in Kosova?

Varga: Caliban's problem is to show that what is happening in the Balkans now is imperialism being imperialism, and that it is so much worse than Serb colonial-imperialism in Kosova that socialists should back Serbia. How can this be done? Throw in a lot of background patter about IMF plans and Gulf oil — enough to create an impression that there is solid Marxist economic theory in the background, and that NATO's war in Kosova is loosely analogous to those IMF plans and the Gulf war — and then concentrate on the bombings! Bombing is imperialism!

Brownstone: What is the specific US motivation for war against Yugoslavia? Yugoslavia's world-famous bananas? "There is no oil like in Iraq." Well then, what?

Caliban: Since the collapse of the USSR the USA "has been out to show that it is the only superpower. Its strategic aim is to exercise 'hegemony' throughout the world — to get its way in any disagreement with other states, big or small".

Brownstone: So this imperialism has no other aim but the exercise of power to show who is boss? Specific economic aims? No. Does Kosova, or Yugoslavia, have special strategic or symbolic importance? No. Is the US concerned, as it was in Indochina in the 1960s and 1970s, to thwart some rival imperialist cartel (the Moscow-led Stalinist bloc in Indochina)? No, on your account imperialism is imperialism is imperialism is imperialism is... Imperialism is power, throwing its weight around.

That may be part of the truth of every imperialism in history, but what distinguishes different sorts of imperialism is drive, motive, objectives, modus operandi. This line, "imperialism is power", like its companion elsewhere in the pamphlet, "war is killing", is too abstract to be an adequate account of reality — or to guide politics with a grip on reality. If power is imperialism, and imperialism is power, that allows you to side against the biggest power, irrespective of the issues. The vast technical-military difference between NATO and Serbia renders Serbian imperialism and everything specific to it unimportant and insignificant. Anti-imperialism narrows to opposing the militarily most powerful imperialism. You side with a primitive, weak (in world terms) and backward colonial imperialism which is attempting genocide, against NATO which, in order to stabilise the European Union's borders, is thwarting it! It is like an idiot, convinced that all thieves and robbers are six foot three inches tall, who hysterically raises the alarm against one of them who is, for his own reasons, really trying to stop a gang of murderous robbers all of whom happen to be four foot eleven inches tall.

Such basics of Marxist analysis as war aims, the preceding history and the entire political context are all faded out. On one side you have a police action executed brutally and clumsily, and on the other attempted genocide – but socialists side with the genocidal murderers!

Caliban: You're just going along with NATO's demonisation of Milosevic. But we've seen it all before. "The end of the Cold War in 1989 was... followed by promises of a new world of progress and peace. Yet, within a year, Saddam Hussein was proclaimed the 'new Hitler'". Atrocity stories were invented. "The multi-million arms business guzzles resources" while babies and old people go without.

Varga: Just proclaimed? Your indignant point-scoring against NATO suppresses the real socialist critique of the NATO powers – that they do not pursue a democratic foreign policy – that they deliberately worked to preserve the Iraqi regime (without Saddam Hussein, they hoped).

Caliban: "Lies are poured out to defend the killing. Then a few years later it is often hard to find anyone to defend the slaughter".

Varga: Everything concrete, specific and real is faded into vast generalities – to hide the specific, real, concrete facts about Serbia and Kosova.

Caliban: Milosevic is no Hitler: and someone far more a Hitler than Milosevic is on NATO's side! President Tudjman of Croatia, leader of "the most right-wing government in Europe since the rule of the fascist General Franco in Spain", who four years ago drove out 200,000 Krajina Serbs from Croatia!

Brownstone: But Milosevic in Kosova was driving out and killing ten times as many.

Caliban: More, NATO's war whipped up nationalist feeling in Serbia and created a risk of the real Serb fascists gaining ground. If Serbia was defeated, reaction in Serbia would gain. "There are real fascists in Yugoslavia today, but they are not in power. One of the terrible outcomes of the bombing is that these people have been strengthened, not weakened."

Brownstone: Therefore we should not want Serbia defeated?

Varga: Here you must be sure to evade the pertinent question: what would "real" Serb fascists do in Kosova that Milosevic was not doing?

Monsters can be made to seem less monstrous by being identified with something known, familiar and not very threatening. The Stalinists used that technique a great deal to pass off features of their police-state regimes which they could not easily deny or explain away. In the same way, *Stop the War* scales down Milosevic's crimes, while appearing to be righteously critical of him, by equating him with the retired British Tory politician Norman Tebbit. "His policies are hard right wing, but he is not a fascist. In fact he is the Serbian version of the Tory Norman Tebbit rather than the Serbian Hitler." Nietzsche got only part of it right: if you fight with dragons you become a dragon. And if you cuddle up to dragons you cease to be able to see that they are dragons.

Caliban: Your view of Milosevic could not but play into the hands of NATO. It had to be fought if the case against the war was to be made. NATO was "demonising" Milosevic for no other good reason than to whip up a war drive.

Varga: Milosevic is not quite "one of us", but he too is the victim of NATO propaganda. That is the message of *Stop the War*. The laws of war propaganda apply to building an anti-war movement, which can be a factor in war! You pick your side and then say what you need to say.

Caliban: The US chief negotiator at the end of the Bosnian war (1995), Richard Holbrooke, described him as "a man we can do business with, a man who recognises the realities of life in former Yugoslavia". "Now he [Milosevic] is demonised in order to provide a spurious justification for a show of US power."

Brownstone: Of course, what could be more spurious than attempted genocide?

IV

Varga: *Stop the War* is careful not to explain that NATO supported Milosevic as the strong man in the region and wanted him to control Kosova. NATO turned on him primarily because they feared that Milosevic's "cleansing" Kosova of 90% of its people would set off what they hoped Milosevic's heavy hand would stop – the destabilisation of the Balkans. By starting on 24 March, at the point of the breakdown of relations between Milosevic and NATO, *Stop the War* can blame the war on the US gratuitously seeking to provoke conflict just so that it can show off its power.

Brownstone: You go mechanically and cheerfully wherever you are taken by the negative thrust of your reaction against "imperialism" – in fact, against advanced capitalism, because what makes the US imperialist in Kosova, but Serbia not (in your eyes), is only that the US is more powerful and more advanced.

Try reading back your approach here to China in the 1930s and 1940s. The Japanese invaded Manchuria in 1931 and China in 1937. Compared to the USA's advanced, primarily economic, imperialism, Japan's was very backward – an archaic militarism engaged in primitive plunder.

Six months before Japan's "surprise" attack on the US base in Honolulu [December 1941], the USA had imposed economic sanctions on Japan that would have stifled it in a short time. The attack on "Pearl Harbour" was not cause but result. Apply the principle that you side against the most developed, strongest, more viable imperialism and with its backward, economically primitive, less viable opponent, ignore "complications" like Serbia's attempted genocide in Kosova or Japan's murderous work in China, and what do you get? You would side with Japan, and denounce the US alone as the provoker of war. You would accuse China, the US's ally after December 1941, of "playing into the hands of the USA" and of helping "imperialism" – economically the strongest capitalist power, and responsible for immense suffering in peace as well as in war. You would "defend" Japan and concentrate all your denunciations of imperialism against US imperialism. Your agitation would centre on such things as US fire bombing Japanese cities, while the Japanese could not touch mainland America. You would make war propaganda against US imperialism and use all the tricks you use in *Stop the War* to counter US accounts of what Japan was doing in China.

In World War Two there were serious Marxists, Max Shachtman and his comrades, who felt that China's liberation struggle had become so tied up with the cause of the imperialism with which China allied, the USA's, that the Chinese nationalists and Stalinists could no longer be supported against Japan. I think they were mistaken. But they would have hanged themselves before they'd have made pro-Japanese propaganda against China as part of their opposition to US imperialism!

For you, Karl Liebknecht's and Rosa Luxemburg's slogan "The main enemy is at home" becomes "The only enemy is at home".

Varga: It's a better story-line to "build the revolutionary party". But it's not all it seems. We'll find later that *Stop the War* sees the real "Great Satan" not "at home", but in the US, as compared to relatively harmless European capitalism.

Brownstone: The good old basic slogan of German social-democracy, "Not a penny, not a man, for this system!", designed to secure independent working class politics in an era of capitalist growth and development, and, thus, to prepare the overthrow of capitalism, becomes: say no whenever the ruling class says yes.

Caliban: Because the world is long ripe for socialism, advanced capitalism is reactionary!

Varga: Paradoxically, this idea – capitalism is ripe for socialism, therefore further capitalist development is reactionary – demands of anti-imperialists that they ally again and again with reactionary forces – Khomeini, Saddam Hussein, Milosevic – in their clashes with advanced capitalism.

From the point of view of the SWP now, it is an historical accident, a leftover from the days when you had a less party-solipsistic view of politics, that you did not side with Stalinism in the Cold War. The logic that makes you support Milosevic, Saddam, or Khomeini would dictate exactly that conclusion. On a world scale you have become Karl Marx's "reactionary

123

socialists"!

Brownstone: And the political cost of your habit of substituting of outside agency, real or imagined, for the real dynamics of class and nation within the situation, is that it bankrupts you again and again, on issue after issue – on Ireland and Israel/Palestine for example, as well as Kosova. It means that in area after area, real history is blocked off, and, in the name of "anti-imperialism" and "revolution", the peoples involved are treated with a condescending metropolitan contempt. Their life and death concerns are only "false consciousness", artefacts of bad men and the demon imperialism (and of the absence of socialists).

Caliban: Our job is not to make a general objective analysis, giving due weight to all relevant factors, as if we are just wise onlookers. The point is to change the world. And to mobilise the forces for that, we must focus the blame on imperialism and capitalism.

Brownstone: Indeed, we must agitate. But if Marxists do no more than agitate, if we do not understand real history in our own independent working-class way, then we can only mirror capitalism's picture of itself, putting bad or negative where official capitalism puts good, or positive. We can not even challenge, still less defeat, the bourgeoisie in the battle of ideas.

E P Thompson famously wanted to save the working people of 200 years ago from the shallow elitist historians – "from the enormous condescension of posterity". Here, it is necessary to rescue the peoples of oppressed and warring nations of today from the manipulative condescension of pretentious, deeply ignorant, kitsch leftists.

For example, the Dayton Accord of 1995 divided Bosnia into two separate zones, 51% to Croats and Muslims, 49% to Serbs. *Stop the War* records this fact, and describes it as "imposed by the US". Responsibility, full and complete, is here attributed to outsiders in an utterly false construction. Yes, the US and NATO "imposed" it. But internal forces created what NATO froze. Any true account of what the UN and, especially, Britain contributed to shaping this would indict them for colluding with Milosevic! If the authors of *Stop the War* were consistent, they would have to say that the old NATO policy of backing Milosevic as the strong man to keep national conflicts under a heavy lid was right, and that NATO's crime now is to have abandoned that policy, "under US pressure".

The SWP's US-focussed anti-imperialism has the curious consequence of pulling punches in their criticism of Britain's terrible role in Kosova and Bosnia in the late 1980s and early 1990s!

Caliban: Moreover, "why has the US bypassed the United Nations?" Doesn't that prove the US is up to no good?

Varga: There is a lot of support for the UN! Don't be afraid to mobilise it!

Brownstone: But do you support the UN?

Caliban: No. "The US and Britain are deliberately ignoring rules they themselves drew up... The UN has never stopped the world being a dangerous place. The new NATO policy will make it even more dangerous." We focus on the USA as the obvious main enemy. Remember the Vietnam anti-war movement? The Dayton peace deal meant driving Serbs, Croats and Muslims from one area to another!

Brownstone: "Meant driving"? Who drove? Primarily, Milosevic's forces, by way of "ethnic cleansing". Should "the West" have tried to stop it? How? Bombs? And what would the authors of *Stop the War* have said?

Varga: Note Caliban's strong nerve here. To denounce the driving out of 200,000 Krajina Serbs as the mark of "the most right-wing government in Europe since Franco", and simultaneously to denounce intervention to stop the killing and driving out of two *million* Kosovar Albanians! That takes a steely determination not to let consistency get in the way of a good "case against the war". After this, *Stop the War* gives us a very belatedly doled-out but central part-fact – a "truth-lie". Dayton "gave Milosevic control over Kosova as 'compensation' for accepting the forced removal of Serbs from Krajina in Croatia". There was then no question of anything else. Milosevic already had control over Kosova. Not to "give" it to Milosevic would mean taking it from him. How? Bombs? This war? But then... not now?

Caliban: The point is to show that NATO is responsible for the terrible things Milosevic was doing!

Brownstone: And so when they acted to stop it, you denounced them and backed Milosevic?

Caliban: But the war was about the fact that "Clinton wants to prove that the US is the world's policeman". "The US has been out to show that it is the only superpower... But other big states are not always willing to go along with its schemes. There have, for instance, been repeated disputes over trade with the West European countries, such as the current 'banana wars', and Japan."

Brownstone: Yes, but how does this fit into what the US and West Europe were doing together in the Balkans?

Caliban: The US "has attempted to pull these [western European] states into line by showing it alone has the military power to act as world policeman, imposing the common requirements of the big states on any smaller 'rogue' state that steps out of line... Now the Kosovan crisis has given it another chance to show it alone is capable of calling the shots in the European Union's own backyard. It reckons that European governments which rely on its military hardware against Yugoslavia will be much less likely to complain at its policies over trade, debt, Monsanto, Middle East oil, or anything else."

Brownstone: You do not explain what it is that the European governments want to do "against Yugoslavia", or why they have to rely on the US's "military hardware" for it rather than using their own. Still, this is the nearest you get to a suggestion of a clear NATO war goal. The USA's real target is not Serbia, but the European Union! The war is "really" about the USA whipping the European Union into line! Kosova is just a "chance" for the US to do that.

Not only is this story a fantasy — it is the old-CP style demonisation of the US to let the local — British, French, whatever — bourgeoisie off the hook.

Varga: Establishing that NATO was acting imperialistically in any more than a general "imperialism of free trade" sense was always a major difficulty. Motives for NATO had to be found other than the upfront business of Kosova. Here the old CP distinction between one's own country and demonic US capitalism was the tack to take.

Caliban: In 1991, with Iraq, the US made sure the Middle East's oil supplies remained in Western hands. In Croatia and Bosnia, the US had another success. Germany "had ignited the Yugoslav powder keg" by recognising Croatia "under a leader who admired the wartime fascist regime of the Ustashe".

Brownstone: That is a plain lie. But in any case, what about the fact that 90% of the people of Croatia had freely voted for independence?

Caliban: "Only the US was able to bring order to the breakaway states — training the Croat army, arming the Bosnian Muslims, bombing the Serbs and finally helping the Croats 'ethnically cleanse' most of the Croatian Serbs." The US has further cemented its influence over Europe by including Hungary, Poland and the Czech Republic in NATO. The Kosova crisis, to repeat, is "another chance to show it alone is capable of calling the shots in the European Union's own backyard".

Brownstone: What evidence do you have for all this?

Caliban: Proof! 'The pro-war *Guardian* gave the game away...

Brownstone: So this is all a matter of secret plans, revealed by the *Guardian* through accidental indiscretion? But if the main issue at stake is the US's desire to impose its will on the European Union, why ever would the European Union capitalist classes — and their newspapers, like the *Guardian* — want to do anything but protest loudly?

Caliban: The *Guardian* gave the game away when it said: "NATO needs to be tested in its new guise and this conflict will do the job as well as any other." The US sees NATO as the key vehicle to impose its will across the world.

Varga: This is the classic Stalinist technique of using bitty quotes from "the other side", without context, using them to prove dark and improbable conspiracies, and "proving" the whole construction by an appeal to readers' general sense that the US must be up to no good! The classic of this sort is called *The Great Conspiracy Against Russia*. It was published in the USA in 1946. Of the two authors, Sawyers and Kahn, one was later revealed as a USSR secret police agent. Published with an introduction by US senator Claude Pepper, it told the story of Russia's recent history as established in the Moscow Trials of the old Bolshevik leaders in 1936, '37 and '38. Bukharin was a blond Machiavelli in a leather jacket, Trotsky with his "pudgy manicured hands", rehearsed his gestures before a mirror. The work was full of snippets of quotes, even from Trotsky — all to lend verisimilitude to enormous lies.

Caliban's politically one-sided and mendaciously selective intellectual shambles is like the staple fare of the western CPs in the high Stalinist Cold War period!

V

Brownstone: The most remarkable political product of what you say is the anti-Americanism: in the good old days, the European CPs would be pseudo-patriotic and anti-American to exploit "the contradictions of imperialism". Before the development in the 1960s of the US anti-Vietnam war movement, the cry in Europe, including Britain, was "Yankee bastards go home".

Varga: And we used to think that "the main enemy" is at home?

Brownstone: You are repeating the fundamental intellectual technique used by Stalinism. You separate the negative Marxist criticism of advanced capitalist society from the positive socialist programme and link it to an alien positive programme, reactionary and historically regressive – support for Serbia in Kosova.

Caliban: But national conflicts can only create suffering. "Every ruler in the region has played the nationalist card, and each time the people who have paid for it have been the ordinary Serbs, Croats, Albanians or Bosnian Muslims." "The Albanian people are spread across six states – Albania itself, Kosova, Montenegro, southern Serbia, Greece and Macedonia. They make up somewhere over a third of the two million people who live in Macedonia. They have demanded separation from Macedonia and to be part of Albania. The break-up of Macedonia would draw in neighbouring states. Bulgaria claims much of Macedonia. Any wider war would draw in the region's two biggest powers – Turkey and Greece."

Brownstone: So best tell the oppressed nations to shut up, endure the status quo, and wait for workers' unity? Here *Stop the War* shares basic political attitudes with NATO: valuing the status quo, the existing state borders, above the rights of oppressed nations like the Kosovars, who threaten to destabilise their own borders and others. It is an echo of what was said at the outset of bombing by one side of the NATO and British establishment – the more statesman-like, patrician, cold-blooded side. Denis Healy, for example. It is a very curious role for socialists to play!

Varga: But *Stop the War* could scarcely avoid playing it.

Brownstone: Elitism here is all-contaminating. *Stop the War* rejects the reports of murder and ethnic cleansing in Kosova. It minimises the then known facts of Serbian ethnic cleansing. It maximises the civilian casualties of NATO bombs. Those were a few dozen or at most a couple of hundred when *Stop the War* was written. The final total was 1,400 according to the Yugoslav government. *Stop the War* flames with rage about those hundreds of casualties, while about the attempted genocide of the Kosovars it is cool, sceptical, and philosophical.

Varga: Another very important point is slipped in obliquely and with admirable skill at the end of Chapter five of *Stop the War*. Philosophically, with the manner of objective historians, the authors throw this in: "Over the centuries the balance between Kosova's two populations has constantly shifted."

Brownstone: So you won't get too upset now, will you? Just another typically Balkan shuffling of the ethnic cards. This is ancient Illyria, sir, that is how things are done there.

Varga: It is important if an anti-war movement is to be built to develop a sense of fatalism, to present the ethnic cleansing of Kosova as already an irreversible fact of history and NATO bombing as only sterile revenge. "Albanians *used to* make up about 90% of the population of Kosovo, and Serbs 10%." The mass cleansing of Kosova is a *fait accompli*.

Brownstone: The rampaging, butchering "cleansers" do their work, and having done it move on... The ethnic cleanser's work is relentless as Fate and irreversible.

Then the basic political grievance against NATO turns out to be that they won't accept it! Instead of letting the Balkan conflicts take their regrettable-but-to-be-expected course, the devilish USA seized on one of them as a "chance" to strike a blow against the European Union!

Varga: For Caliban, the life of one of the members of the chosen Serb "übermensch" nation is worth very large numbers of the inferior, Albanian "untermensch" people. This is a shameless use of the double-standard or the lie-by-omission, a favourite war-propaganda technique of the Stalinists in war, Cold War and peace. The Kosovar Albanians come a poor second to the Serbs.

And why? Because everything comes second to "building the party" via "building the anti-war movement". At the National Union of Teachers conference, 2-5 April 1999, this priority was translated into the argument that the Albanian Kosovar entity was no more. Therefore, to concern ourselves with Kosova was futile. Our only concern should be that bloody NATO be given a bloody nose. *Workers' Liberty* supporter Patrick Murphy reported: "One of our comrades asked the SWP's most senior NUT person why they had insisted on dropping self-determination for Kosova from the motion. Up until this week, he assured her, it was their position to support Kosovar rights. However, that was now an abstraction: the Kosovars had been driven out; there was no Kosova to speak of and probably never would be" [WL55].

Caliban: We care about the Kosovars! In our pamphlet, we challenge the imperialists' good faith. "Who really cares for the refugees?... The government and the media use the suffering of Kosovar refugees as the excuse for their bombing." But Britain won't let refugees in! "As NATO bombs were launched on the Balkans" the Home Secretary tried to deport a Kosovar refugee. But "happily" the Appeal Court threw out the deportation order.

Brownstone: So, just as there is said to be more rejoicing in heaven over one sinner saved than over hordes of the steadily righteous, the authors of *Stop the War* show more concern for the plight of one Kosovar Albanian in Britain than two million in Kosova!

Caliban: The enemy is at home! What he does here is more important than what is done overseas. And what hypocrites the *Daily Mail* and the *Daily Star* are! Until recently they were boors, baiting Kosovar Albanian refugees – now they worry about the fate of Kosova's Albanian children! The *Mail* wants to let them in! "Disgustingly hypocritical!"

Brownstone: My enemy's enemy is never as bad as my enemy is; petty crimes of my enemy dwarf enormous crimes of my enemy's enemy.

Caliban: The enemy we can get at is the one at home!

Brownstone: Internationalism in the hands of political idiots becomes deranged parochialism!

Varga: Note the skilful demagogue's trick of inflating the less important details to evade the big things – here, the fate of a comparatively small number of refugees in Britain gives them more scandal and generates more indignation than what is happening to two million in Kosova.

Brownstone: The good old slogan of Liebknecht and Luxemburg, "The main enemy is at home", is used to justify shameless apologetics for terrible things far away and to camouflage the inverted chauvinism of siding with Milosevic and wanting him to win even when it means death for an unknown number of Albanian Kosovars.

Caliban: The refugees in Britain are something we can rouse people on – without helping NATO imperialism! The people who let themselves be lined up behind NATO out of sympathy with Albanians should confine themselves to the Albanians here at home!

Varga: Softies and "humanitarians" are a problem in making "the case against the war". All you can do is try to give them a proper sense of perspective on Kosova. *Stop the War* has a boxed-off section specifically written for softies. "Nobody could fail to be moved by the suffering of the refugees fleeing Kosova."

Brownstone: Nobody but the authors of *Stop the War*! In fact, this, halfway into the pamphlet, is the first definite reference in the pamphlet to the fact that Serbia is doing anything out of order in Kosova, or that the war involves anything but the US gratuitously using "a chance" to show Europe who's boss. Even here the pamphlet gives no indication of who (the Serbian state) has been driving Kosovars to become refugees. This fact will be left to the last page of the pamphlet, when the reader will be suitably prepared to accept that it is of secondary significance.

Caliban: "Their fate is tragically similar to many others in a world where economic crisis and war are commonplace."

Brownstone: Socialists must be resigned and fatalistic about such things and denounce the bourgeoisie which for its own reasons is less resigned, as the only enemy! Wait until socialism changes everything!

Caliban: "In the same week that every newspaper produced graphic pictures of the Kosovans' torment, around 200,000 refugees were driven from their homes in Angola."

Brownstone: NATO is not concerned about Africans, therefore, we, the readers of *Stop the War*, should not care about Kosova Albanians!

Varga: The technique here is to use general cosmopolitan guilt to defocus and numb concern about Kosova. Two million? Pah! What is that in the great sea of suffering under capitalism? If the Kosovar Albanians had any decency or feelings of solidarity with the people of the Third World they would spurn NATO's help! If they were anti-imperialist they would want Serbia to win.

Caliban: Of course you can't expect such people to have an overview: but we are not limited to the outlook of the unfortunate Albanians.

Brownstone: No — you are free to adopt the outlook of Serb colonial-imperialists in the name of abstract anti-imperialism!

Varga: Tact is everything here. Do not give even approximate figures for Kosova. The population of Pristina (200,000) is of course well known. But that was NATO bombs, remember? Unavoidably, a picture of Kosova is slowly being built up. But that can be controlled. The reader can, so to speak, be walked backwards through Hell, becoming gradually more aware of where she is in the flickering light. *Stop the War* doles out bits of truth about the broader picture as she is backed past it.

The beauty of the walking backwards technique is that every additional detail can be made to seem its opposite. You are given a late-in-the-pamphlet firm statement about Kosovar Albanian suffering — only to be told, having been softened up, that it is commonplace in this hell-ridden capitalist world. You are not to worry too much about it or you will fall for "NATO" propaganda and double standards.

The proper socialist attitude here is to be blasé and fatalistic. Revolutionary socialists must not let themselves get angry. A numb holier-than-them smugness about capitalism and its "commonplace" crises, crimes and wars is better!

Caliban: That way you won't play into anyone's hands. *Stop the War* has the courage to fight the one-sidedness, distortion, narrow-minded manipulation, and dishonesty of the British press and politicians...

Varga: ...with their own weapons. For why should we leave the best tunes for the devil to play? The Stalinists understood that! The psychology here is that socialists must compete with the bourgeoisie not by pitting truth against lies and half-lies, but by constructing a better "story" using lies and half-truths where that will help the good work.

VI

Caliban: We do not support Milosevic. We support the opposition in Serbia. What scares Milosevic and all the other rulers is the sort of united movement that was seen in the 1980s, where workers of all nationalities begin to direct their anger at their rulers and not each other.

Brownstone: There were no chauvinists among the strikers? If national and communal conflicts would oblige us by vanishing, we could have a good trade union struggle? Yet we have, even now, some good trade union struggles. Without an agreed political solution, they have never solved anything.

Caliban: They are a start!

Brownstone: Marxists do not just hope for that "start" to develop into political action capable of changing society. We put forward a programme. What is yours for the national conflicts in the Balkans? You side with the oppressors against the oppressed!

Caliban: We side against the great worldwide oppressor!

Brownstone: Blind negativism! As part of it you side with the local oppressor! You pretend to think that you are living up to the socialist principle that you side with the oppressed against the oppressor. In fact, what guides you is not who you side with, but who you side against. But there is no such thing as a revolutionary politics that is purely negative. Serbia was not fighting for liberation from colonial enslavement, or for anything but the right to be a colonial oppressor of the worst kind. Yet you said: Let Milosevic have his way in Kosova — for fear of worse. You apologised for swinishness, and made arguments for submitting to it on the grounds that to act against it would "provoke" (or, in old CP parlance, "play into the hands of") something worse. Settle for this horror because — you say! — it is the lesser horror! After all, what was Kosova? For you, Kosova was only a word — not two million people faced with death or displacement. An inconvenient word.

Caliban: In 1991 and 1996 Milosevic's position was threatened by the opposition. In March 1991 tens of thousands of students and workers protested on the streets of Belgrade — against government repression and censorship. At its height, a quarter of a million occupied Belgrade city centre and brought the city to a halt for five days. They chanted "Slobo must go".

Brownstone: A central part of the real picture is suppressed. Some reports say that the anti-Milosevic demonstrations also called for action against the Kosovar Albanians! Laura Silber's reports for instance. The Serb opposition is awash with rancid chauvinism – a fact *Stop the War* will slip in later on, as a mere reservation.

But in any case the Serb opposition could not, even if it wanted to, act in time to make a difference to the Kosovars!

Caliban: Your problem is that you have no faith in the Serbian working class!

Brownstone: Your problem is that you are a self-deceiving hypocrite! And an irresponsible one. Marxists advocate unity between the workers of the oppressed and oppressing nations on the basis of a programme of consistent democracy – that is, of securing the interests of the oppressed. Not *Stop the War*. You do not mention the Kosovar workers' action in 1991 – stay-down-the-mine strikes in defence of Kosovar autonomy within a federal Yugoslavia. Or the moving and inspiring solidarity of the employed Kosovars with the unemployed, victimised by Milosevic – donating a proportion of their incomes to support others. Even your focus on working-class action is selective.

Varga: This selectivity, too, requires strong nerves and rigid self-control against sentimentality and squeamishness and inconvenient universalising tendencies. The working class of an oppressed nation "allied to imperialism" is not the same as the working class of an oppressor nation! For Caliban, the Kosovars have become part of a "bad people", a people made bad because of their place in the "international balance of forces". They are so lacking in anti-imperialist feeling that they accept imperialist help to fight off the assault of a vastly stronger power, their colonial masters, intent on genocide!

Caliban: Tanks and troops crushed the opposition. Milosevic feared being toppled by revolution, like Ceaucescu in 1989. Six hundred demonstrators had to be released from jail.

Brownstone: Why do you paint a picture of recent past opposition in the Serbian state that ignores the Kosovar Albanian question and the opposition's attitude to it?

Caliban: Because we have our priorities right! True, the main nationalist leader was Vuk Draskovic, who, "disastrously", was a worse nationalist than Milosevic himself. But Milosevic also faced workers' opposition: "Labour unrest is the greatest threat to the Serbian government," wrote Laura Silber in the *Financial Times*.

Brownstone: That might be true. And the politics of the labour unrest? Unless the "restless" workers accepted a class, an internationalist, a consistently democratic programme, what immediate difference would their action, or their victory, make to the Kosovar Albanians? This is a crazily Serb-centred approach: the Albanians must wait, or, as things were when *Stop the War* was written, flee or die.

Caliban: "Even as late as spring 1991, as Yugoslavia's bloody war got under way, some 700,000 workers went on strike in Serbia to demand higher wages."

Brownstone: And in Kosova workers went on strike for political reasons against the abolition of Kosovar autonomy!

Caliban: "But, tragically, there was no socialist leadership which could argue to unite workers' anger over living conditions and wages with opposition to nationalism."

Brownstone: Opposition to nationalism? To nationalism, yes. But not, if the "socialist leaders" are Marxists, to national rights! Consistent democracy, including the right of self-determination for nations, is always a part of our basic programme. The striking Serb workers could not be taken forward politically to working-class politics unless they would accept such an approach to Yugoslav national conflicts. The workers of the different nations – for example, of Serbia and Kosova, both of whom had strikes at this time – could not be united against nationalism except on the basis of a democratic, working-class programme on the national question, one that proposed a viable framework for mutual accommodation and co-existence.

Your whole approach depends on the idea that there were no real national grievances, only spurious conflicts generated by bad politicians and imperialist impositions. But there were real and pressing issues of national rights – and not only for the Albanians! Your approach is boneheaded sectarian socialism – in the service of Serb chauvinism!

Caliban: "In 1993, at the height of nationalist frenzy, there were strikes in Serbia and Croatia", and anti-war demos in Belgrade. "Milosevic was nearly toppled again in 1996. Mass protests in Serbia took place every day for 100 days from November."

Brownstone: In terms of the war and the Kosovar Albanians, what is the point of all this?

129

The Kosovar Albanians must wait for the Serbs? They must wait – under the ground or across the borders – for the Serbian opposition to win and then for the victors to outgrow their nationalism and chauvinism? For now, they must die or let themselves be driven out? This is to let anti-NATOism drive you to the point of the most extreme Serb chauvinism and reaction! The Albanians must gladly die rather than fight and risk destabilising the Balkans. They must die rather than form an alliance with NATO against Serbia to avoid Kosovar Albanian extirpation; die rather than bring NATO's bombs raining down on Serbia. They must die for... Serbia. The addle-headed anti-nationalists turn into vicarious Serbian chauvinists!

You claim that "the rulers of each part of Yugoslavia turned to ethnic rabble-rousing in an effort to divert... class feeling into scapegoating". But such lordly even-handedness is, like all even-handed blanket condemnations of nationalism, back-handed support for the dominant nation, in this case, Serbia. And how do you explain that every "part of Yugoslavia" did allow itself to be turned into "ethnic rabble"? Did Stalinism have anything to do with it?

Caliban: In the 1950s and 60s Yugoslavia "was regarded as a stable and essentially peaceful part of Europe". After those decades of harmony, what happened in the late 1980s and the 1990s was "the result of economic crisis and of manoeuvres by outside powers and local rulers".

Brownstone: In the fight against imperialism, we must not let the question of Stalinism distract us. *Stop the War's* "history" of modern Yugoslavia has the distinction of mentioning Stalinism only obliquely, and of implicitly praising it.

Varga: Here there is a profound difficulty. The national question is a real, autonomous force. In old-style pre-Stalinist Marxism, Marxists were always concerned to put forward a programme of consistent democracy on this question – the right of self-determination without regard or respect for existing state boundaries. But any of that here will derail the necessary simplicities. Remember the line: the US has just seized on Kosova, a terrible tragedy but one "tragically similar to many others in a world where economic crisis and war are commonplace", indeed a routine one by Balkan standards, to show off its might. We need a story about the Balkans that dispenses with the national question!

Caliban: Economic crisis led "Yugoslav leaders" to encourage outside economic investment. Worse crisis. The IMF dictated cuts. "Yugoslavia was being torn apart by deep crises imposed by the market, and intensified by the bankers." But Yugoslavia was not yet torn apart. Workers responded by attacking "their own bosses". 365,000 workers took part in 1,570 strikes in 1987; there were enormous demonstrations in Belgrade the next year. Four thousand Serb and Croat factory workers marched seven miles in protest at an International Monetary Fund austerity diktat. They largely ignored a small group of Serb nationalists calling for the blood of Albanians.

Varga: This selection of facts is meant to suggest that on the national-democracy front, at least, things had been fine under Tito Stalinism. In fact it proves nothing. It is streamlined and simplified. It lacks both the political and historical dimensions and as we will see, misrepresents the dynamic of things for reasons of an *a priori* political "line". But it seems to provide a barebones "economic-analysis" "Marxist" explanation – and that is what matters here. For *Stop the War*, the key point to get across is that the national question in Yugoslavia is not something real, autonomous.

Brownstone: The analysis is narrowly economistic and therefore misleading. Yes, the strike is the elemental form of working-class action. To relate to workers in such conflicts, even the tiniest, is the beginning of wisdom for socialists. Those socialists who develop a hoity-toity attitude – "we are political, not 'economistic'; we are on a higher plane" – eviscerate themselves. Yet this elemental form of class struggle can be allied to many ideologies – from Peronism to Catholicism to every sort of nationalism. Politics is decisive. *Stop the War* fades out the dynamic national question in Yugoslavia. And with remarkable fortitude and restraint, you fade out strikes and other working-class actions in Kosova – some of the most significant labour action in former Yugoslavia!

Caliban: That proves we are not economists! We focus only on such strikes as serve our broader case! The Kosovar Albanian strikes were tainted by nationalism!

Brownstone: They were the highest form of industrial-political action in ex-Yugoslavia – and for a progressive and democratic cause, against colonial oppression.

Varga: This looks like an internationalist ideal realised – until bad men and IMF economics destroyed it! But if it both idealises Stalinist Yugoslavia and obliterates history, then that is good and desirable for *Stop the War's* immediate objectives. For *Stop the War*, it is better to present Stalinist Yugoslavia as a society free of ethnic tensions and conflicts – in fact, to build on official Titoite ideology – in order to blame outsiders, namely the the IMF and NATO.

VII

Caliban: Then the "banker turned politician Milosevic stepped in to divert the anger away from the government by whipping up hatred against Albanians living in Serb-run Kosovo... Milosevic put forward a simple answer to the economic crisis brought about by the madness of the market – blame the Albanians."

Brownstone: Yes, Milosevic used Serb chauvinism. But you present a conspiracy theory of national and ethnic division. The IMF (and later Germany, by recognising Croatian independence) introduce evil from outside. Nationalism "inside" is an artificial thing – nothing but a tool for demagogues and conspirators to resort to. Why those demagogues should succeed is not explained, other than by the absence of "socialist leadership".

The basic fact of the late 1980s was a Serb-chauvinist offensive for Serbian dominance in Yugoslavia. There had been an upsurge of Croatian nationalism at the beginning of the 1970s, but Serb nationalism was later the catalyst for all the other nationalisms that destroyed Yugoslavia. The Yugoslav army and state apparatus became, effectively, a tool of the Serbian republic within Yugoslavia. That gave the whole process its dynamic. That was the proximate cause of the break up of Yugoslavia. Without Serbia's drive for dominance, the nationalisms of the other Yugoslav nations would not have made the sort of patent sense that led 90% of Croatians to vote for secession in 1991.

Caliban: No. Nationalism was only a demagogic tool of the bosses. "Milosevic was not alone in such vile tactics. His mirror image in Croatia was Franjo Tudjman. Their scapegoating led to horrific conflict."

Varga: Don't blame Milosevic too much! Others were as bad! We have walked backwards into new facts grudgingly doled-out, but they have been skilfully skewed out of their own perspective and into that of the makers of "the case against the war".

Caliban: "The people of the various ethnic groups did not live separately from each other, each in one republic or region. There was a large Serbian minority in Croatia as well as Bosnia. Croats also lived in Bosnia. Albanians lived in Serbia and so on."

Brownstone: Here the fact that Albanians lived in Serbia mainly as a compact 90% population of a distinct region – an internal colony! – is hidden. Why? To have a fairy tale of an ideal – Tito Stalinist – Yugoslav past!

Caliban: "When the rulers of each republic talked about Croatia for the Croats or Serbia for the Serbs, it inevitably led towards violence and ethnic cleansing."

Brownstone: False abstract symmetry that is concretely very pro-Serbian! It was Serbian nationalism that destabilised Yugoslavia.

Varga: Having now, by eliminating hard facts and story-cluttering detail, and cutting out anything that would contradict the "line" and propagandist intention; having misrepresented the dynamic with the unmistakable purpose of minimising Milosevic's responsibility, we can get down to some hard facts – selected facts.

Caliban: "When Tudjman's supporters attacked Serbs at Borovo Selo, Serbia/Milosevic unleashed his Chetniks (right-wing monarchist Serbs) to attack Croats."

Brownstone: Ah, who attacked first? Who fired the first shot? Remember, Tudjman is worse than Milosevic.

Caliban: "When war developed..."

Brownstone: "Developed?" Who waged war? For what purposes? *Stop the War* strives to give the impression, without flatly stating it, that Croatia attacked Serbia. In fact, both Slovenia and Croatia voted overwhelmingly for independence, and Milosevic then attacked both nations to try to maintain Serbian domination over them.

Caliban: "When war developed in the early 1990s, the US and Britain backed Croatia against Serbia. They were supporting the most right-wing government in Europe since the rule of the fascist General Franco in Spain!"

Varga: This is a masterly touch! Switch focus from the issue – the national conflict – to something not relevant, (unless the argument is that somehow Serbia made war on Croatia in order to defeat Tudjman's right-wing politics!) What is right-wing where, as in Serbia,

Stalinist "red" and nationalistic-fascistic brown intermingle? In fact this is a Stalinist definition of right-wing.

Brownstone: Just as for decades, the USSR was taken to define the "left", here Serbia is. If Milosevic is left, it is because of his and Yugoslavia's greater residue of Stalinism.

Caliban: The West made Tudjman the "good guy", when the "nationalistic frenzy of Serbia and Croatia boiled over into war, carving Bosnia up in 1992".

Brownstone: No mention of the fact that the Bosnian war was initiated and shaped by a Serbian drive to conquer and "ethnically cleanse" as much territory as possible for a "Greater Serbia" — or of the fact that the West then maintained an arms embargo against the Serb-beleaguered Bosnian government.

Caliban: "Tudjman strengthened his position after four years of war because he had the West's backing and NATO launched air strikes on Serb armies. Right-wing Serbs had killed Croats and Bosnian Muslims..."

Brownstone: Unconnected to Milosevic, who, we have been told, is not as right-wing as Tudjman, and assuredly "not a fascist"? In fact the wars for a Greater Serbia were organised and directed by Milosevic's government.

Caliban: "Right-wing Serbs had killed Croats and Bosnian Muslims, most notoriously at Srebrenica. But it was Tudjman who went on to carry out the greatest ethnic cleansing of the war in ex-Yugoslavia. Backed by Western firepower, he ordered an assault on the Serbs of the Krajina region of Croatia. Some 200,000 Serbs fled."

Brownstone: In fact, there were many more Bosniac and Croat refugees from Serbian terror in Bosnia. But what follows from the justified condemnation of Tudjman? That it is Milosevic's turn now in Kosova? That is how things are in the Balkans... But, support Milosevic?

Varga: Again, note the strong nerves needed for this sort of work. Indignation at 200,000 expelled four years ago — displayed in the service of those who, as the authors write, are engaged in trying to drive out those of the two million Kosovar Albanians that they will not kill.

Caliban: "The wars in ex-Yugoslavia were terrible. But no side had clean hands."

Varga: Note the technique: *Stop the War* has "made the case against" all but Milosevic, and that is a "clever" negative way to make a case for Milosevic.

There is nothing quite so useful in skirting over difficulties as the truism. "Serbian, Croatian and Muslim leaders [were] all out to use the war in their own interests." The judgement is both banal and unfair to the Bosnia Muslim leaders, but immensely useful in making the pro-Milosevic case "against the war". Everybody was equally bad, and so poor Milosevic should not be singled out.

Caliban: "The West excused its intervention as providing protection for the Bosnian Muslims."

Brownstone: In fact, the UN and particularly Britain helped Milosevic against the Muslims. *Stop the War*'s Great Satan, the USA, was then somewhat at odds with the countries like Britain, who were keenly colluding — under the UN flag — with Milosevic.

Varga: *That* cannot be *Stop the War's* line! This "case against the war" must exonerate Milosevic by condemning others as being as bad or worse. The Bosnian Muslims have to be bad too.

Caliban: "Their leader, Alia Izetbegovic, was equally guilty of whipping up nationalism during the war. That encouraged atrocities like the murder of hundreds of Serb civilians in Sarajevo by Muslim paramilitaries."

Brownstone: As history this is grossly unfair. It is a remnant of the SWP's scandalous indifference and neutrality during the Bosnian war.

Caliban: History? It is the making of current history that interests the SWP!

Brownstone: As the Stalinist professor said: what is history but current politics and organisational needs read backwards?

Varga: The root here is blindness to national democracy and to national rights. The pretence that Stalinism solved "the Balkan problem" merges with the elitist idea that things like nationalism and religious conflicts are just the work of "bad men" who have their way in the absence of a "socialist leadership", a good counter-elite, which can magic such things away by focusing on wage struggles.

A Serb nationalist makes use of the SWP's placard on a "Stop the War" demonstration

Caliban: "Every ruler in the region has played the nationalist card and each time the people who have paid for it have been the ordinary Serbs, Croats, Albanians, or Bosnian Muslims."

Varga: A plague on all their houses!

Brownstone: Except where one house is in conflict with the US or NATO, the "Great Satan"! Then you enlist on Milosevic's side! Sectarianism towards the national question turns, at the touch of US/NATO intervention, into the most shameless apologetics for Serb chauvinism and propaganda on behalf of those who are attempting genocide!

VIII

Varga: No account of the Balkans now can do without some interpretation of Balkan history. The problem for *Stop the War* is how to avoid letting inconvenient questions get an airing during this process, like the history of Serbian imperialism, or the real historical foundations of the national conflicts. *Stop the War* provides a chapter on "How past interventions sowed the seeds of bloodshed". It cannot be a history lesson. It must be a tendentious pretend-naïve quick tour. Blame "outside" intervention for everything!

Caliban: "As today, at each stage [the great powers] have claimed to be standing up for the rights of smaller nations in the region."

Brownstone: So that shows that standing up for smaller nations is a bad idea? But has there ever been an "intervention" whose immediate objective (for NATO's own reasons, certainly) has been to stop the destruction of almost the entire population of a distinct national and geographical entity? Has there been anything even remotely like it?

Caliban: "Every intervention has brought misery, creating new divisions between ordinary people."

Brownstone: Creating? The crime of the "interventionists" has been to drive the state borders through the living national entities. This made the national divisions more poisonous, but did not create them or the difficulty created by the intricate interlacing of the Balkan peoples.

Varga: Caliban strips the "ordinary" people of their national-ethnic identities and reduces them to blank pages on which either bad or good people write their messages.

Caliban: "Britain backed the seizure of Kosovo and the formation of the Kingdom of the Serbs, Croats and Slovenes in 1919-20."

Brownstone: Your date is wrong. The Serbs seized Kosova in 1913 and won it back as part of the victor camp in 1918-19.

Varga: "The seizure of..." Who did the seizing? Serbia. And Trotsky rightly called it an act of Serbian imperialism.

Brownstone: For all its "anti-imperialism", this is an ultra-elitist, metropolitan-centric way of portraying the world.

On the one hand the big powers are responsible for everything; on the other, when for once in a blue moon they act to make horrors like Milosevic's less horrid, nothing matters but to oppose them. This writes the smaller peoples out of history.

Caliban: In World War Two "fascist Ustashe forces in Croatia systematically killed Serbs and Jews".

Brownstone: True. But why isn't there any account of the immediately more relevant bloody Serb reconquest of Kosova in 1945, which, for bloodshed and repression of the "natives", rivalled the French re-establishment of authority in Algeria at the same time?

Caliban: But while the "Chetniks turned on Croats... a communist – Tito, who was half Croat and half Serb – succeeded in building a multi-ethnic anti-Nazi movement".

Brownstone: A communist! At last! Communist here is like "revolutionary" – it is good. But Tito presided over the reconquest of Kosova and its repression for more than two decades!

Varga: Tito was of Croat-Slovene parentage.

Caliban: We tell the truth about Tito! He "used the language of socialism, but maintained a strict regime of state control, with its own privileged ruling class".

Brownstone: Now, having backed two-thirds of the way through the pamphlet, we get, hidden away as a bullet point fact in a chapter about outside intervention, one of the central facts of the present conflict. Tito "granted Kosovan Albanians certain national rights".

Varga: Yes, don't be too precise. It limits what you can then say!

Caliban: "Milosevic reversed this as he drove to succeed Tito."

Varga: Evade the whole framework of national reality by blaming Milosevic's personal ambition! In fact, he latched on to an erupting movement of Serb chauvinism.

Caliban: However, "the West's intervention in the Balkans during the 1990s made the situation worse".

Brownstone: Yes – by collusion or quasi-collusion with Milosevic in Bosnia.

Caliban: No. "[The West] enshrined the idea that different ethnic groups who have often lived side by side now have to be forced to live apart, policed by NATO forces."

Brownstone: As distinct from "being forced" to live together or being butchered? Who is the undefined agent: who wants to force them? Whose policy did the West endorse? The role of Serbian imperialism is buried here. So is the underlying role of Titoist national policy.

Caliban: "For a century, revolutionary socialists have put forward the alternative of workers' unity in the Balkans across national boundaries."

Varga: Yes, but how? On the basis of what solution to the long-festered national antagonisms? What are the details? For tradition and "authority". *Stop the War* goes through the semblance of invoking Trotsky's pre-World War One writings on the Balkans, where he was a war correspondent in 1912-13.

Caliban: Trotsky wrote that "European diplomacy... manufactured the states that today occupy the Balkan peninsula... to convert the national diversity of the region into a regular mêlée of petty states... The new boundary lines have been drawn across the living bodies of nations... Every one of the Balkan states now includes within its borders a compact minority that is hostile to it. Such are the results of the work carried out by the capitalist governments."

Brownstone: What was Trotsky's programme on the national question? What does this quotation say about *Stop the War*'s presentation of nationalism as whipped up by bad men? For

Trotsky it is a result of national oppression inherent in the existing states.

Varga: In fact this quotation from Trotsky is used only to give authority to *Stop the War's* description of "the West's" effect on the local peoples and their states. "Trotsky's description of the West's role has come true again and again." All outside interference ("the West") is here conflated to make maximum use for today of Trotsky's old condemnations of Austro-Hungary and Russia. It is a way of sinking the concrete truth of the present and of recent history into earlier history and into abstract historical generalisations.

Brownstone: And in what way, from the point of view of over 90% of the people of Kosova, is Serbian rule less "outside intervention" than NATO's? Given that NATO's action had Kosovar Albanian backing, it was the least "outside" of the outside interventions.

Caliban: They have no right to ally with imperialism!

Brownstone: Who has a better right to define what they see as imperialist, or not, than the Kosovar Albanians themselves?

Caliban: "When the First World War broke out, the Serbian revolutionary Lapcevic stood up in the rabidly pro-war Serbian parliament and denounced the fighting. He said that Serbia 'must cease to be a tool of the Great Powers and pursue instead the goal of a Balkan social-ist federation'. He was against the oppression of the all the Balkan peoples, but he argued that to concentrate solely on the national question without regard to the wider issues of imperial-ism and its wars would lead to disaster."

Brownstone: The key word here is "solely". In fact, the programme adopted by the Balkan socialists in 1910 regarded the creation of a consistent democracy as the solution to the national imbroglios as an irreplaceable tool for making international working class unity pos-sible.

Caliban: The Communist International's 1920 manifesto declared that in the Balkans: "Imperialism has created a series of smaller national states. It rules them through banks and monopolies and condemns them to unbearable economic and national hardship, endless con-flicts and bloody collisions." "The Bulgarian revolutionary Kabakchiev argued that, although there were over one million Bulgarians split up between other states and divided off from Bulgaria by imperialism, it was necessary to go beyond nationalism."

Brownstone: Yes, but how? By solving the national question democratically!

Caliban: "The only way out is a Balkan socialist revolution. The great powers have ripped the region apart and prepared the ground for mass murder and terror. Revolutionaries have been the voice of sanity, of friendship across boundaries and of class unity."

Varga: The equivalent of that recently has been the repeated support by many big powers, including Britain and specifically on the Kosova question, for Milosevic as the "strong man" to keep the area quiet for capitalism. It is the Dayton accord, and the Rambouillet formula's denial of independence to Kosovar Albanians. But from Caliban, all that − the basic, long-term political course of the big powers − attracts no criticism. His anger is directed exclu-sively against a subordinate and anomalous phase of big-power policy − the 1999 attempt to coerce Milosevic − and thus, more sharply, against the Kosovars who dared to disrupt the big-power settlement and in self-defence and in pursuit of their national rights.

Brownstone: Rambouillet, however, was a great deal preferable to Milosevic's attempt to clear Kosova of its population! *Stop the War's* position is to replace Dayton and Rambouillet not with a democratic, national, anti-colonialist regime but with Serb freedom to commit genocide. Without working-class unity, there will be no Balkan socialist revolution; and with-out a consistently democratic programme on the national question, there will be no working-class unity.

Varga: *Stop the War* conflates the socialist level with the democratic − "socialism is the answer to the national question" − in such a way as to eliminate the democratic basis of working-class unity. And that, in turn, eliminates the possibility of working-class socialism! Their own sectist shadow gets in their light.

Brownstone: Worse. The future socialist unity of the peoples is counterposed to the defence, or even self-defence, of the oppressed and those facing extermination now!

Caliban: "Serbians cannot be free for as long as their country oppresses Kosovo. Kosovo cannot be free if it becomes a pawn in NATO's game and its liberation [sic] is taken up cyn-ically by the US, Britain and the rest."

Brownstone: Very impartial and foreseeing and balanced! You do not mention the more obvious and urgent fact that Kosova cannot be free – or even exist as a nation – unless Serbian genocide is stopped.

Caliban: Since when has an imperialist power helped oppressed people other than when it hopes to use them as pawns?

Brownstone: Since when have socialists refused to support national liberation movements because they had such connections? For example, German imperialism helped Irish nationalist revolutionaries during World War One. It helped Lenin get to Russia in 1917. The Kosovar Albanians are not pawns being used as an excuse by the USA to enslave Serbs and others in the region.

You state blandly that "Kosovo cannot be free if... its liberation is taken up cynically by the US, Britain and the rest". What do such words mean from people who fanatically resisted all attempts to get the "peace movement" you controlled to include calls for Kosovar rights and getting Serbian troops out of Kosova? They mean something different from a routine advocacy of political independence. They mean, for you, that the Kosovars do not deserve to be free, or even to live, "if their liberation is taken up cynically by the US, Britain and the rest". You wind up with an unmistakable though unvoiced demand that Kosovar Albanians must sacrifice themselves to stopping the European Union from being intimidated by the USA!

Caliban: "Serbians have to support the right of Kosovar Albanians to self-determination, to decide their own future, and Kosovar Albanians have to be for harmony with Serbia and for an end to ethnic tensions. Their unity and respect for each other's national rights are the only way forward to lasting peace and progress."

Brownstone: Balance and impartiality again! That could have been written 10 years, or fifty years ago, with any peoples you like substituted for Serbs and Albanians. What about the situation now, the issues and choices now? You have not raised – indeed, you have fought against raising – any proposal about Kosovar Albanian rights. You oppose the call for the genocidal Serb army to get out of Kosova. Your "balanced" statement is the equivalent of arguing around 1944 that the onus was on the European Jews to work for harmony with "Germans". You blame the Kosovar Albanian victims "equally" with their Serbian murderers and would-be murderers.

IX

Varga: Note the walking backwards technique again. Now, on page 22, it has been made "safe" to refer to self-determination for Kosova. Self-determination is a desirable element in the socialist future – just as friendship and harmony across borders in general is – but for now the lack of self-determination for the Kosovars is only one of countless problems in the Balkans, all ultimately due to big-power machinations. It does not have sufficient importance or relevance to imply any sympathy with the Kosova Liberation Army fighting for self-determination.

The pamphlet has a boxed-off section, "Who are the Kosova Liberation Army?" First, we get something resembling the truth. The KLA began in the mid 1990s. Before that, "most Kosovar Albanians had responded to their position as second class citizens by backing the non-violent movement led by Ibrahim Rugova".

Brownstone: Except that "second class citizens" is a prettification of Serb persecution in Kosova for the previous decade – let alone of the attempted extermination under way as *Stop the War* was written.

Varga: Then this: "But the West ignored their plight. The US-backed Dayton Agreement of 1995 declared Kosovo an integral part of Serbia."

Brownstone: Exactly like *Stop the War* – for now, as distinct from a future when there will be few if any Albanians left in Kosova, for which *Stop the War* bravely advocates future "self-determination".

Varga: So at Dayton, the big powers should have insisted on Kosovar rights? Or is *Stop the War's* grievance that the big powers now depart from Dayton by insisting (at Rambouillet) on autonomy for the Kosovars within Serbia and on the Kosovars' right not be killed and driven out?

If NATO's "concern" for Kosova were a mask for a drive to enslave Serbia, then this exposure of their inconsistency and hypocrisy could help establish that fact. But here the "exposure" is used to disqualify the NATO powers from playing any other role in Kosova than to leave Milosevic to carry through the Serbian-chauvinist logic of Dayton and to mask the truth about what Serbian imperialists are doing in Kosova.

Caliban: "Milosevic responded [to Kosovar guerrilla action] just as US backed governments responded to similar movements in countries like Turkey – with 'search-and-destroy' military operation that killed civilians."

Varga: Ah, yes, so many people accept such things as normal. Why get excited over the Kosovar Albanians?

Brownstone: But what do socialists say about Turkey's repression of the Kurds, for example? We support the Kurdish resistance, despite its bad politics. All this has only one possible sense to it – NATO should be consistently swinish; it has no business, no right, to complicate the simple schemata of certain socialists able to see only the heaviest blacks and the cleanest whites.

Varga: Now we get a skilful – and even gleeful – twist in the use of the "objective or hostile authority" or eyewitness. Foreign Secretary Robin Cook "denounced the KLA as 'terrorists'". Madeleine Albright "hinted" at bombing the KLA too.

Brownstone: And if they had? What would Caliban's line be then? According to the method employed so far in *Stop the War*, our concern is such questions is only to detect what the interests and policy of "imperialism" is, and then invert them. The principle that all that matters is the interests and policy of imperialism is exactly like the attitude of the great capitalist states to Kosova, or to massacres in East Timor or Africa – only the conclusions are inverted.

Caliban: "They refused to support Kosovar independence even as the bombing began."

Brownstone: Like *Stop the War* – which, in addition, makes propaganda for Serbia against NATO and against the Kosovar Albanians!

Varga: Note this brilliant tactical zigzag to the "left". Rambouillet stipulates autonomy for Kosova under Serb overlordship. NATO started bombing in order to impose that settlement. *Stop the War* advocates – no other conclusion follows from what it says – giving Milosevic a free hand to exterminate Kosovars – and at the same time criticises Rambouillet and NATO for advocating less than full independence for Kosova! Maybe that shrewd thrust will inhibit a few lefts who will think that the distance between autonomy and independence is greater and more important than the distance between autonomy and massacre!

Brownstone: And if NATO had supported Kosova Albanian independence? Wouldn't the destabilisation of the region which you fear, and they fear, perhaps have been the result? Would *Stop the War* denounce them for it? Is the suggestion here that "even" the NATO bombers don't back the KLA programme? Or conversely that NATO should support "independence? In which case, shouldn't *Stop the War*?

Caliban: "This has not, however, stopped the KLA continuing to look to the US. It is in danger of becoming the plaything of the NATO big powers in ways that can only harm Albanian and Serbian workers and peasants alike."

Varga: You must play every angle you can imagine! The KLA are bad because they are "terrorists" (as we know on the authority of Robin Cook and Madeleine Albright's condemnations of them), and also because they have welcomed Cook's and Albright's assistance to save their people from annihilation.

Here we have the immensely variable and useful technique of using prefabricated, imprecise words – "plaything", without indicating what "game" is being "played" – reinforced in iron by determination to obscure and hide what is actually going on.

Brownstone: How could the Albanian workers and peasants in Kosova be harmed by the KLA's alliance with NATO worse than by being subjected to mass killing and displacement? What harm compared to what Serbia is doing to the Kosovar Albanians can conceivably come to the Serb people from it? What exactly are the KLA and the Kosovars, fighting for their very existence, obliged to do to serve the interests of Serbian workers and peasants, the overwhelming majority of whom are with Milosevic for now? Sacrifice themselves? Commit altruistic suicide for the greater good of anti-imperialism (and the prosperity of Serb imperialism)?

Varga: *Stop the War* quotes a strikingly naïve assertion from *Tribune* that no Serb civilians have been killed by the KLA. Considering the reality of ethnic conflict and ingrained, hate-clogged nationalism, that would indeed be remarkable. "This is simply not true", insists *Stop the War*, thereby reinforcing an impression of morally-upright concern for truth in every detail.

Brownstone: The same schoolmasterly scruples and heroic anti-imperialist energy that served so well in *Stop the War*'s exhaustingly severe and righteous discussion of the Holocaust!

Caliban: "Killing Serbs has been part of the KLA's guerrilla strategy."

Brownstone: Killing Serbs? Soldiers? Paramilitaries? Police? How could it not be? And, in an ethnic conflict like this, how could it not be Serb civilians too?

Varga: That is the nature of such things. It is almost always part of national liberation movements.

Brownstone: From people here engaged in a propaganda war against the Kosovar Albanians on behalf of the state organising and fomenting mass murder and mass displacement, isn't this to risk looking simply obscene?

Caliban: The KLA has "targeted Serbian security forces, but it has also attacked civilians by throwing grenades into Serb cafés".

Varga: You see? Milosevic may have "horrible policies", but the KLA − an army of the 90% majority people in Serbia's colony − are at least as bad. How can you defend the Kosovars, even from genocide, if they do such things?

Brownstone: Of course, chauvinism and murder beget chauvinism and murder in communal conflict. If the absence of such horrors were a precondition, then we would never have supported any national liberation movement anywhere, ever! Socialists should judge the overall picture; and judge it politically. Decisive for socialists, democrats and consistent anti-imperialists is the fact that the Kosovars, the vast compact majority in Kosova, were faced with being driven out or killed − and entitled to defend themselves. They were entitled to ally as they needed to, without necessarily being defined by their allies.

Varga: For *Stop the War,* all these questions are incidentals, to be fended off or marginalised as seems best. Essentially, the pamphlet and *Socialist Worker*'s coverage was assembled in the belief that with suitable propaganda a large anti-war movement could be built, in alliance with pacifists, confused old anti-US or anti-German chauvinists like Tony Benn and Dennis Skinner, and the many lost tribes and sects of Stalinism and kitsch Trotskyism.

Brownstone: Not since October-November 1939, when the Stalinist Communist Party of Great Britain started to build a pro-Hitler-Stalin campaign for "peace" − meaning, "let Hitler win" − has anything like it been seen.

Caliban: "What began as very small protests [over Vietnam] snowballed into mass demonstrations that even affected the mood of the US soldiers in Vietnam. Opposition to wars has always started with a minority of the population revolted by the barbarity they see before them.... Socialists connect the struggle against war with struggles against poverty, bad housing, racism and all oppression..."

Varga: All the bad news that's fit to print, except that which damages our government's enemies...

Caliban: "... Then we will be fighting a class war − the only war that can end war."

Varga: This is a very clever touch for, in fact, *Stop the War's* own approach is not according to the general guidelines it outlines. *Stop the War* is fighting not class war but, on the propaganda front, Serbian ethnic war against the Kosovar Albanians. As a means of "getting" at NATO.

Brownstone: *Stop the War* was a sterile attempt to create an ersatz anti-war movement, arbitrarily, mechanically, and on the basis of lies. This passage conveys the only unadulterated truth in the whole pamphlet − in what it reveals of the thinking at the heart of the whole strange business, the attempt to lie into existence a mass anti-war movement.

Varga: The right emotional note needs to be sounded. In *Stop the War* there is a picture showing soldiers holding a wrapped up human being over a camp fire. The caption says they are Belgian soldiers roasting a live Somali child in 1992...

Brownstone: Indignation about the Somali child in 1992 − if the caption is to be trusted − is here put to the service of the butchers of Kosovar Albanian children in 1999! In World War Two and in the Cold War both sides made "anti-imperialist" propaganda, both sides exposed atrocities − of the other side. The Germans made much anti-British Empire propaganda. They printed telling accounts of the pioneering British concentration camps in South Africa during the Boer War! They also made a great fuss over the bodies of thousands of Polish officer POWs killed by the Stalinists in 1939-40 and found in the Katyn Forest in 1943. Both sides told much truth − about their enemies. Independent socialists tell the truth about both sides.

Caliban: "The 20th century is ending as it began − punctuated by war."

Varga: For its final chapter, *Stop the War* chooses the blandest, broadest appeal − to naive pacifist sentiment.

Brownstone: What they actually purvey is nihilism and fatalism against the Kosovar Albanians – the Kosovar Albanians who had a right to defend themselves and wage a war of liberation – and the right to the backing of honest socialists when they did it.

Caliban: "They say their wars are against tyranny and evil, and for democracy and liberation. The reasons change over the years. But each time lies are pumped out to mask the truth of what all wars are about – power, control and the ability of the world's rulers to carve up the globe and make profit. And in every war the rich and powerful of each nation send ordinary working-class soldiers to die for them."

Brownstone: Then there are no wars of liberation? There are no just wars? From *Stop the War's* point of view, as stated here, Serbia should not shoot down NATO planes.

Varga: Now, on the last page, when the reader has been led backwards right to the end, for the first time language appropriate to what is happening in Kosova is used – but so tilted as to minimise Serbia's attempted genocide in Kosova as just another workaday horror of capitalism. "The Kurdish minority in Turkey face oppression every bit as savage as that meted out to the Albanians in Kosova."

True, the Kurds are savagely oppressed – though there has not, as far as I know, been an attempt to drive out the entire Kurdish population or wipe them out by systematic murder and displacement. Not even here, on the last page, does *Stop the War* make plain reference to the likelihood of the whole Kosovar Albanian population being driven out or butchered – as they certainly would have been had the Serbian drive in Kosova continued.

It is also true that Kurdish nationalist groups have accepted aid from the CIA against Iran and Iraq. Why didn't the SWP then start supporting Iran and Iraq against them?

Caliban: "But Turkey is a member of NATO and a key ally of the US and Israel. So the West arms Turkey."

Brownstone: So the big powers are hypocrites? Yes, they are murderers, accomplices to murder, gangsters and shameless liars and hypocrites. And the underlying moral and political rationale for your stand is best summed up in the demand that they should be consistent hypocrites?

We shouldn't believe them or trust them? Of course not! And we should take the same approach to *Stop the War*! You use your general indictment of capitalism to excuse, minimise and make invisible the specific horrors in Kosova.

Afterword

O N one level, to anatomise the techniques of a work like *Stop the War* might seem to be beside the point. Its faults come not from honest ignorance, muddle or confusion of thought. The muddling up and confusion of thought themselves come from something else: from the need to justify a "line" arrived at arbitrarily according to someone's "bright idea" that a big anti-war movement would be good for "the party" just then.

The point is that the prevalence of "Apparatus Marxism" and of an "Apparatus Marxist" culture over a very long time helps make possible both the taking of such arbitrary party-solipsistic decisions as the SWP leadership's decision to build an anti-war movement in defence of Slobodan Milosevic – and that is what it was! – and the tissue of muddled reasoning and nonsense that is *Stop the War*.

It makes it acceptable. It educates people not to look too closely at what exactly is said, or what the real implications – as distinct from the party-useful immediate implications – of what is said and done are. The degeneration becomes cumulative. It becomes seemingly irreversible. Attempts like this article to stand against it come to seem either irresponsible pedantry – "You don't want to fight imperialism! You don't want to build a revolutionary party!" – or a worthy but hopeless attempt to control the waves and tides.

This examination of the SWP's grotesque tissue of apologetics for the most savage regime in recent European history, at the point where it had embarked on a systematic attempt at genocide in Kosova, points to how things really stand here: for Marxism as a guide to both honest analysis and revolutionary action nothing less is at stake than the choice: "to be or not to be". Unless the poisonous swamp is drained, then real Marxism in politics will over time become an impossibility.

We have put the pamphlet *Stop the War* on the Alliance for Workers' Liberty's website at www.workersliberty.org

Tony Cliff and Max Shachtman part 3

By Paul Hampton*

What attitude should be taken towards the Communist Parties ?

CLIFF'S final prong was that bureaucratic collectivism disorientated revolutionaries in their dealings with Stalinist Communist Parties, especially those in the West after the war. This did not appear in the original article – it is grafted onto the revised version. Shachtman had written:

"Stalinism is a reactionary, totalitarian, anti-bourgeois and anti-proletarian current *in* the labor movement but not *of* the labor movement... where, as is the general rule nowadays, the militants are not yet strong enough to fight for the leadership directly; where the fight for control of the labor movement is, in effect, between the reformists and the Stalinists, it would be absurd for the militants to proclaim their 'neutrality' and fatal for them to support the Stalinists. Without any hesitation, they should follow the general line, inside the labor movement, of supporting the reformist officialdom against the Stalinist officialdom. In other words, where it is not yet possible to win the unions for the leadership of revolutionary militants, we forthrightly prefer the leadership of reformists who aim in their own way to maintain a labor movement, to the leadership of the Stalinist totalitarians who aim to exterminate it... while the revolutionists are not the equal of the reformists and the reformists are not the equal of the revolutionists, the two are now necessary and proper allies against Stalinism. The scores have to be settled with reformism – those will be settled on a working class basis and in a working class way, and not under the leadership or in alliance with totalitarian reaction."[1]

Cliff claimed that if this policy was followed in the West, it would strengthen right-wing social democracy and would not prise rank and file Communist workers from their leaders. Duncan Hallas had argued in 1951 that it was not the programme or leadership but rather the composition of a party which determined its class character[2]. For Hallas, therefore, Communist Parties were workers' parties, and revolutionaries should utilise the tactic of the united front towards them. This political assessment of the Stalinist parties, was actually worse than the harder, Cannonite section of the "orthodox" Trotskyist movement. Shachtman argued that the Communist Parties were more than just agents of Russian foreign policy (a common conception amongst Trotskyists); they also sought to set up identical regimes to the USSR if they gained power. This was borne out by the experience of Eastern Europe and China, and later confirmed in Cuba and Vietnam. Therefore the usual policy of the united front did not mechanically apply to Stalinists. The originator of this assessment, Shachtman showed, was Trotsky himself, in one of his last articles:

"The predominating type among the present 'Communist' bureaucrats is the political careerist, and in consequence the polar opposite of the revolutionist. Their ideal is to attain in their own country the same position that the Kremlin oligarchy gained in the USSR. They are not the revolutionary leaders of the proletariat but aspirants to totalitarian rule. They dream of gaining success with the aid of this same Soviet bureaucracy and its GPU. They view with admiration and envy the invasion of Poland, Finland, the Baltic states, Bessarabia by the Red Army because these invasions immediately bring about the transfer of power into the hands of the local Stalinist candidates for totalitarian rule."[3]

It is true that Trotsky had argued earlier in 1940 that the SWP should critically support the Communist candidate in the presidential elections (in the absence of a genuine workers' candidate), but even more "orthodox" American Trotskyists like James P Cannon were

---

* Parts 1 and 2 of this article appeared in *Workers' Liberty* nos. 62 and 66

opposed to doing so. Of course Trotsky was trying to address the real problem that the Communists had tens of thousands of members in the US in 1940, a figure that had shrunk considerably by 1950. Shachtman's hostile attitude towards the Stalinists did not stop his group from calling for a Socialist Party-Communist Party-CGT government in France (because the Stalinists were not on the verge of taking power). His Stalinophobia did not extend very far in 1950, as he debated Earl Browder, the former CP leader who been expelled from the party in mid forties. This was the debate where he turned to Browder, in the course of discussing the number of ex-Communist leaders who had been killed by the GPU, and joked, that "there, but for an accident of geography, sits a corpse"!

The crucial test was the attitude taken towards the McCarthyite witch-hunt. From the outset of the anti-red drive in 1946, the Workers' Party opposed it categorically, distinguishing between the leaders of the CP and the rank and file members, and argued for a independent political fight by the working class and its organisations against Stalinist influence. And its propaganda for socialist democracy was a legitimate and principled line to distinguish itself from Stalinism. One of the few serious reasons given for the dissolution of the ISL into the Socialist Party in 1958 was that a new pole of attraction was needed to regroup the left, including those ex-members of the American Communist Party who had left in the wake of Khrushchev's revelations about Stalin in 1956. This, together with the fracturing of CPs along national lines (as well as their decline on membership), was clearly a material factor to be taken into account when dealing with these organisations. Yet Cliff presented Shachtman as holding to the same attitude towards the Communist Parties regardless of circumstances.

Cliff on politics: "All that glisters is not gold'

SHACHTMAN initially followed Trotsky in defining Russia as more progressive than capitalism, because of nationalised property, but later came to characterise Stalinism as barbarism. Cliff criticised Shachtman for failing to draw the requisite political conclusions from his sociological analyses. Again Cliff borrowed from the arsenal of orthodox Trotskyism, alluding to the dispute within the SWP in 1939-40, and to Shachtman's failure to call for the defence of the USSR when Russia was attacked by Nazi Germany in 1941.

Cliff never understood the 1939-40 dispute about Russia's attack on Poland and Finland. Shachtman had then argued that socialists could not read off their attitude to wars simply from the character of the regimes involved — look, for example, at the wars between Italy and Ethiopia in 1934-35, or Japan and China in 1937 — but rather they had to analyse concretely the politics of the combatants involved, because (to paraphrase von Clausewitz), war is a continuation of politics by other means. Cliff parroted the catch-cry of inconsistency, but because the same argument could be thrown back at him, he took a very different attitude to the wars in Korea and Vietnam, which both involved, at least at the outset, a conflict between American imperialism and a backward Stalinist state. (In fact the political issue in these wars was really about national liberation not Stalinism.)

Cliff was well aware that for Shachtman the "defence" of the USSR was analogous to the struggle for colonial independence, i.e., relative to other considerations, and that the involvement of the USSR in the second world war was not primarily about the leading imperialists fighting together to get rid of nationalised property. The USSR entered the war in 1939 with imperial designs on parts of Eastern Europe, and became an integral partner on the Allied side against the Axis in another inter-imperialist conflict. The victory of Hitler's rapacious imperialism would indeed have been a disaster for the workers of Europe, but the consequences of Russia's expansion of empire after 1945 were hardly less oppressive. Shachtman had never said socialists had to support the USSR in every war with other imperialist powers, but he left the door open for its "defence" under certain circumstances. After the war, and given the further expansion of Stalinism, this door was firmly closed.

During the 1950s and 1960s, it is true that some members of the WP/ISL lost their political bearings and were drawn into what they saw as the lesser evil, of supporting democratic US imperialism against the USSR. For example, leaders such as Irving Howe left to form the journal *Dissent*. But to do so meant they had to break with the organisation, as indeed Shachtman effectively did when he dissolved the ISL into the Socialist Party in 1958. No doubt Cliff had in mind Shachtman's muted left cover for the CIA-inspired Bay of Pigs invasion of Cuba and his support in later life for America's war in Vietnam. But

Shachtman's personal evolution is not a verdict on the Third Camp tradition which he helped to develop, particularly as these errors were rightly criticised at the time by others in his tradition, who maintained their hostility to both US and Stalinist imperialism. The argument that bureaucratic collectivism was inherently unable to provide a perspective for socialists is not borne out by the record. Draper summed up this perspective in 1949:

"The basis for the disorientation of the proletarian forces consists in this: that these rival exploiting systems are not clearly recognised as enemies on an equal footing... It is on an analysis of the new conditions that the politics of Independent Socialism is founded — 'Neither Washington nor Moscow' — and it is on this that the socialist struggle against the war is based... We declare that, as in the first and second world wars, support for either camp amounts to a betrayal of the interests not only of socialism and the working class but humanity."[4]

"Neither Washington nor Moscow" — the familiar catch-cry of Cliff's publications for years and used before him by the Workers' Party to sum up the relationship of the international working class to Western imperialism and Russian Stalinism. The "Third Camp" slogan was a synonym for independent working class politics. The WP/ISL adopted a "plague on both your houses" approach to all sides, including the USSR, during the second world war, concentrating on the "main enemy at home', American imperialism. They analysed the spread of Stalinism into Eastern Europe under the control of the Red Army, and opposed it vigorously. They analysed the way in which both the labour movements and the capitalist classes in those countries were smashed, as they had been in Russia after 1928, and unlike the mainstream Trotskyists, harboured no illusions that these events were so-called "deformed workers' revolutions which had taken place without and against the activity of the workers' themselves. Later, they drew attention to the phoney nature of the "unions" in the Stalinist states, being rather instruments in the running of a system which allowed no normal, free trade unions. Their perspective, developed in the light of experiences in 1956, would have been more or less adequate during the period of the decline of Stalinism, including the war in Afghanistan, towards Solidarnosc and during the revolutions of 1989-91.

"In the anti-Stalinist revolution, therefore, we vigorously support all tendencies, struggles and steps toward a revolutionary democratic opposition to the regime...

"The leading social force in the anti-Stalinist revolution, however, is the working class. The experience of both Hungary and Poland has shown that the revolutionary working class spontaneously organised its forces into Workers' Councils as its revolutionary instrument against the state, and that these Workers' Councils tended to assume the character of dual power challenging the old state or assuming its power after the shattering of the old state."[5]

Conclusion

WHY did Cliff slander Shachtman? Within the Trotskyist milieu he was accused by Grant of following "bureaucratic collectivism", and this impression was buttressed by Draper in a friendly review of Cliff's book in 1956: "We have often pointed out that the 'state capitalist' theory sometimes shades into versions which make it virtually identical with our own. This tends to happen where the 'state capitalism' which is seen in Russia is analyzed as being basically different from 'private capitalism' that it tends to take on the characteristics of a new social system, which is not the same as any other system, and which is labelled as hyphenated-capitalism only as a matter of terminological taste. Cliff's analysis does not begin this way, but it tends to wind up so."[6] This was over-generous: Cliff had contributed nothing original on the inner workings of Stalinism, but taken an attractive name-tag and turned it into an empty phrase.

Cliff slandered the views of Shachtman and his comrades because they were the main competitors of his "state capitalism" as the alternative to the workers' state label. A combination of misrepresentation, oft repeated, together with a certain plagiarism all those years ago, served to rub out the real issues. The crowning glory of the British SWP, a 50-year tradition built around "state capitalism" is a sham, built on a mythology about bureaucratic collectivism. This theory was not without its problems, but they should be discussed honestly and on their merits. As a body of work, bureaucratic collectivism was a substantial contribution towards an understanding of the USSR, Eastern Europe and China in their formative years, and should be one of the reference points for those who want to revive and renew the real Marxist tradition.

Notes

1. Shachtman, "A Left-Wing of the Labour Movement ?", *New International*, September 1949.

2. See Hallas, "The Stalinist Parties", *Socialist Review*, July 1951, in Hallas (ed) 1971. Cannon wrote: "It has been our general practice to combine in general day-to-day trade union work with the progressives and even the conservative labor fakers against the Stalinists. We have been correct from this point of view, that while the conservatives and traditional labor skates are no better than the Stalinists, are no less betrayers in the long run, they have different bases of existence. The Stalinist base is the bureaucracy of the Soviet Union. They are perfectly willing to disrupt a trade union in defense of the foreign policy of Stalin. The traditional labor fakers have no roots in Russia nor any support in its powerful bureaucracy. Their only base of existence is the trade union; if the union is not preserved they have no further existence as trade union leaders. That tends to make them, from self-interest, a little more loyal to the unions than the Stalinists. That is why we have been correct in most cases in combining with them as against the Stalinists in purely union affairs." Cannon, 19th October 1940. Printed in Evans, L. (ed.), *James P. Cannon: Writings and Speeches, 1940-43 — The Socialist Workers' Party in World War II.* (1975: 88-89).

3. Trotsky, 'The Comintern and the GPU', 17th August 1940. First published in *Fourth International*, November 1940. In Breitman (ed.) *Writings 1939-40*, (1973: 350-351).

4. ISL 'Capitalism, Stalinism and the War', *New International*, April (1949: 116, 126)

5. ISL Theses, *Labor Action*, 15th July (1957: 6-7)

6. For some proof of the connections between Cliff and the Shachtmanites, see the testimony of Ken Coates and Stan Newens in *Workers' Liberty*, 18, February 1995. Draper (1956), *Workers' Liberty*, No.49, September (1998: 43)

Other reading on Cliff, state capitalism and the SWP:

"The Great Gadsby" (an obituary of Cliff), *Workers' Liberty* 64-5.

"Cliff's state capitalism revisited", *Workers' Liberty* 56.

FORUM

Capitalism: neither decline, nor progress

SOME time in the late 80s various fragments of the Healy/Lambert tradition of catastrophist Trotskyism met in all seriousness in Paris for a conference on the theme "Have the productive forces grown since the War?" Chris Reynolds is correct to reject this kind of dogmatism, which flies in the face of reality and by which capitalism has been in an epoch of continuous decline since 1914. He is also correct to reject attempts to maintain the notion of decline by redefining the term and to insist on an analysis that starts from capitalism as it is rather than from our hopes of its collapse or the recitation of past classic texts.

However, his own 'New Forces, New Passions' (WL 63) suffers from some of the things he justly criticises in others. Substituting the concept of capitalism's still-progressive role for that of its decline and Lenin's *Development of Capitalism in Russia* for Trotsky's *Transitional Programme*, Chris's analysis is one-sided and fails to take account of contradictory aspects of contemporary capitalism that qualify his picture. He also spends much of his article dealing with the history of the "decline" position and its dangerous political consequences; but that cannot necessarily form a basis for rejecting every such theory. So, while I think he is correct to reject the "decline" position, his own position is equally not a rounded description of capitalism in its current stage.

My own view is that post-war capitalism has been able to maintain dynamism and growth despite downturns — which makes the theory of decline at best confusing, if one uses the word in any meaningful sense. However this occurs only at the cost of introducing new fragility, contradictions and potential instability into the system. Doug Henwood puts this well when he writes: "Marxism has been ill-served by a lot of quasi-Keynesian talk about 'stagnation'. Growth rates and investment levels may not be what they were during the Golden Age of the first post-World War Two decades, but still, the system has been in many ways both more turbulent and more universalising over the last 20 years than at any time since before World War One."

Modern capitalism is *both more turbulent and more universalising*. Some symptoms of this mixture are: increased competition, an open international regime allowing the free movement of capital, a shifting international division of labour, and rapid changes in technology and techniques of production. Taken together these things led to an increased speed of change, the need for flexibility, and rapid and continuous restructuring and innovation.

The underlying driving forces of these changes are not themselves new to capitalism, but over the last 20 years have been proceeding at a faster rate and in new forms. They in turn give rise to the development of new working classes around the world to which Chris Reynolds correctly attributes such significance. Let us examine briefly a few of the consequences of this:

Waste and the environmental crisis: Capitalism is becoming more wasteful. In order to maintain a high rate of turnover of capital and maintain markets which might otherwise be saturated, the rate of product innovation must rise and product cycles shorten. This has been made possible by more flexible production processes. Planned obsolescence, the creation of fashions and the constant introduction of marginal changes to designs use more and more resources, not to meet human needs but to try to ensure that the accumulation of capital is uninterrupted. A striking example is the computer industry, where there is typically a gap of less than six months between the introduction of new product ranges yet thousands of perfectly functioning machines are scrapped by businesses each year in order to keep up with what are often minimal changes to hardware and software.

These demands in turn contribute to an environmental crisis, which is a striking confirmation of the contradiction between the private ownership of the means of production and the needs of human survival. Attempts to resolve this crisis by means of market mechanisms (e.g., taxation) are doomed merely to reproduce this contradiction in a new form.

Unproductive expenditure on marketing: One result of faster product innovation and increased competition is that certain types of unproductive expenditure (non-value creating costs here incurred in the process of realising surplus value) have had to grow. The costs of advertising reached $200 billion a year in the US in 1998, four times what it was 20 years before. This is necessary for the large capitalist firm to compete, yet represents a cost which has to be paid for out of its profits.

The role of financial capital: $1.2 trillion worth of foreign exchange transactions take place every day. One week of this is the equivalent of US GDP and one month's worth equals the total world product. Less than 10% of this amount is required to finance trade in goods and services. The remainder is pure speculation, which is about as turbulent as it gets!

Similarly, speculation on a generally rising stock market — ultimately underpinned only by confidence in a bright future and the hope that the state will intervene in the case of major crashes — has come to provide the basis for a whole range of financial commodities — mortgages, pensions, credit, insurance etc. The consequences of a major crash would be to ruin a large section of the population in the advanced economies, who have become dependent on credit and indirectly on speculation for maintenance of their standard of living.

Uneven development and de-industrialisation: Perhaps most importantly for Chris Reynolds' analysis, the development of "new forces" and "new passions" which arrive with the expansion and development of capitalist industry is neither universal nor does it exclude a regression in other sectors of the world economy, which has a negative impact on both the constitution and consciousness of the working class. *Rather they are part of the same process of the restructuring of capital flowing across the world in search of profitable outlets.* Thus large areas of the globe (e.g., most of Africa, parts of Asia and Latin America) remain left out of the growth of industrial capitalism. Many traditional sectors in industrialised countries are in terminal decline due to their unprofitability and the unwillingness of the state to support them. This last phenomenon – sometimes called "de-industrialisation" – affects such divergent areas as the British coalfields, the US "rust belt", the eastern half of Germany and most of the Russian economy.

The restructuring of capital is thus accompanied by a restructuring of the working class. Alongside the emergent trade unionism and labour politics of the newly industrialising countries, we see also the destruction of traditional strongholds of industrial concentration, trade unionism and class consciousness. All sorts of phenomena then appear, which serve to undermine tendencies towards social solidarity: work in the semi-legal/drugs economy; self-employment; the growth of neo-fascist and extreme nationalist movements; and, last but not least, the struggle for survival.

This is only one aspect of the social contradictions which have intensified alongside the increasingly open world economy and the growing gap between rich and poor, both within and between different countries. (See the table "A divided world" in *WL*63.) Many elements of social crisis are growing precisely because capitalism is expanding.

Capitalism does not just therefore "augment the raw materials for socialism" in a linear manner as Chris suggests. Noting these contradictions in passing ("As well as augmenting the raw material for socialism, the development also augments the wealth, power, resources and skill of the ruling class."), he fails to acknowledge that they have any implications for his overall analysis of capitalist development, asserting instead too broadly that "on none of Lenin's eight points [in *The Development of Capitalism in Russia*] has development ceased or gone into reverse". While we may argue about the relative weight of "augmenting" and "reversing" the development of these raw materials, it is necessary at least to recognise that capitalism is at the same time destructive and creative if one is not to fall into an analysis which is incomplete and unbalanced in seeing capitalism just creating the raw materials for socialism.

Paul Hampton (*WL*64-5) and Hillel Ticktin (*WL* 66) point to some of the same phenomena I have outlined (de-industrialisation, growth of finance capital, growth of unproductive expenditure) as indicators of capitalist decline. However, these facts do not necessitate accepting their version of the theory of decline. They accept the facts of capitalist growth – though Hillel Ticktin refers to them as "success indicators based on nominal growth" and Paul Hampton sees them as "better associated with the forced adaptation of capitalism [to working class pressure] than its vitality". Yet they argue that capitalism is in decline because it comes to undermine its own laws of motion, the law of value becoming increasingly meaningless as a social and economic regulator in this period. The driving force behind this is capital's need for the socialisation of production and labour, which has the effect, even in the absence of a working class takeover of the economy, of making capitalism "increasingly a hollow shell waiting for its overthrow". The capitalist class realises this and consciously takes steps to retard or counteract the encroaching socialisation.

There are many problems with this position. Firstly, it seems to see socialisation (concentration and centralisation of capital, the spread of interdependent social relations, the development of and the growth of the working class, the "development of non-market forms") as an almost automatic force in capitalist development resulting from the growth of the productive forces rather than a by-product of the drive of capital to create the best conditions for its accumulation and the expansion of value. What are perfectly sensible actions from the standpoint of capital as a whole, albeit at the cost of increasing social contradictions (e.g., deindustrialisation, restriction of the size of the state sector and the penetration of private capital into areas previously reserved for social production), here become transformed into attempts by capitalists to stave off the detrimental effects of socialisation in hollowing out the hold of the law of value.

This socialisation then results in the growth of forms transitional to socialism which increasingly dominate the economy. Thus according to Hillel Ticktin ('The Political Economy of Class', *Critique* 20-21), "Nationalisation, 'central planning', large bureaucratic apparatuses are all forms used by capitalism which are *inherently non-capitalist.*" [My emphasis.] (He says they are not socialist either. But to say they are transitional forms is for his theory a tautology which tells us nothing about their dynamics.) The capitalists fight back to preserve the system from erosion by these forms – though quite why they should if they can augment their wealth by other means is unclear. This only makes sense if these forms are somehow necessarily in conflict with the interests of capital.

We see here the truth of Chris Reynolds's comment that Hillel Ticktin starts from an idealised picture of a pure capitalism. Large bureaucratic apparatuses within large capitalist firms were an essential part of the form of capitalism known as Fordism which dominated between the 1920s and the 1980s. While such apparatuses do require unproductive expenditure (and thus have been broken down as information technology has developed), nothing about them is inherently in contradiction with the needs of capital. State ownership per se does not prevent nationalised firms participating in market relationships or operating according to the law of value, though the fact that it was usually unprofitable sectors that ended up being nationalised has disguised that fact. That the capitalist state, for example in certain European countries in the 60s, has tried to intervene (usually unsuccessfully in the long term) via planning within the framework of capitalism in order to overcome some of the contradictions of capitalism does not make these measures somehow non-capitalist. On this basis all state intervention that does not simply enable the operation of the market is somehow non-capitalist and a transitional form. Yet in all periods of capitalism state intervention has existed and been necessary to ensure as smooth an operation of the system as a whole as possible, though its extent and forms have changed – partly, but only partly, as a result of working class pressure as Paul Hampton notes.

Taking forms such as nationalisation as "inherently non-capitalist" leads us to a position like Ted Grant's whereby "where we have complete statification, quantity changes into quality, capitalism changes into its opposite". (*Against the theory of state capitalism*, 1949) Hillel Ticktin does not go so far, partly because he sees capital actively trying to fight back against the inevitable tide of socialisation. However, in the absence of its overthrow by the working class, we instead move towards a hollow shell no longer dominated by the process of capital accumulation but rather by transitional forms and arbitrary processes that are no longer those of capitalism. While in Grant's and Kautsky's pre-1914 theories capitalism collapses at this point, with Hillel Ticktin we remain stuck in this state in something that is not quite a new form of society but is not really capitalism either. What then are its dynamics, historical role and laws of functioning?

Does this present a credible picture of the operation of capital today? I would say not. Capitalism *is* becoming more universalising as Chris Reynolds claims. We are seeing the extension of market forms and the operation of the law of value to new areas of the globe and new areas of human activity. Further, some of the phenomena Hillel Ticktin and Paul Hampton describe do not involve the negation of the law of value in the way that they claim. We shall look at one example: the operation of monopoly and the gap between price and value.

The assumption that the operation of the law of value is increasingly restricted is supposedly demonstrated by the growth of monopoly and an increasingly arbitrary relationship between value and price. Both the existence of monopoly and the divergence between value and price have been characteristic – to varying degrees – of capitalism as a system throughout its history. Marx notes that if the value and price of a commodity are equal, it is by coincidence.

Let us look at one example. The labour costs of a pair of Nike trainers is less than 5% of the final selling price. This discrepancy makes possible the vast salaries paid to Nike bosses and sporting celebrities who give the product their endorse-ment. The distinct character of the product, jealously guarded and zealously promoted, gives it the features of a monopoly in that it can be sold well above its value (though Nike does face competition – hence the large advertising budget). Where does the surplus come from? What are the mechanisms by which this is possible? Do they indicate that the law of value is no longer operating?

Clearly, one of the major factors here is the super-exploitation of the workforce that produces the shoes in Third World countries. Such production is associated with a number of features of earlier stages of capitalism: the production of absolute surplus value (lengthening of the working day), relatively unsophisticated and low cost technology and, until now, in the absence of effective trade unionism, the reduction of wages to around the minimum required to keep the workforce alive (i.e., the value of labour power without the addition of what Marx calls the "historical element" which arises as the result of working-class bargaining power). Rather than not being regulated by the socially necessary labour time embodied in the commodities, it is precisely the driving down of that quantity in real terms among the producers that permits the existence of massive monopoly profits and such a large divergence of value from price.

The other side of the equation is the need to find a mass market (the goods are not luxuries), which would not be possible from the producers themselves given their restricted purchasing power. Instead the existence of the world market makes it possible to sell the goods in other markets where large sections of the population are able to pay the prices demanded, due both to the existence of a large "historical element" in their wages and the currently easy availability of consumer credit. The size of this market ultimately constrains the size of the monopoly profits generated so that prices can never be totally arbitrary.

The surplus profits are thus created at the expense of both consumers and producers and this set-up is fragile in that it requires a large amount of unproductive expenditure to sustain it. This example shows that, while monopoly profits can only be made at the expense of workers or other capitalists, this need not imply that the law of value ceases to act as an enabler or regulator of economic activity. Thus increasing concentration of capital does not necessarily lead to a shrinking of the operation of the law of value.

The notion that human labour can be reduced by automation throughout the capitalist system to such an extent that labour time ceases to function in such a way is also wrong, though it was noted as a theoretical possibility by Marx, for reasons to do both with the nature of social labour and technology and also with the necessary economic functioning of capitalism as a whole. (This requires a more detailed analysis at another time.)

The Hillel Ticktin-Paul Hampton theory of decline points to some real and significant phenomena but wraps them up in a mechanical theory of a declining law of value, encroaching socialisation and transitional forms. Such a theory of decline ultimately ends up with a teleological view of capitalism advancing towards socialism but never quite getting there.

Before summing up, it is worth pointing to some – perhaps surprising – similarities between the analysis of Paul Hampton and Hillel Ticktin and that of Chris Reynolds. Both believe it is necessary to provide one overall label – progress or decline – for the current stage of capitalism. Both see capitalism as increasing the potential for socialism through socialisation of labour and production. Both see that socialisation as the key feature enabling us to characterise the current phase of capitalism – one sees it as pointing to the progressive tasks it is carrying out, the other to it as the key characteristic of capitalist decline. Labels are then attached as a result of over-general analysis and then become the important thing.

I would question whether such characterisation of "the nature of the epoch" abstracted from an analysis of contemporary capitalism as a totality is of much use today. It is certainly not necessary in order to conclude with Paul that capitalist relations of production form a fetter on the development of the productive forces (even though they are expanding), with Chris that the objective preconditions for socialism exist today or with Hillel that the gap between capitalist reality and socialist potential is growing.

Capitalism as a system has always operated in such a way as to develop the productive forces in its own brutal, wasteful and irrational manner, to contain obstacles to its own successful functioning, and to develop new ways of overcoming them which in turn lead to new contradictions. It is possible for capitalism to be both "more universalising and more turbulent". Yet there is no final crisis towards which capitalism inevitably develops – Lenin remarked long ago that there is no economic crisis with no way out for the bourgeoisie and Marx demonstrated that the devaluation of capital in a crisis cleared the way for renewed development. The question rather is what are the costs for the working class and humanity as a whole and what opportunities capitalist development provides for the development of socialist consciousness. This does not require us to apply questionable generalisations about progress or decline.

Bruce Robinson

A one-sided view of capitalist progress

I DON'T disagree with what Chris Reynolds says about progress ('New forces and passions' _WL_63) but I think it is one-sided, in two respects.

Firstly there are, I think, two distinct notions in Lenin about the progressive or reactionary character of "imperialism, the highest stage of capitalism". One is the notion of "moribund" capitalism – that is, the idea that capitalism has exhausted its capacity to develop the forces of production (forced to adopt collectivist forms like monopoly, etc.). Chris rightly argues that if this were so the 20th century would be inexplicable. Capitalism continues to this day to do "progressive" work: developing production, innovation, and so on. Moreover, I would add that it would be impossible to function in the world without some notion of progress in human affairs.

I suffer from a condition, diabetes, which a hundred years ago would have killed me in a few months; it kills few people now, and the drug which keeps me alive is artificially produced. On this level, to complain that capitalism is not progressive would be tantamount to saying that it makes no difference to me whether I am alive or dead.

But there is another, related but separate, view of progressive/reactionary in Lenin's argument. He, along with other revolutionaries, objected to those who supported the First World War with arguments which saw the world through the prism of the previous century. In nineteenth century Europe, nationalism and the drive towards the creation of nation states had been progressive on various levels: sweeping away obstacles like tariff barriers to the development of capitalism; rousing the people into a political force; carrying with it ideas of democracy and freedom; proposing secular, and to some degree popular, sovereignty against the divine rights of kings or what remained of them. Lenin and others argued that by the beginning of the 20th century, in Europe, this progressive work had been exhausted. The side to capitalism which is expansionist, predatory, aggressive, etc was dominant. It was expressed through militarism, a bureaucratic state, conquest, and war. The advanced capitalist nation state, and the nationalism it employed to bind the working class to the bourgeoisie, was reactionary.

This view of what is reactionary or progressive is not tied to or reducible to the matter of capitalism's ability to develop the forces of production; it links to a view of capitalist development rather differently. There is a point in capitalist development where its expansionist logic becomes increasingly dominant, and the bourgeois state's economic and political ambitions are bound up with this "imperialistic" drive.

This idea has two possible meanings. 1. That there are imperialisms other than capitalist ones (an idea I agree with). 2. That advanced capitalism is not necessarily imperialist.

In saying that advanced capitalism is necessarily imperialist, I do not mean to say that only the most advanced capitalist states are imperialist. Rather, that there is an expansionist logic to capitalist development which leads nation states to imperialist ambitions.

It seems to me that the opposition to the First World War by the revolutionary left was based primarily on an assessment of the "stage" of capitalism, not measured by productive development etc., but politically – these were bureaucratic, militaristic states. Chris is right that post-1945 bourgeois democracy is on a different "grid" to the variables around in 1914-18. But this doesn't change matters fundamentally, as is clear if you imagine a hypothetical war between more-or-less equal European states today and what we would say about it.

This is important in understanding Marxists' opposition to the First World War. I don't think the revolutionary argument in 1914-18 was derived purely from a detailed assessment of the national question. Take Belgium. Lenin was quoted in *Workers' Liberty* during the Balkans war to the effect that a war over Belgium's national rights, even by big capitalist powers, would be all right – or Marxists would be sympathetic to it – were it not for other small nations.

But this interpretation seems to me to turn the real train of thought on its head. This was not: we would support these states going to war over Belgium... But there are other small nations' rights involved so we can't support the war. It was: we are opposed to the war; these people (the social chauvinists) say they support it – with disastrous consequences for the international workers' movement – because (for instance) of Belgium... But they are liars and hypocrites, which is clear if you think for a moment about other small nations they couldn't care less about. The argument about Belgium is derived from a position of opposition to the war, taking up the detailed defence of those who supported it. It was not the basic rationale for opposing the war. (Granted, because of the nature of the time it's hard to disentangle these issues, but I hope my point is clear.) A more recent analogy: we opposed both sides in the Iran-Iraq war. Both sides oppressed Kurds and others. But our opposition was not simply because of the oppression of national minorities, but because of the nature of each regime – more precisely, because of the politics of which the war was a continuation, within which national oppression of minorities was an element, but not the only one.

Secondly, there is another side to any discussion of "progress" which I think is important. The modern use of the word emerged in a nineteenth century context in which not only human affairs were considered to consist of an inexorably progressive march forwards (with capitalism as the glorious destination) but everything else was, too. Darwin's theory of evolution was widely interpreted – and still is – as an account of an inexorable rise of "better", "more advanced" species in nature, with conscious humanity as its culmination. This, however, is nonsense. Human beings are not "more advanced" or "superior" to apes, or for that matter cockroaches. We have simply evolved differently; every organism is well-adapted to its own conditions, and if it isn't it dies out. There was no inevitability to the appearance on Earth of our species. (Evolutionists argue the toss about whether intelligence, and especially consciousness as we experience it, is inevitable, but that seems to me a separate issue, although the argument against certainly wins on points.)

Does this matter? Yes. The progressivist view of nature implies some special place for human beings in the universe, which ultimately implies God. (It's a version of what in philosophy is known as the "anthropic principle", that the universe must have a purpose or human beings would not be here to wonder what it is). It is an anti-materialist view. We should draw a sharp divide between the notion of "progress" in human affairs and a general notion of progress in nature.

Clive Bradley

Kosova and East Timor: an Australian view

EAST Timor was discussed at a September meeting of the National Committee of the Alliance for Workers' Liberty. It was noted that there were discussions on troops in WL Australia. The minutes then state: "Doubt there will be disagreement on UN troops here [Britain] – after Kosova debates: don't call for peacekeeping troops; don't necessarily denounce them. The implication was clear – we shouldn't have had a problem in Australia – the British debates on Kosova had already sorted out the issues. Unfortunately, the advice offered – don't call for peacekeeping troops; don't necessarily denounce them – put WL Australia on the wrong side of the debate on East Timor.

The request for troops had come from the East Timorese leaders. After fighting alone for 24 years, and after the overwhelming popular vote for independence, were they not entitled to invite in a military force, to protect the population from the Indonesian army and the anti-independence militia gangs? For the largest left party in Australia, the Democratic Socialist Party, it was clear that the East Timorese leaders did have this right. Furthermore, the Australian government was ignoring the East Timorese request, so the DSP, in solidarity, itself raised the call for troops to be sent.

The WL Australia position amounted to saying to the East Timorese: "We know that Australian/UN troops will save many of your lives. Secretly, we hope troops will be sent; if they are sent we will not call for their withdrawal. But we can't be seen to support the sending of troops. That would destroy our revolutionary reputation."

Yet the AWL had rightly castigated the British SWP for its indifference to the fate of the Kosovars. So how did the position of WL Australia on East Timor relate to the Kosova debates in Britain?

These debates are surveyed in "The left during the Balkans war", by Sean Matgamna (*WL* 62). The responses to the war fell into two main categories: 1. the main issue was Serbian ethnic imperialism in Kosova, 2. the main issue was the military action by Nato. There were those who attempted to give both issues equal prominence, but Sean argues that they tended in practice to fall into the second category, because "Stop the Bombing" was their only concrete slogan. The effect of this slogan was to demand that Milosevic be given a free hand, despite "support" for the Kosovars with calls of "Down with Milosevic" and "Independence for Kosova".

However there was another "Third Way" – don't have any concrete slogans! This (seriously) was the position stated by Hillel Ticktin in *WL* 56: "The first thing for socialists to realise is that we have very little role. There is no socialist movement on the ground. That leaves us with putting forward our socialist programme. The left must not degenerate into supporting the nationalism of either side. That includes the nationalism of the oppressed Kosovars." The interviewer contended that, "We should say whether we believe the British government should lift the arms embargo and give the Kosovars guns to defend themselves," to which Ticktin responded, "I don't think socialists can give advice to a bourgeois government." The interviewer replied: "This is not advice. Socialists should simply say what we want done."

Yes indeed! So, did the AWL want military assistance to be given to the Kosovars or the East Timorese? Apparently not, if the assistance took the form of Nato ground troops or the Australian army. But it would be nice if some unspecified agency transported arms to Kosova and East Timor and somehow supplied the resistance movement, despite the opposition of the Serb or Indonesian military.

Trying to make this incoherence into a political virtue, Sean states: "Watching the agony of the Kosovars – or the East Timorese – naturally produces in decent people the urge to shout out 'instructions' to the rulers: essentially it is an ineffective cry of protest and, subconsciously, a belief in word magic. It is like the shouts of the mother who from a distance helplessly watches her child stepping out in front of a speeding car. It is a call for saviours on high. Its only effect is to express our real weakness and add to its political confusion – about what the role of socialists must be and what revolutionary socialist politics is – that will forever keep us weak."

So "send ground troops" was a pitiful cry of helplessness, but "arm the Kosovars" or "military assistance to the East Timorese" was clear headed revolutionary socialist politics? In the case of East Timor, the resistance leaders had already specified that the assistance they needed was troops. The DSP rightly demanded that the troops assist the East Timorese as allies rather than act as an overlord, but the demand by WL Australia for "military assistance" without troops was downright fakery. There is little doubt that the Kosovars also required more than hypothetical rifles. If anyone believed in word magic it was those who imagined that the call "arm the Kosovars", when specifically not addressed to Nato, helped the Kosovars in any tangible way. Even sillier is the implication that decent people, who shout if their child steps in front of a speeding car, will forever keep "us" weak – the clear headed socialists who would keep quiet and go straight home to conceive another child!

In Australia, decent people insisted on "confusing" the issue by expressing solidarity with the people of East Timor. Trade unions (illegally) stopped the movement of goods to and from Indonesia. Large rallies were held in all the state capitals. The key demands were for recognition of the independence of East Timor and for a military force to be sent to defend the East Timorese. It was obvious that the United States would not send any troops, because (as William Cohen stated with crystal clarity) US national interests were not involved.

Were these decent people "foolishly" demanding an Australian war with Indonesia, as one AWL observer alleged? Perhaps some were, but the main thrust of the rallies was to "simply say what we want done", namely an Australian or UN force sent to East Timor to assist the independence movement. How to face down Indonesia and avoid a war was the government's problem. It was certainly no solution to assure the Indonesian government that they could veto the deployment of troops in East Timor. The Foreign Minister (Alexander Downer) suggested sending unarmed peacekeepers, but this was shot down by the Australian military. The commanders demanded and got a government commitment to seek "robust" rules of engagement. Indonesia finally yielded to economic and diplomatic pressure and consented to the entry of the Australian-led UN force.

The overwhelming majority of people at the Australian rallies were reformists, according to Sean's definition. That is they believed that the state, "with enough pressure, can be influenced to do what people of good will want". Isn't that exactly what happened? The explanation is contained in an Australian labour movement song from 1891 – " the ballot is a thing they did not have to reckon with when George the Fourth was king". Sean also defines the revolutionary belief

A WORKERS' GUIDE to

IRELAND 95p + 50p p&tp

From
PO Box
823,
London,
SE15 4NA

that the state,"is a class state, which, even when – for its own reasons and with its own methods – it does something desirable, is not our state". OK, so the Australian government acted for its own reasons, which included a desire to stay in office. But eventually it did, partially and unreliably, what people of good will wanted. Shouldn't we aim to create our own state? Of course, but thousands of East Timorese had an immediate and urgent problem of survival. In these circumstances, mindless maximalism was the height of irresponsibility.

The reason that WL Australia opposed a "troops in" position on East Timor, was that this was seen as the equivalent of calling for ground troops in Kosova. The AWL had supposedly established that to call for ground troops in Kosova was to abandon working class politics in favour of political support for Nato. Calling for ground

troops in Kosova was alleged to be advising Nato how to conduct its war against Serbia. Similarly, calling for troops in East Timor would be advising the Australian government how to... er... ? There was no war with Indonesia. Advising the Australian government on how to stabilise the region? No. It was telling the Australian government to abandon its long-standing policy of accepting Indonesian rule over East Timor. So the parallel with Kosova was questionable. If the parallel did hold, then it would establish nothing more than a requirement to look afresh at the Kosova question. In rational politics, a "precedent" can never be a reason for refusing to properly consider the current problem.

The claim, that calling for ground troops in Kosova automatically implied political support for Nato, was never proved.

Roger Clarke

We need a critical appreciation of Benjamin

ESTHER Leslie's article on Walter Benjamin ('Tragedy, Progress and Struggle' *WL*66) is welcome and I hope, along with her, that his work can be rescued from the academics who have done him to death in recent the years. There are, however, a number of problems with Benjamin's work, some of them quite fundamental, that Esther Leslie's article doesn't touch on. Unfortunately, I haven't had the opportunity to read her book yet, so if any of the points I now raise are discussed there then I offer my apologies in advance.

First of all there is, I believe, within Benjamin's work, but particularly in *The Work of Art in the Age of Mechanical Reproduction* a utopian view of technology and a correspondingly hazy notion of progress. Benjamin seems to say (though he is never very clear) that changes in the way artworks are produced and received (particularly films) have changed our way of seeing the world ("the mode of human sense perception") and this in turn develops within us a more critical stance to the world around us. This is muddled and pretty much unsupported by any evidence. Two points need to be made:

1. There is no evidence that the way we perceive the world changes other than by a slow, lengthy, and complex process of evolutionary adaptation. In the few generations that have lived since the advent of photograph and film (1896) such fundamental change is impossible – a much greater time-scale is required. It may be that film has released human perceptual capacities that have been underused (somewhat akin to the blind person who develops an exceptionally sharp sense of hearing) but this is hardly a new mode of perception. In fact the examples that Benjamin offers are somewhat pedestrian – the use of close-ups, rapid editing techniques and slow motion in film hardly require any major perceptual leaps by the viewer and can be accommodated for quite comfortably by our existing visu-

al apparatus (which we have inherited from our hunter-gatherer forebears). In other words the new faster, more intense visual input of the modern, technological age has simply heightened our already existing capacities.

2. The idea that changes in our mode of perception through photography and film (assuming that the idea is correct) also results in a critical attitude to the world is also questionable. To give a concrete example, which Esther Leslie mentions, how does watching a film by Sergei Eisenstein, with its extensive use of montage, develop within the viewer the idea or desire to then go out into the world and, one hopes, change it? I would argue that there is nothing intrinsically within montage that is revolutionary, or that changes our ways of perceiving the world. Montage as practised by Eisenstein and others is basically a technique and, as such, can be used in a number of ways. It is, therefore, politically neutral. What is inspiring about *Battleship Potemkin* is its theme and subject matter.

However, powerful and striking montage techniques can also be employed to pursue the most reactionary purposes as they were in *Triumph of the Will*, the Nazi documentary by Leni Riefenstahl, and *Napoleon* by Abel Gance ("a Bonaparte for budding fascists" according to leftist film critic Leon Moussinac who, nevertheless, greatly admired the techniques and aesthetics of the film). Goebbels, the Nazi head of propaganda, was a great admirer of Eisenstein but the Nazis weren't the only ones who recognised the possibilities of montage: it can also be found, admittedly in a bowdlerised form, in a number of Hollywood productions and is also, sometimes, used in such outwardly commercial formats as as pop videos and advertisements. The great man himself saw montage, usually, in terms of technique. In 1937 he referred to montage as a "powerful component of film composition" and his writings (admittedly somewhat rambling) devote a lot of space to concrete applications of montage techniques to specific filmic problems, including for example, the numerous exercises he set his students at the Moscow Film Institute (VGIK).

This last point leads me on to another, wider, issue and that is the way that the left has often regarded cinema. Esther Leslie writes that "cinema had at least the potential to generate a critical, politically based culture" but, like Benjamin, she's a little short on examples: she mentions only Charlie Chaplin and Eisenstein. Both deserve enormous credit for their work but it has to be noted that in the Soviet Union Eisenstein's films were never that popular. Even *Battleship Potemkin* ran for only a few weeks in Moscow's cinemas. Western films, on the other hand, were big box office attractions (Mary Pickford and Douglas Fairbanks being particular favourites). My point is that not that cinema couldn't be part of a wider "critical, politically-based culture" (though I find the phrase somewhat vague) but that the left has too often formulated notions

about what a political or radical cinema should be in a manner which has been restrictive and often disastrous, resulting in films which nobody in their right mind would want to go and see. As examples I would cite *La Chinoise* by Jean Luc Godard, anything by the French-German film-makers Straube and Huillet, *The Riddle of the Sphinx* by Laura Mulvey, and almost any film which attempts to apply notions of Brechtian "alienation" or "distanciation" (a sure guarantee you will be bored to death – and incidentally another overworked "theory" that cries out to be critically re-examined).

The connection with Benjamin is that his theories have often been cited as support for a so called revolutionary or alternative or political cinema. Benjamin's advocacy of popular, accessible art is surely welcome, yet his notion that the new technology and techniques associated with film and photography result, somehow automatically, in new ways of seeing the world is fundamentally flawed.

John Cunningham

For a democratic-secular state!

LOOKING at your website article on Israel, I think you write off too easily the idea of a democratic secular state to solve the problem of Israel and the Palestinians. You consider it either as a utopian scheme or as a call for the military demolition of Israel by the neighbouring Arab states. Either way it is not an option, and you call for a two-state solution, an Israeli state next to a Palestinian one.

Under present conditions, a two-state 'solution' would mean the Palestinians getting a few tracts of land, the bits that they presently control plus a few others. The Israeli government would give to the Palestinians – by analogy – the sink estates of Peckham and Hackney, Thamesmead and a few other run-down areas of London, and keep the rest of the capital for itself. More importantly, partition would reinforce the growing reactionary trends in Israel – fascistic, fundamentalist tendencies in both Judaeism and Islam. This would drive deeper divisions between Jews and Palestinians, and would lead to exclusivist sentiments within both

states, with dire consequences for those who don't "fit in" – Arab Israeli citizens, Christians, etc.

Partition is a reactionary solution. The partition of Ireland led to priest-ridden societies north and south; the partition of India led to huge massacres and continual tension between India and Pakistan. Similar reactionary consequences will follow a partition of Israel and the setting up of a Palestinian state. Is that what you want, because that's what will happen.

No, however "utopian" it seems, a democratic secular state is a sensible idea. It means one in which all its inhabitants can live within a single state with no religion or nationality receiving favoured or detrimental treatment. In short, the demand that Israel behaves as a proper bourgeois republic.

And if that sounds utopian, does not the idea of socialism seem "utopian" at the moment? But that will not prevent either you or I from calling for it.

Paul Flewers

A three-volume set on the 'Militant tradition' from Workers' Liberty

• Part 1: Marxism and the labour movement (£5.00 plus 70 pence post) contains the founding document of our tendency, What we are and what we must become, written by a minority in Militant in 1966
• Part 2: Trotskyism and Stalinism (£2.50 plus 50 pence post) contains an analysis of Militant on the Russian war in Afghanistan and a critique of Grant on the Colonial Revolution
• Part 3: Leninism and Opportunism (£2.00 plus 50 pence postage) contains article on Militant in Liverpool, the LPYS, 'Panther' and Ireland.
Buy separately or the set of three, post free, for £7.50 from:
AWL, PO Box 823, London SE15 4NA. Cheques to "AWL"

REVIEWS

Neither capitalism, nor Stalinism, but dreamworld?

Susan Buck-Morrs
Dreamworld and catastrophe: the passing of mass utopia in East and West

STALINISM and capitalism in the 20th century, according to Susan Buck-Morrs, were driven by parallel "dreamworlds". "Stalin's First and Second Five Year Plans amounted to the largest technological transfer in Western capitalist history... [Most] design and layout [of new factories]... was American, probably one-half of the equipment installed was German. Of this, a large amount was manufactured in Germany to American design on Soviet account. In quantity, American-built equipment was probably second and British third..."

It was paid for by selling artworks previously owned by the Russian aristocracy. One Raphael painting alone, now in the National Gallery in Washington DC, covered half the cost of the contract under which Arthur McKee and Co. of Cleveland built the new industrial city at Magnitogorsk.

Most movie screenings in the USSR up to 1930 were of foreign, mainly US films, while after 1930 the USSR film industry deliberately mimicked Hollywood techniques.

While capitalist states construct their "sovereignty" and their "wild zone of power" by counterposition against an enemy in space (other nation-states), Stalinist states, so Buck-Morrs claims, construct theirs by counterposition against an enemy in time (the old capitalist world). The two systems were not only intertwined, but also "co-dependent" in their difference. "'Good' was defined as the other of the other... entwining them in a dialectical death embrace."

After 1991 she watched the reintegration of Russia into the capitalist world market with horror. "Again and again, the scene was of new extremes of class difference. Chic women shopped at Western department stores and exclusive boutiques, while old women and veterans begged in pedestrian tunnels. The cavernous Institute of Philosophy where we continued to meet was half-deserted, as researchers took on several jobs to survive."

She opposes the "standard wisdom that capitalism is desirable and inevitable, the normal natural arrangement of social life", and "the myth that multinationals have the same rights to their 'private' property, consisting of the earth's natural resources and society's collective labour, as do individual citizens to a pair of shoes or a refrigerator".

She wants to find space for new "oppositional cultural practices". But, to find that new space, she feels she has to back out of the world of "industrial modernity". A half-stated undercurrent in her argument is advocacy of small-scale, low-tech development against "the capitalist heavy-industry definition of economic modernisation", which she indicts Stalinism for "adopting". But how would she ever have got to Moscow to do her studies without heavy industry to produce the aircraft to get her there, and the metals and other materials for those aircraft?

Politically, her reason for some confidence about rescuing "the utopian hopes that modernity engendered", amidst what she takes to be the definitive collapse of all the 20th century's "mass utopias" and "dreamworlds", is the idea that the collapse of Stalinism has also "taken away the unique formula for legitimating the peculiarly American form of domination. This special kind of imperialism that insists it is no imperialism cannot continue to exist if the political enemy ceases to exist".

But arguments about enemies in space and enemies in time were never the material base of US capitalist, or Stalinist, power. In fact, the Vietnam war was justified to the US public as holding the line for the "free world" against the menacing *future* of "communism", and US military action in the Gulf and ex-Yugoslavia has been legitimated as upholding a new human-rights world order against throwbacks from the *past*. Russia's invasions of Czechoslovakia and Afghanistan were justified to the bureaucratic elites (the only section of society the rulers might have bothered about justifying them to) as defending the space of the "socialist bloc" against threatened Western footholds and incursions.

A ruling class with solid material bases for its power will always construct a more-or-less adequate system of ideological hegemony – social existence determines consciousness, as Marx put it. US-led capitalist power will not crumble just because particular ideological devices have become obsolete.

Despite her professed Marxism, Buck-Morrs reads history upside-down – with ideologies and rhetorics as the base, and material production as mere superstructure. Oddly, but logically, and despite her earnest desire to challenge "standard wisdom", she also downgrades the power of critical thought to change society.

"For critical intellectuals from the East, the existence of a non-socialist West sustained the dream that there could be 'normalcy' in social life. For their counterparts in the West, the existence of the non-capitalist East sustained the dream that the Western capitalist system was not the only possible form of modern production. Of course we each knew that our hopes were not realised in any perfect way by the other side. But there mere fact of the existence of a different system was proof enough to allow us to think the dream possible..."

In other words, the collapse of the Cold War counterposition between capitalism and Stalinism has ruined, not capitalist ideological hegemony, but those whom Buck-Morss calls the "critical intellectuals", i.e,. the salaried, tenured, university-accredited radicals.

It ruined them because they were not critical or intellectual enough. Not critical enough: their criticism was limited to counterposing one variant of established exploitative power to another. Because they did not have Marx's notion of ideas

becoming a material force when they grip the masses, they could operate only on the margin of accomplished facts.

Not intellectual enough: although at odd points in the book she notes sharp changes around the end of the 1920s, she assumes that the post-1930 system was a legitimate flower from the bud of the 1917 workers' revolution. She seems to have read no Trotsky, citing him only at second hand. She does not mention the Left Opposition, or later writers such as Max Shachtman, Hal Draper, Joseph Carter, and CLR James – she ignores them.

Colin Foster

Democracy's demons

J Arch Getty and Oleg V Nauvov (eds)
The Road to Terror: Stalin and the self-destruction of the Bolsheviks
Graeme Gill and Roger D Marwick
Russia's Stillborn Democracy? From Gorbachev to Yeltsin

MARX noted in *The Eighteenth Brumaire of Louis Bonaparte* that the bourgeois crisis of mid-nineteenth-century France was resolved in the cry: "Rather an end with terror than terror without end." Stalinism was an end with terror, as a new book of light commentary and heavy reproduction of documents confirms.

In *The Road to Terror*, Getty and Naumov assemble a wide array of top-secret dossiers, letters, police reports, confessions, confirmations and transcripts of meetings recently made accessible by the opening of previously closed once-Soviet archives. They detail Stalin's role as architect of the terror and its purges throughout the 1930s, culminating in the trials and self-liquidation of the entire old guard of Bolshevism in 1937-1938.

They also establish the insecurities and loyalties that conditioned a pathology of political capitulation that structured the *nomenklatura*'s sorry suicide in these dismal days of revolution's unambiguously final, decisive defeat.

Getty and Naumov are too politically and interpretively oriented to the surface phenomena to do much more than skim over the dimensions and character of the terror, but the 200 documents they reproduce are an invaluable addition to the English-language evidence on Stalinism's campaign of brutal suppression. In that historical process lay the obliteration of Soviet civil society and of the possibility of proletarian democracy that Lenin, Trotsky, and the original Bolsheviks struggled to create out of the contradictions and chaos willed to them by Tsarism and coercive capitalist containment during World War One.

They failed, and the tragic result was Stalinism's terror-driven end. Fifty years later the defeat of democracy was re-enacted in the almost

farcical contest pitting the Stalinist reformer, Mikhail Gorbachev, against the market puppet and clown prince of democracy, Boris Yeltsin.

Stalinism's suffocation of any possibility of proletarian democracy – and more than a half century of degenerate constraints on institutions such as trade unions or discourses of political opposition and alternative – reduced socialism and its philosophical and strategic orientation to little more than textualisations of ritual adherence. And so the struggle for a new proletarian order in 1985-1995 Russia was stillborn.

Gill and Markwick explore the farce of this stillborn democracy, detailing the new terror without end that reigns in a Russia where "bourgeois" denotes a style of rapaciousness rather than a formed class and civil society is up for grabs, to be bought outright or secured through violence. "Profits", declared one commentator with characteristic abandon, "it's too early for that – we're still dividing up the property." And that property was the collective enclosure of the Revolution of 1917, however degenerated, the social inheritance of a working class that never managed to see its way out of the blind alleyways and truncated terrain of socialism's original primitive accumulation.

The struggle for democracy in twentieth-century Russia has occurred twice, the first time as tragedy, the second as farce. Whether this second, market-society defeat, farcical in its Yeltsin deformity, will prove more debilitating, on a world historic scale, than the first revolutionary effort of 1917, squashed by Stalinism, remains an open question.

Gill and Markwick are not sanguine about the possibilities for Russian democracy and they tend to put their eggs in the basket of the good leader, someone other than Yeltsin. Their book is dated in this respect, but Marxists will appreciate that the way out of tragedy/farce lies, not with a President, but with larger class forces. These have yet to be mobilised in the new Russia. When they are democracy's demons will be vanquished, its proletarian promise realised.

Bryan Palmer

How Stalin armed Hitler

Edward E. Ericson
Feeding the German Eagle

THE bulk of this volume is an examination of the economic talks between Nazi Germany and Stalin's USSR in 1939-41, while Stalin remained "neutral" and Hitler was at war with the West. They ended with the German attack on the Soviet Union, on 22 June 1941. As Ericson puts it, "Nazi Germany turned to bite the hand that had fed it for the past twenty-two months."

Hitler described the signing of his pact with Stalin on 23 August 1939 as "the saddest day" of his life. But without his trade deals with Stalin, the Nazi war machine would have been in extreme difficulty. For example, Nazi Germany relied on the USSR for supplies of rubber, without which there would have been no tyres for aircraft or other military equipment.

As Ericson concludes: "Without Soviet deliveries of... four major items (oil, grain, manganese and rubber)... Germany barely could have attacked the Soviet Union, let alone come close to victory. Germany's stockpiles of oil, manganese, and grain would have been completely exhausted by the late summer of 1941. And Germany's rubber supply would have run out half a year earlier.... Hitler had been almost completely dependent on Stalin to provide him the resources he needed to attack the Soviet Union."

Stalin thought he could buy off Hitler by providing all he asked for: "[in June 1941]... the Soviets were doing just about everything they could to meet the German demands. Warehouses... were filling up faster than the German and Soviet transportation systems... could handle." "The pace continued until the eve of battle with a Soviet express train, carry-

ing 2,100 tons of desperately needed rubber, crossing the border only hours before the invasion began!" German technicians and engineers were also working on the Soviet naval fleet right up to the German invasion, when they were allowed to leave.

The Soviet negotiators, however, were hard bargainers. They were in a better position. The USSR had other trading options, whereas Germany had nowhere else to turn. The Russians were difficult for the Germans to deal with because their orders came from the Kremlin, often directly from Stalin himself. Frequently they had to wait for the next telegram from Moscow. The Nazi state left its representatives more relaxed and autonomous – largely free to argue as they wished, and afterwards to "sell" the results of the discussions to Hitler on their own terms.

Karl Schnurre, the chief German Foreign Office negotiator was discussing with the Soviet Trade Commissar Anastas Mokoyan, in December 1939 when: "Mikoyan said he couldn't take a decision – 'it was a matter for Molotov' – at which point Molotov himself suddenly emerged from a curtained-off archway in Mikoyan's office. After a short discussion, Molotov, in turn, said he could not decide, it was really a matter for Stalin... "; who then appeared, smoking his pipe, from behind a curtain, and negotiated with the Germans himself.

The book's main use for socialists is to dispel any remaining myths regarding the "anti-fascist" role of Stalinism. The author's occasional description of the Stalinists as "Bolsheviks" does grate somewhat.

Matt Heaney

A half-critique of Cuba

Peter Taaffe
Cuba: Socialism and Democracy

THIS book is a pseudo-debate between Peter Taaffe of the Socialist Party and CWI (formerly-Militant) in Britain and Doug Lorimer of the Australian Democratic Socialist Party (DSP) and, I guess, an attempt to check the recent rash of Castro-worship in the Scottish Socialist Party, with whom Taaffe maintains a strained relationship.

The DSP, following the lead of the American SWP, rejects Trotsky's theory of permanent revolution, preferring Lenin's blurred and outmoded formula of a "democratic dictatorship of workers and peasants" as the programme for revolutions in countries of less capitalist development. It endors-

es Castro's leadership largely uncritically, and sees Cuba since 1959 as a socialist state.

Taaffe subscribes to permanent revolution, and is thus more critical of Castro. Yet Taaffe shares fundamentally the same framework as Lorimer, believing that Cuba under Castro is, as Russia under Stalin and China under Mao were a deformed workers' state, historically more progressive than capitalism, and in some senses (nationalised property, planned economy, welfare gains, absence of a bourgeois class) part of the socialist alternative. More critical of Castro than the DSP, the CWI (in a pamphlet by Tony Saunois) constructs a mythical version of Che Guevara with which to associate itself. Despite some telling points, Taaffe never manages to nail Lorimer's Stalinoid politics.

Why isn't Cuba socialist? The 1959 revolution was not made by the Cuban working class but by the guerrillas of the July 26th Movement (J26M). There were no Soviets in Cuba in 1959 and the general strike the previous year had been a failure. There were no signs of workers seizing the factories, establishing committees for workers' control. There was no proliferation of independent unions challenging the Batista regime. The J26M was neither rooted in the working class, nor advanced a socialist programme.

The Castro regime, pushed into a corner by US imperialism, did indeed overthrow capitalism in Cuba after 1959, but only to construct a form of exploiting society on the model of the Stalinist USSR. Castro constructed a one-party system. Only supporters or members of the Cuban Communist Party can stand in elections. The trade union movement, purged after 1959, is now bound hand-and-foot to the state. Dissident political groups, even those opposed to the US blockade, cannot exist legally.

The welfare system in Cuba before the 1990s was indeed better than Batista's, and on a par with the best of equivalent capitalist states, such as Costa Rica and Taiwan. But Cuba was already one of the richest countries in Latin America before 1959. In the 1980s it depended on an annual $5 billion subsidy from the USSR, as well as on the exploitation of Cuban workers and peasants. After Russian support was withdrawn in 1989, the economy collapsed, to be drip-fed only by the recent expansion of tourism and business ventures.

In foreign policy, the Cuban state whistled to the tune of the USSR, supporting the invasion of Czechoslovakia in 1968 and the crushing of Solidarnosc in 1981. In Africa, Cuba switched from the Eritrean national liberation movement to supporting the Derg in Ethiopia. Closer to home, Castro failed to condemn the slaughter of students in Mexico in 1968, gave his stamp of approval to the recently ousted PRI regime, even when it committed electoral fraud in 1988 to stay in power, and failed to back the Zapatistas. Socialists support Cuba's right to self-determination, and oppose the US blockade, but that does not commit us to silence on Castro's anti-working class policies at home or abroad.

Taaffe mentions some of this, but does not draw the threads together. Chapter Four asks: "Is there a privileged elite?" and shows that the Castro leadership has all the attributes of a ruling class.

Taaffe evades the fundamental problem for his position — how can a "workers' state" have been created without the active intervention of the working class? — and expresses a "workers' statism" that dare not speak its name.

The extent of Taaffe's illusions is indicated in passing when he implies that Hugo Chavez, the Venezuelan leader who recently orchestrated the oil price rises through the OPEC cartel, might be the new Fidel Castro. He also writes that it was wrong to support the Russian invasion of Afghanistan in 1980. True, but what about some political accounting for the nine years in which Taaffe's tendency supported the Russian troops!

Paul Hampton

But still, it moves

Dava Sobel
Galileo's Daughter

IN 1610, Galileo Galilei, as Bertolt Brecht put it, "abolished Heaven" — by proving the Earth was not the centre of the universe and that the Church's entire theory of the cosmos, based on Aristotle and Ptolemy, was false. By pointing his telescope at the moons of Jupiter, he proved the celestial spheres were not immutable. Some Church astronomers refused to look. Eventually he was accused of heresy.

Dava Sobel, author of *Longitude*, recently dramatised on Channel Four, has written a fascinating biography of the man Einstein called the father of modern science. She has chosen also to deal with Galileo's relationship with his eldest daughter, a nun known as Suor Maria Celeste — a relationship preserved through the daughter's rather beautiful letters to her father during her adult life. But it is the story of the father which is most gripping.

Galileo provided physical evidence for the view of the universe of Copernicus, namely that the Earth was not the centre of it, but moved around

the sun. It was revolutionary not only because it was true, but because it represented a sharp break with medieval science, which depended on the textual authority of ancient thinkers; instead, Galileo looked to observation and the evidence of his senses. He had already disproved, if not to clerical satisfaction, such Aristotelian theories as that objects of different weight fall at different speeds and that ice floats because it is flat.

The Catholic Church considered the notion that "the Earth moves" contrary to Scripture, but at first the Copernican system was permitted to be discussed "as a hypothesis". When Galileo produced his magnum opus, *Dialogue on the two world systems*, in which a Copernican thrashed an Aristotelian, however, the Inquisition decided he had gone too far and forced him to recant. Galileo did recant, promising that Copernicus was wrong. His books were officially prohibited by the Church, a ban not lifted for two hundred years.

One of the many interesting things in Sobel's book is that she places this conflict in a clear historical context. The Pope, Urban VIII – who in his days as a Cardinal had been friendly to Galileo and enlightened on the matter of Copernicus – had inadvisedly taken sides in the Thirty Years War in Germany, and was under pressure from critics to prove his ability to defend the Catholic faith. Galileo was thus something of a scapegoat.

Galileo was not an anti-religious thinker; far from it. Sobel shows in considerable detail how, throughout his life, he tried to reconcile his discoveries with his belief in God. Thus the threat he received from the Inquisition was not a purely physical one. Sobel goes into some depth regarding Galileo's trial in 1633, even reproducing verbatim reports of it. She is sympathetic to his decision to capitulate, in part because he was old and sick, in part because he was concerned to prevent the banning of his book, but mostly because, from her account, he rightly felt he had broken no Church law in any case: he had presented the Copernican case, as they had insisted, as an unproven "hypothesis" only.

This is therefore a far cry from Brecht's version in which Galileo's capitulation is a betrayal of the struggle for truth against medieval obscurantism (or at least is seen as such by his followers).

She makes no suggestion, either, of any ideological conflict between Galileo and his favourite daughter. Maria Celeste's letters are used to bring to life seventeenth century Italy – in particular the terrible plague which swept the country in the 1630s.

Other accounts of Galileo's life suggest he was, among other things, an inveterate womaniser. Sobel says almost nothing of this, presenting instead a man who was ill for almost his entire life. I think there is a tendency here only to tell us sympathetic things about the great scientist.

But she has tremendous skill in explaining Galileo's path-breaking ideas, not only about the Copernican system, but a wide range of other matters, including his final treatise on motion, which paved the way for Isaac Newton (who was born the year Galileo died).

Gerry Bates

Genome alone?

Steven and Hilary Rose (eds)
Alas, Poor Darwin: arguments against evolutionary psychology

ALAS, Poor Darwin, assembling articles from biologists, sociologists and others, takes exception to the excessive claims of evolutionary theory (EP) – the theory that human behaviour must be understood in terms of adaptations caused by natural selection (so that we are, basically, palaeolithic hunter-gatherers).

Geneticist Gabriel Dover swiftly dispatches the gene-centred version of evolution put forward by Richard Dawkins. Stephen Jay Gould defends himself from the "slurs and sneers" of American philosopher Daniel Dennett in his book *Darwin's Dangerous Idea*. Anne Fausto-Sterling gives a feminist response to EP (which stresses incessantly the evolutionary origins of differences between men and women, locating them in "reproductive strategies"). Ted Benton puts contemporary debates in a historical setting, with some fascinating quotations from Alfred Russel Wallace, Darwin's co-founder of the theory of natural selection, and a socialist and proto-feminist.

The discussion is wide-ranging, not least, as the editors note, because there is more than one target: EP and behavioural genetics are slightly at odds with each other (the one stressing human "universals", the other concerned with differences between individuals). To anyone new to the numerous subjects, this plethora of issues is no doubt daunting, but it makes for a rich discussion.

There are differences between the views offered here, and some are more interesting than others, but a central thought emerges which is important and well-made. The

disclaimers of the evolutionary psychologists and, more generally, of those who want to emphasise biological evolution as the cause of social patterns – their tendency to dismiss their critics as bewildering nitpickers or unreconstructed "environmental determinists" – blurs the fact that their supposed insights into human behaviour are offered as indicators for social policy.

They concede complexity of causation, the fact that DNA is both complicated and still largely mysterious, and so on, but their headline arguments enter popular culture shorn of caveat.

I'm sure the advocates of EP, the "selfish gene", etc, will think they have been, in turn, caricatured and unfairly attacked – and they would, I think, on occasion be justified. But these essays at least demand a serious response.

In a sense there is an emerging common ground. As Stephen Jay Gould says in his essay, there are insights provided by EP which could be fruitful, if its advocates were a bit more laid back and cautious. Marek Kohns excellent recent book, *As We Know It*, attempts to rescue EP from the political right; Chris Knight's *Blood Relations* draws on EP to make some intriguing speculations about the origins of culture. A greater creative engagement with EP, rather than pure dismissal of it, is in order.

Commenting that it is perfectly reasonable to investigate evolutionary factors in human nature, Steven Rose then rightly adds: "The problem with [EP] is that... it offers a false unification [of the levels of analysis] pursued with ideological zeal." (p247)

Thus these essays remain, on the whole, concerned with providing ammunition against the enemy. For this reason, I suspect *Alas, Poor Darwin* will prove invaluable for social scien-

tists who hadn't noticed EP creeping up on them and have suddenly found themselves ambushed.

Edward Ellis

Global police and the multitude

by Michael Hardt and Antonio Negri
Empire

TONI Negri was the most celebrated intellectual of Italy's "ultra-left" in the 1970s. He was jailed in 1979 for "armed insurrection against the powers of the State"; won freedom in 1983 by getting elected to Parliament; fled to France in 1983; and has been back in jail, in Italy, since 1997.

His new book, *Empire* written with an American academic, Michael Hardt, analyses the world of "globalisation". They see it as all-encompassing, oppressive, but containing potentials for liberation.

"The strategy of local resistance misidentifies and thus masks the enemy. We are by no means opposed to the globalisation relationships as such... The enemy, rather, is a specific regime of global relations that we call Empire. More important, this strategy of defending the local is damaging because it obscures and even negates the real alternatives and the potentials for liberation that exist within Empire. We should be done once and for all with the search for an outside, a standpoint that imagines a purity for our politics... The multitude, in its will to be-against and its desire for liberation, must push through Empire to come out the other side."

But the primary impression I am left with upon reading *Empire* is that Marxists are liable to forget that there are processes of legitimation of capitalist society necessary to reinforce its juridical rule, because Marxists already accept that capitalism (and so its rule) is self-perpetuating in the very mode of production itself.

Negri and Hardt subject this forgetfulness to a critical examination and find that the global legitimation of domination is very different today from that which Lenin found when he produced his theory of imperialism. What defines *Empire* is not US rule per se but the propagation of imperial, not imperialist, concerns.

Processes of justification for intervention make the popular demands for peacekeeping forces to "do something" in the hot-spots look like a voluntary basis for popular assent to bourgeois hegemonic rule.

As evidence for this the authors cite the moral rights of intervention that are generated when NGOs and global peace-keeping institutions work hand-in-glove with one another to constitute the moral impetus for a global police force represented in organisations like NATO.

The liberal pluralist's wet dream does what Marxists always thought it did: better protect capitalism.

And so there are some useful things in this book for us to take note of. For example, an explanation

of the recent US expeditions in the Balkans as a patent plunder of material resources for the machine of imperialism has and does cover for some gross remnants in the left that repeatedly fail to distinguish between the transparent cases of securing expanding markets, and those in which the domination serves long-term strategic interests.

Nevertheless, whether that reinforcement of strategic interests is but a delayed form of increasing proletarianisation is unclear in the book.

And that is the other major premise of *Empire*. Globalisation, according to Negri and Hardt, cannot be characterised along the orthodox trajectory as the highest "stage of imperialism". Rather, it must be defined as a qualitatively new form of capitalist domination.

The political implications of *Empire* are ambiguous. The resistance to *Empire* by "the multitude" when that "multitude" has been contrasted to "the people" earlier in the book only by its "deterritorialising power" – that is, the impossibility of old-fashioned nationalism – [is unclear] especially considering the fact that the authors think that globalisation "should not be understood in terms of cultural, political or economic homogenisation". Globalisation, like localisation, should be understood instead as a regime of the production of identity and difference, or really of homogenisation and heterogenisation (p.45). Does not this regime fundamentally weaken these new subjectivities, sought after as points of resistance by the authors, against the terror? They grant this possibility themselves.

There are other things, I think, that must also be rejected. Negri and Hardt attempt to support their theory of Empire with an utterly superficial commentary on the arguments between Lenin and Luxemburg and Hilferding. This particular section of the book will be infuriating to most Marxists.

Nevertheless, the authors' discussion of the relationship between nationalism and populism is particularly insightful and worth reading. Further, the "crisis of modernity" that many philosophers rely on as argument against Marxism and which is usually construed as the "death" of any overarching authoritative reference – no God, no Nature, no Communist Party, no History – is refreshingly absent here. Negri's and Hardt's Marxism does not collapse into a heap in the face of a shrill announcement of so many funerals. Bio-political sovereignty is the substitute edifice of modernity, still alive and voracious as ever.

Melissa White

157

Contributors

Clive Bradley
Is a freelance television scriptwriter.
John Bloxam
Was the organiser of the "Bennite" Rank and File Mobilising Committee in the 1980s.
Susan Carlyle
Has worked as a stage manager, teacher, social worker and now, artist. She was for a dozen years a Labour councillor in Tower Hamlets.
Jim Denham
Is a welfare rights advisor.
Paul Hampton
Is a school teacher.
Nick Holden
Is a freelance web designer.